THE ZOMBIE GUIDE TO PUBLIC SPEAKING

2ND "DEAD"ITION, RE - ANIMATED

STEVEN S. VROOMAN

Copyright © 2015 Steven S. Vrooman

A MoreBrainz Project
Seguin, TX 78155
stevenvrooman.com

All rights reserved.
ISBN: 1515337790
ISBN-13: 978-1515337799

FOR HUFF,

*who first taught me
to combine
public speaking and pop culture*

FOR MICHELLE,

for everything else

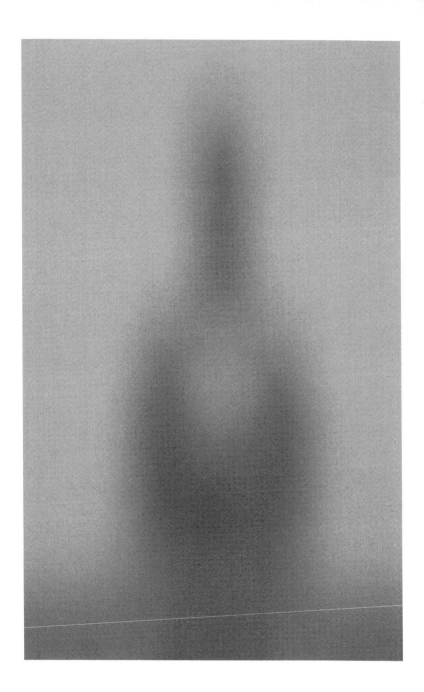

Table of Contents

Introduction:	
Pretending that We Are Doing a Lot of Work	**9**
Introducing the *MOPSBOTS*	11
A Note on Revision	13
Reanimation	17
A Note on the Illustrations	**18**
Part One:	
Reclaiming Speaking's Soul	**19**
Chapter 1: Failing	**21**
Greetings and Good Wishes	24
Shortcuts	26
The Dilemma	30
Chapter 2: Anxiety	**35**
Channel Your Nervous Energy	40
Forget Performance	43
Conclusion	45
Chapter 3: Depression	**49**
The ABCs	56
I Still Feel Like a Failure, Vrooman	59
Conclusion	63
Chapter 4: Ditch Your Speech	**65**
Extemporaneous Speaking	67
Repurposing the Outline	68
Why I Hate Notecards	75
Part Two:	
Reanimating the Bones	**77**
Chapter 5: Organization	**79**
Connectives	80
Movie Trailers	84
Link/Mario Picks Up The Key/Sword/Amulet/Rock	88
Chapter 6: Introductions and Conclusions	**95**
Introductions	96
Conclusions	104

Chapter 7: Visual Aid Architecture	**113**
Strategic Ambiguity	115
Managing Focus	120
Organizers	125
There is No Spoon	130
Professionalism	136

Part Three:	
Resuscitating the Flesh	**141**
Chapter 8: The Uses and Abuses of Sources	**143**
Drive-By Quoters	145
The Horrible Cycle	147
Zombie Statistics	150
A Final Caution about Citations	162
Chapter 9: Narrative	**165**
How to	170
Chapter 10: Numbers	**177**
How To	180
Chapter 11: Humor	**187**
How To	192
Chapter 12: Figurative Language	**201**
Travels with Feynman	204
How To	206
Wizard Powers	215
Dungeon Master's Guide	221
Chapter 13: Slideworks	**223**
Textual Data	224
Numerical Data	229
Images	240
Audio and Video	263

Part Four:	
It's Alive! Alive!!	**265**
Chapter 14: Argument Basics	**267**
Flipping the Enthymeme	268
Structures and Errors	279
Chapter 15: Argument and	**289**
the Double Hierarchy	**289**

Hierarchy and Transcendence	290
The Checkers Move: Shifting Hierarchical Allegiance	296
New Hierarchies	302

Chapter 16: Delivery and Credibility — 305

Energy	306
Credibility	308
The Details	310
A Few Concluding Thoughts on Group Presentations	315

Conclusion: Looking for Brains	**319**
References	**321**
Acknowledgments and Thanks	**337**
Photo/Art Credits	**341**
About the Author	**345**

Introduction:
Pretending that We Are Doing a Lot of Work

If this book were just a satire, it would grow old pretty quickly: First, stumble to the front. Second, raise your arms. Finally, groooooaaaannnnn.

No, this book is not a joke. It is a deeply researched analysis of why most public speeches don't accomplish our goals and what we can do about that. As I was writing it, a professor of pop culture as well as public speaking, I became obsessed with the ways that the scary, brainless interaction that passes for speaking is so similar to scary, brainless zombies.

Plus, zombies are fun. Most of you would rather be fighting zombies than giving a speech. I want this book to be readable, and maybe the zombie references will help. When this book's drafts were inflicted on students for feedback and revision, one of the positive comments was that this was the first textbook one particular student had ever finished.[1] Another said that this book was not dry like most books, but was, in fact, moist. Gross. Full circle to the rotting corpse theme, I guess.

You shamble up to the front of the room. The audience groans and shuffles around. Everyone is looking for brains. There are none to be found. All suffer from the living death of boredom and lack of engagement.

One of the scary things about zombies is that they look like people, your neighbors, family, colleagues and friends, but they are not. At least one person in most zombie movies

---

[1] All teachers complain that their students don't read enough for class. I once had a student whose response to this was: "I stopped reading books when they stopped putting pictures in them." Well, take a look inside this one, buddy. Checkmate.

will make the mistake of thinking there is still humanity in someone and get chomped for it. This is also what is scary and sad about most speeches. Everyone looks human. But there are no human connections. Our minds disappear into a glaze of Power Point.

In *Dawn of the Dead* (Romero, 1978), the zombies come to the mall. Survivors have this to say about it:

> *Francine*: What are they doing? Why do they come here?
>
> *Stephen*: Some kind of instinct. Memory of what they used to do. This was an important place in their lives.

We do the same thing with speaking. We brainlessly show up to the same places, go through the same motions, use the same kinds of slides, and repeat the things that seem to matter even when they don't.

Once, working with students who were learning to teach, I was frustrated with their insistence on churning out Power Points which bulleted *everything* that looked like a list in their assigned chapter, including obviously pointless things like a list of four different ways you might record an interview (tape recorder, phone, etc.). After accusing them of failing, of recreating the same terrible lectures they'd been subjected to their entire lives, most admitted that what they wanted their students to learn that day was very different than what they put on their slidedecks. It was just hard to imagine doing anything else but shamble through the chapter, looking for ~~brainssss~~ lists that would look like, well, a familiar Power Point.

All too often we show up to meetings or events or class, pretending that we are doing a lot of work. And when the audience claps and we sit down, for a minute all of us feel that it was all right, that we really did all just endure something together that was worth it. A second later, that feeling is gone, and we wonder what happened to another day or another afternoon and wish, like we did when we were ten, that somehow school would be cancelled and we could, just for a day, choose again to do something cool with our time.

Most speeches fail. We pretend that this is okay, that it is not a terrible waste of everyone's time.

There are two fantasies for the probably doomed survivors in a zombie tale. The first, that there is somewhere safe to run or helicopter to, is not possible for you. You are reading this book because you can't escape the hungry monsters. You have to give speeches. The second fantasy is that there is a cure. Fortunately for you, this turns out to be true. You can reanimate your audience. But it will not be easy.

Introducing the *MOPSBOTS*

Public speaking, at its best, moves people and creates change. But when was the last time you were enthralled by a speech? No phone, no wandering attention, no thoughts of lunch? Speaking has become an inert show, a droning on in front of a flickering failure of visual aids. We have already given up before we stand up to give a speech. No one cares, not even you. Public life has been reduced to a "let's just get this over with" mentality.

Too strong a judgment? Look at the faces in the room around you next time you are sitting in an audience and tell me I'm wrong.

We need to resurrect this dead thing called speaking.

Even if speaking is not dead, at the very least it is often

a kind of soulless thing, shambling around. It is the hollow appearance of something that goes through the motions but is really slowly rotting. There are reasons for this. It's not just "modern society" or "this new generation's attention spans" or anything like that. Almost a hundred years ago, Stratton (1920) laid the blame with the speakers: "It should be a rule that before a man attempts to speak he should have something to say. This may apparently not always be the case" (p. 122).

I have been teaching, speaking and coaching on this issue for more than twenty five years. I have amassed a large collection of textbooks in that time, and I wrote this book because not only were the ideas in those books not helping my students get better (and would have no appeal to an out-of-school professional looking to better their skills), but in many cases they were advising things that were downright counterproductive. We'll call these books *MOPSBOTS* (My Old Public Speaking Books On The Shelf), robots mopping up facts, zombie books, shambling through the same shared decade-repeated lists perhaps to look like, well, a familiar book,[2] bloating, with their revisions, to well over 500 pages.

Back in graduate school, when we were learning to teach public speaking, the common joke was that books on communication were about making the obvious seem complex by inducing the memorization of lists. Then we could use those lists to make multiple choice tests. What is really important gets lost in that janitorial model of education. Why *that* list? Why *those* questions? If we all fake it long enough can we pretend our class is valuable?

This book will try to drill down to get to what is most

---

[2] A "familiar," mythologically, is a demon, you know.

INTRODUCTION

important and what can actually make you better.

A Note on Revision

This book has two new chapters. Seven chapters have been extensively altered. All of this, from the first-ever public speaking textbook chapter on depression to the extensive use of *Dungeons & Dragons* references in the figurative language chapter to a huge new selection of images,, is designed to make the book more interesting and useful than the first edition was.

In addition, this "re-animated" version of the 2nd "dead"ition has newly improved, higher resolution artwork and photos.[3] Even though this is the *third* book I've published, culminating from thousands of hours of work, I still had more to learn.

Don't you?

There were things about image scanning and editing and pdf exporting I still didn't know.[4] I learned a lot in doing an entirely different sort of project, helping my partner in awesome, Michelle Johnson, publish her book, *Doodled Blooms: A Hand Drawn Coloring Book of Fantastical Flora*. And that's the thing about revision. You don't know what you don't know until time and situation change radically enough for you to see it.

We have long been taught that revision is important in writing. Most of us resist that message with the irrational

---

[3] The pre-re-animated versions of the 2nd "dead"ition, with their pixelated images and green cover art, will henceforth, at least in my mind, be called the bootleg edition, or perhaps the shadow edition.

[4] And if you've seen the menu systems in GIMP and Inkscape, you understand that.

fury of a Tiefling Warlock casting Infernal Wrath.[5] But few of us are taught the importance of revision in public speaking. The classic public speaking class design, which was old when I was learning how to teach the class, *MOPSBOT* in hand, in 1995, was to have students simply do four speeches over the course of the term, usually informative, persuasive, group and some kind of entertain/special occasion thing.

This allowed the class to cover different kinds of speaking styles, but it meant that students usually only got one shot at each thing.

Sometimes it feels like if we just go up and "wing it" we will be great on the first try. Maybe so, delivery-wise, at least, if you like to live dangerously. But research? Visuals? Audience adaptation? That stuff doesn't benefit from another round??

When I was accepted to speak at TEDxSanAntonio, I was initially leery of being assigned a "curator," a personal coach who would help you though many stages of revision, including at least three group practices where you would have to adapt to the feedback of all the other speakers and their curators.

Did they not know who I was? DOCTOR Vrooman! Did I really need a coach?

Yes.

Jeff Adams, my coach, helped me to improve my speech in a number of ways. Here he is on the next page. Say "Hi" to Jeff everyone.

---

[5] You didn't expect the *D&D* references so soon, did you? #CriticalHit

INTRODUCTION

What you can see now as the final TEDx product (Vrooman, 2014b) is vastly different from what I started with. It is sooooo much better than it would have been without Jeff and all the others who gave me feedback.

I adapted this experience to my own Professional Speaking class in the summer of 2015. They gave one speech over and over again. We all provided feedback to push the speeches in new directions. I would require them to do things like ditch their entire introduction and make a new one or come up with all new supporting material or images on visual aids. This was all so they could choose their very best stuff by the end.

THE ZOMBIE GUIDE TO PUBLIC SPEAKING

I can say that all of them had a final speech that was orders of magnitude better than their first, and not just because of lessened nerves and delivery practice, which gets better no matter how you slice a public speaking class: you speak a lot, you get better. They were more confident in their material and their material was more interesting.

Revision is usually frustrating, though. If you don't have a Jeff Adams around or a class which forces you to revise, you should get help. Find a partner in class or in the office and "curate" each other. If all else fails, record yourself on your phone, upload it to social media and ask how you did.[6] But, as frustrating as it is, it is worth it in the end. As one of my students this summer wrote:

> I personally spent a lot of time researching the content for my speech. But every time I thought I had found something good, we would have to throw it out for the next one. I would then spend the next 30 minutes raging about how I hated this class and I was convinced that Vrooman was a little demon that laughed himself to sleep at night knowing he caused us unlimited amounts of anxiety. However, after seeing through the cloud of sleep deprivation, I knew that what he was doing was for the best. By the time our fourth persuasive speech came around, I was confident that I had picked the right content.

A curator, friend or teacher, if nothing else, holds you accountable for doing what you know you need to do to get better.

---

[6] This is an "in emergency, break glass" kind of suggestion, as social media feedback might be, shall we say, intense.

INTRODUCTION

Reanimation

In the first popular Hollywood zombie film, *White Zombie* (Halperin, 1932), Bela Lugosi's character, aptly named "Murder," can turn people into zombies. The plantation owner character tries to possess a woman he desires by having Murder zombify her, but he ends up concluding, "I thought that beauty alone would satisfy. But the soul is gone. I can't bear those empty, staring eyes."

Can you bear, when speaking, so many bored faces?

Only you, when you are the speaker, can change that. If the audience is not paying attention to you, it is not them. It's you.

You are failing.

But don't lose hope. It happens to all of us. If we understand the reasons we fail, we can build a better chance of success.

A Note on the Illustrations

Sam Johnson-Vrooman drew the zombie pictures for this book. He'd drawn the cover images for the first edition, but one of my goals for this edition was more zombies. So each chapter has at least one.

We'd like you to color them. Public speaking is stressful. And coloring pictures is great for stress relief (Santos, 2014).

We'd also like to see your work. If you are feeling it, please Instagram or tweet them @MoreBrainz with #ColorMeUndead. Or you can share with "MoreBrainz" on Facebook. There's already a few out there in that hashtag. Take a look.

Please?

I just ran into a student the other day who said she'd colored them all in but didn't feel like sharing. Boo!

Sharing is caring, people.

PART ONE

Part One:
Reclaiming Speaking's Soul

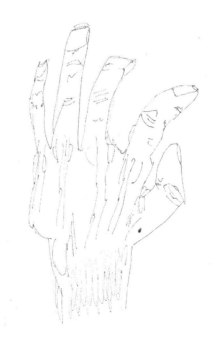

THE ZOMBIE GUIDE TO PUBLIC SPEAKING

CHAPTER 1

Chapter 1: Failing

You are a zombie. At the podium. Trying not to groan. Someone once told you to imagine them all naked. Someone else told you . . . told you . . . told you . . . . darn! You can't think of it now, you're so nervous. The one thing, too! The one trick that would have helped you get through this thing. And! Y o u !! F O R G O T ! ! !

So you look down, start reading a paper or a Power Point, and try to just go through the motions. You know no one is listening or caring, but you just do it all anyway.[1] How many times have you done this? Maybe every time? You know it is not working, but, well, hey, that's what you gotta do, right?

You are the zombie, played for humor in the movies, bumping repeatedly into something, getting nowhere:

> Zombies will try to scale any surface no matter how unfeasable or even impossible. In all but the easiest situations, these attempts have met with failure. Even in the case of ladders, when simple hand-over-hand coordination is required, only one in four zombies will succeed. (Brooks, 2003, p. 14)

Zombie films, which always seem to be social commentary, may be, in the end, critiquing this aspect of human behavior most of all: we just keep doing the same pointless things over and over again. And when you clump all of us listless speakers together, we can be called a school

---

[1] Hopefully no one is throwing tomatoes at you, like the poor guy on the facing page.

or business or a society.

We seem to take a terrible pride in this, at times. One of the most common arguments I get from people who disagree with the ideas in this book is, "Well, that's just not the way we do Power Points in _____," or, "No one has the patience for storytelling where I work." What that says to me is that we know there is a better way to communicate but that we purposefully avoid it in order to fit in. This is the story of Rick and Glenn in the "Guts" episode of *The Walking Dead* (McLaren, 2010), draping themselves in zombie viscera for camouflage. I've seen people in meetings drape themselves in the leftover guts of old ideas in order to fit in, not because they believe in them.

Why do we keep failing in this way?

Communication, especially in the areas of public speaking and persuasion, is often the study of failure. How often do you really listen to another person? How often has someone gotten you to change your mind? Yet most *MOPSBOTS* (My Old Public Speaking Books On The Shelf – did you even bother to read the Introduction?!?) will tell you something different. The first chapter of Brydon and Scott's (1994) book is about "Becoming an Opinion Leader." I guarantee no other book on the subject's first chapter is called "Failing."

So much of communication is failing. If you are like Foss and Foss (2003) predict, when you are told you are mistaken, you are most likely going to reject that and strengthen your initial position, exactly the opposite of what the speaker or writer was trying to do.

We are very familiar with this phenomenon in everyday life. Adler and Towne (1996), in their interpersonal communication textbook, list a series of defense mechanisms people employ when face-threatening acts, or messages that challenge our self-image, are received. Let's try it out. Here are some statements this book will argue:

- Most PowerPoint presentations you have created were counterproductive.
- There is never a good reason to memorize or read a speech word-for-word.
- Humor is appropriate and needed for every single speech on every topic.

You probably disliked reading at least one of those statements. See how many of Adler and Towne's (p. 374-376) defense mechanisms went through your mind:

1. Attacking the critic > **verbal aggression** > "At least I didn't write a crappy textbook."

2. Attacking the critic > **sarcasm** > "I'm so glad you're always right, Vrooman."

3. Distorting critical information > **rationalization** > "Teachers MADE me do it that way." (Logical, but untrue)

4. Distorting critical information > **compensation** > "But I'm a good writer." (Distracting, irrelevant strength)

5. Distorting critical information > **regression** > "I'm just not ever funny." (Playing helpless)

6. Avoiding dissonant information > **physical avoidance** > ~reader skips this section of the book~

7. Avoiding dissonant information > **repression** > "La, la, la; I'm not listening!"

8. Avoiding dissonant information > **apathy**> "Who cares? Public speaking is stupid anyway."

9. Avoiding dissonant information > **displacement**> ~reader closes book, yells at the dog~

Interpersonal communication teaches us that we filter information through our emotions, which explains a great deal about why we resist persuasion. Unfortunately, to the extent that we know that (and, really, that's not exactly a surprise to you, is it?), our strategy usually is to try to get people to focus on "just the facts" and set feelings aside. This is not only impossible, but it is also a bad idea.

Greetings and Good Wishes

Gregory Bateson (1972) argues that most communication is "greetings and good wishes," or, perhaps "telling people that you are not angry with them" (p. 12). Think of the "Hi, how are you doing?" ritual when you pass others in staircases. Or, lately, just "'sup" and "'sup." Here's me (Vrooman, 2014b) demonstrating that:

CHAPTER 1

When someone stops and gives details, this is usually a problem. But if I just walked by silently, you'd assume I was mad or having a bad day, and perhaps you'd wonder if it was about you. We have the exact same conversations about nothing important with our friends and family most of the time. The conversation is important even though what makes it important is often unsaid, and the information itself is not particularly noteworthy. Gesture and posture and tone of voice often matter more than words. For Bateson, as mammals, we are not really built for information exchange. We are built for community.

What if he's right? What if human beings are fantastically poor at information processing? What if we always revert to emotion and relationship first?

This is the first reason why we often fail at communication, in everyday life and in speeches. We try to find and present information *just right*, but that might literally be the last thing on the audience's mind.

If Bateson is correct, this explains much, and his notions are supported by scholars of rhetoric and persuasion from various fields. Thousands of years ago, Aristotle (1994) posited the first multi-channel model of persuasion when he suggested that ethos (source credibility), pathos (emotion) and logos (argument) interacted equally to produce a persuasive effect. More recent multi-channel models simplify the three parts into two.

Shortcuts

The Elaboration-Likelihood Model (ELM) and Heuristic-Systematic Model (HSM), both of which emerge in the early 1980s, describe two routes of information processing, the central/systematic and peripheral/heuristic (Chaiken, 1980; Petty & Cacioppo, 1981). Central/systematic is thinking, which we would like our audience to do. Booth-Butterfield (2009a) calls this central-route thinking WATTage. Wait a few paragraphs and I'll tell you what this acronym stands for, but the metaphor is kind of cool on its own: your mind, when thinking, burns. Thinking is energy, measured in watts, like the light bulbs going off over a cartoon character's head when an idea strikes (Like lightning! More light metaphors!).

But, yeah, people don't like to do that so much. So much effort, so much energy. The peripheral route uses heuristics/cues, mental shortcuts which avoid deep thinking. Some examples are:

- source attractiveness (Petty, Kasmer, Haugtvedt, & Cacioppo, 1987),
- source voice characteristics,
- mood,
- number of arguments, (Gelinas-Chebat & Chebat, 1992),
- perceived expertise,
- length of message (Chaiken & Maheswaran, 1994),

CHAPTER 1

- consensus (whether the rest of the audience seems to be agreeing) (O'Keefe, 2008)

Thus, if you are attractive and have a long speech other people seem to like, someone might be inclined to just agree with you but wouldn't do it in any deep or lasting way.

Here's a whiteboard version of all of this:

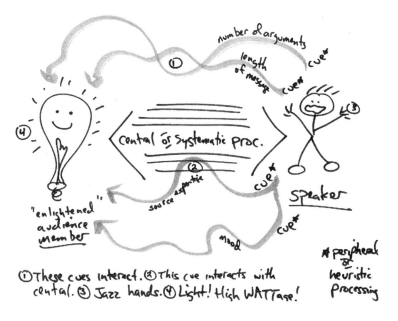

① These cues interact. ② This cue interacts with central. ③ Jazz hands. ④ Light! High WATTage!

* peripheral or heuristic processing

We are cognitive misers (Fiske & Taylor, 1991), which means that we are generally unwilling to think about things (like zombies!). We are inclined to use peripheral/ heuristic cues to judge a presentation, and a great many of those are source- and emotion-based. Two variables, our *ability to process* and our *motivation to process*, help determine to what extent we move past simple peripheral decision-making and engage our brain (Chaiken, 1987; Petty & Cacioppo, 1981). And this is what Booth-Butterfield (2009a) means by

"WATTage": "WATT" is the "willingness and ability to think" (p. 77). A bit more poetic than "ability and motivation to process," I guess, which would be the sad AMTP as an acronym. Here's his (2009b) description of our thinking under both conditions:

> When you possess both high willingness and ability to think, the light of your mind brightens to full intensity and illuminates everything in the room of your mind. With this high WATT mind, you can see details, cracks, and facets and you can contemplate them for all their nuance, subtlety, and worth.
>
> By contrast at low WATT, the light of your mind barely burns and you see less in the room of your mind. Now, you focus only on bright shiny pieces. The room of your mind is illuminated not by the light of your thinking, but by the bright light of those external ideas. You draw light from those ideas.

I wonder, reader, which your mind is doing now? All these citations in this chapter. Do they make you want to just peripherally say, "Well, sure, I guess. Probably right." That would be a low WATTage peripheral response. I guess it's hard to blame you. Or, are you really thinking about how you are thinking? If so, what tipped you over into the central/systematic route?

All of this kind of fits Bateson's ideas, but ELM and HSM researchers generally argue that any persuasion that we experience from peripheral cues (like the friendship messages Bateson cares about) will be shallow and short-lasting in comparison to systematic, central processing.

CHAPTER 1

That contradicts Bateson! Now I need some WATTage from you. Think about it: let's say I'm wearing a T-shirt for an obscure band that you happen to love. At a personal level, this might be the start of a friendship. The shirt is a cue that matters more than whatever I say in greeting. But for the ELM/HSM, it is a simple, surface-level cue that we rely on to make a judgment because listening to ideas is too hard.

Which is it?

When Victor Landa, one of the TEDx San Antonio emcees, introduced me as a speaker, his final word to the audience is that I wore really cool shoes. Here they are, my vinyl snakeskin Vans:

You have been reading (or, at least, *skimming*) my book for 29 pages now. Do the 4043 words thus far tell you more about me, or do those shoes?

I just don't think that we can discount those kinds of personal details. And that's true for Kenneth Burke (1969), who argues that *identification*, the quick, almost magical personal connection that people can make, is the most important part of persuasion. Another philosopher has argued that the basic mechanism of communication is not ideas, but the merging of the experiential horizons of people (Gadamer, 1994). We find connections between each of our personal stories.

One way to resolve this issue is to understand what kinds of experiments the HSM and ELM researchers perform. In almost every case, subjects watch a commercial or read a print advertisement. In those conditions, people are indeed cognitive misers and any relationship with the voice on the commercial is fleeting.

In the case of a speech, though, there is a chance to build at least a few minutes of a relationship between speaker and audience. Our dilemma is how to do that most effectively.

The Dilemma

Our dilemma, in a world of expanding information overload we don't really want to spend the effort to process, is to deepen our relationship enough with the audience to make them *parallel* process, to use those less intellectually deep peripheral cues to engage with the message, not retreat from it (Chaiken, 1987), but without shortchanging our central message so much so that we no longer have any content and are only in the business of entertainment.

It really is the same thing that zombie movies are able to do. Along with all the gore and scares and humor and drama, which work at the peripheral level, you have a stack of social critiques that we are willing to absorb because we are engaged with the entertainment, like the consumerism message of *Dawn of the Dead* (Romero, 1978) or the smartphone critique at the beginning of *Warm Bodies* (Levine, 2013). Only because it's funny am I willing to hear

CHAPTER 1

someone critique my phone use.

If our dilemma is to find the right HSM/ELM middle ground, to *entertain-connect* instead of *entertain-distract*, how exactly do we build that into our preparation? Is it enough to simply find various ways of asserting, "I am here. I care about this. I care about you. I need you to care about this too"? It can't be, because that only deals with the motivation to process issue. I can connect and entertain, but if I am still a cognitive miser at heart, I'll smile and think of something else while you are speaking.

How do I increase the ability to process?

The first, foundational element here is to make things simpler. But if it is all simple, I have no motivation, only ability. There is no personal or cognitive reward for paying attention. Some things have to be simple, but not all things. Just think, for a second, about how complex entertainment is. Can you tell me the character arc of the protagonist of your favorite TV show from the first season to the last? I bet you could give me a LOT of detail about Olivia Pope if you wanted to, with plenty of complexity. What is simple is a long, seemingly endless shot of grasses undulating in a lake. But when I show *Solaris* (Tarkovsky, 1972), which has such a shot, in film studies, students revolt. Motivation and ability sometimes compete.

The second, and harder element, is to understand that lack of ability to process is not the same thing as an audience who simply doesn't get it because the material is too hard. We can break it down and slow it down so that everyone can learn it, but the difficulty here involves habits of cognitive miserly thinking that reduce even the most able audiences' abilities to understand.

The trick here is with two processes Evans (1989) found in his research with how people respond to arguments. We use *selective scrutiny* to judge whether or not a conclusion or claim seems plausible, and we pay little attention to the evidence or reasoning presented. So if I argue that aliens exist, visit Earth and abduct people, you will make a quick judgment of whether that seems like a good idea or stupid idea, and then you won't listen to anything else I might say.

You can see how this is true of arguments you discount, but Evans' real contribution is with his *mental model* process. Whether I agree or disagree with the claim, I will create my own model of what premises might support that claim. So if you think the alien thing is ridiculous, you might assume I'm going to give some first-hand accounts of people you think were probably dreaming. If you think the alien thing is plausible, you might think about how many billions of stars there are and how many planets there are likely to be and the overall statistical likelihood that we are not alone in the universe, etc. All the while, you are <u>not</u> listening to my ALL! NEW! EVIDENCE! and SUPER! CREDIBLE! NARRATIVES!

It's not that we have an inability to process in general, but as Areni (2003) has found, using both the ELM and Evans, "self-generated propositions dominate" (p. 360) our thinking. *We have a hard time stopping the processing of our own ideas long enough to get to yours.*

How do I break someone out of this mental rut? The people who make commercials know part of the answer. I have to surprise or shock or give you something weird and unexpected that pushes you out of your selective scrutiny and mental modeling. This kind of thing is usually experienced as a complexity. There is something confusing, and we pay attention to figure it out. All stories and jokes begin this way.

Thus, even though we might be tempted to assume that simplicity is connected with ability and complexity with motivation, it is better to think of them as two different

CHAPTER 1

interlocking processes. Always simplicity and complexity are in tension. So are motivation and ability. Our job is to make sure we are taking care of all of those things at all times.

What you, reluctant reader, *must* understand before we move on is that such a thing is really really really hard. It is a delicate balance at the best of times, and when you add an audience full of complex and different people, it can sometimes be impossible.

Everyone seems to act as if we know exactly how to do it. And yet you've likely spent your life only pretending to listen to them.

But before you close the book on this first chapter on failure, here's something for those of you feeling like failures, feeling hopeless. Rich Petty came up with the ELM as an undergraduate political science major while he was taking a psychology class for fun (Booth-Butterfield, 2011). It became the central research project of his later academic life and he's convinced us all that his ideas have merit. That's a lot of WATTage from a lot of people. Persuasion is possible. But it is never easy.

THE ZOMBIE GUIDE TO PUBLIC SPEAKING

Chapter 2: Anxiety

Max Brooks (quoted in Eaton, 2006) is scared of zombies, so he writes about them:

> They scare me more than any other fictional creature out there because they break all the rules. Werewolves and vampires and giant sharks, you have to go look for them. My attitude is if you go looking for them, no sympathy. But zombies come to you. Zombies don't act like a predator; they act like a virus, and that is the core of my terror. A predator is intelligent by nature, and knows not to overhunt its feeding ground. A virus will just continue to spread, infect and consume, no matter what happens. It's the mindlessness behind it. (p. 57)

I think communication anxiety is exactly like this when you feel it. It's a kind of irrational creeping thing that slowly surrounds you and makes the few tools you have for fighting it off seem paltry in comparison to the simple vast, dumb weight of it.

Whether you call it speaking anxiety, communication apprehension, or stage fright, the majority of people experience it to some extent. In research on thousands of college students over almost half a century, McCroskey and his various colleagues have found that 70% had either high or moderately high anxiety. Only 5% have low anxiety (Richmond & McCroskey, 1995).

This is a big issue. For many of you, it is THE issue.

I teach college classes and was a competitive public speaker who put himself through school with a debate scholarship and money from speech contests. But still, before every semester begins, the night before the first day of classes, I need to watch horror movies, about zombies especially, to be able to sleep. I have had vivid nightmares my entire life, so I am used to dreams where the monsters are after me. I can sleep through them[1]. But the ones about showing up in the wrong class, having forgotten my pants or my books, etc., *those* are the ones that keep me up at 3am.

Some experience this anxiety to such an extent that it affects the choices they make in their lives and careers. I've had students whose sweat would geyser out of the glands on their forehead, have to visit the trashcan to vomit before speaking, or wear additional padding for anti-urine protection. I've had students who could finish their speeches only when a friend in class came up and stood beside them.

The *MOPSBOTS* (time out: do you remember what that acronym stands for, Cognitive Miser?) have a generally anemic answer to this problem. Here are some sample suggestions for overcoming your nerves:

Grice & Skinner (1998):
> Know how you react to stress. Know your strengths and weaknesses. Know speech principles. Know it looks worse from the inside. Know your speech. Believe in your topic. View speech making positively. Project confidence. Test your message. Practice. Learn from experience.

Lucas (2001):
> Acquire speaking experience. Prepare. Think positively. Visualize. Know that most nervousness

---

[1] I kind of look forward to them. Does that make me weird?

is not visible. Don't expect perfection.

Sprague & Stuart (2000):
Put your fear in perspective. Prepare and practice. Use relaxation techniques. Use positive self-suggestion. Seek professional help.

Fraleigh & Tuman (2009):
Select a topic you know and enjoy. Start preparing early. Take care of yourself. Visualize success. Use relaxation techniques. Volunteer to speak first.

There are some good ideas there (volunteer to speak first) and some scary ones (seek professional help), but I think most people would look at that list and conclude, "That's not enough!"

It's not. Most people face some level of speaking fear all their lives. If projecting confidence was so easy, we'd all do it, right? And often our jobs ask us to speak with little preparation time on things we don't care that much about. What then?

The most pernicious element here is the faulty causal equation made by teachers and bloggers and coaches who know that:

But that doesn't mean that the reverse is true:

This is the mistake made by people who are in the middle

of the normal curve of anxiety described by McCroskey, and a lot of them wrote *MOPSBOTS*. There are two problems with this. First, causality doesn't work that way. Just because watching depressing movies might make you sad does not mean that watching happy movies will make you feel better. Second, the assumption behind how the diagram works is wrong. The anxiety caused by lack of preparation is *additional* to the normal level of anxiety that seems to always be there, the tip of an iceberg of nerves:

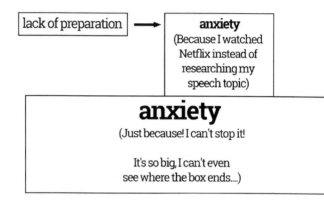

It frustrates me that preparation is the dominant suggestion in the *MOPSBOTS* lists and in innumerable "How To Fix Speaking Anxiety in 7 Steps!" blog posts that swipe from them, because it betrays a lack of understanding and empathy about how anxiety works. And if it connects with depression, as in the next chapter, they have even less to teach us. I had a student once who would do all the work, but because, in the end, she was sure it wasn't perfect, would toss it and come to class nervous and "unprepared."

Although Dan Roam (2014) suggests that "worry dissolves instantly on contact with planning" (p. 242) and draws pictures of anxiety being drowned with a bucket or

CHAPTER 2

hiptossed away by a zen guru, we know that's not the whole story.[2]

In a lifetime working on speaking anxiety for myself and others, and in my years working with thousands of nervous students, I have found two things that work better than most. The rest of this chapter outlines them. But often the trick comes from the outside. I make students do ridiculous things in front of class. I make people fail, repeatedly, publicly. And we have a good, or, at least, not the *worst* time doing it. Students participate because I make them. If you can find someone who can make you do some things to push you out of your comfort zone, it makes it easier, like the lifeguards at kids' swimming lessons who push or drop the kids off the diving board because they just can't choose to do it on their own. If you can be your own lifeguard on this, more power to you, but maybe, like in the old game show, it's time to phone a friend.[3]

Until then, try one of these . . .

---

[2] He does admit that planning "doesn't actually remove the psychological roots of worry," which is good, but he assumes that preparation can "replace anxiety with meaningful action" (p. 242), which is not really the case. The fact that he calls it "worry" instead of "fear" or "anxiety" is telling. Worry is a kind of anticipation of bad outcomes. And sure, anxiety has that element, too. But I'll bet if I could do a science fiction-y experiment on you and have you stand up to give a speech while I controlled your mouth and body and made you perform a perfect speech you still wouldn't want to go up there and do it with everyone looking at you. If you are high enough on the anxiety scale, you still wouldn't like it!

[3] Some activities you might do to create a push here are outlined in a continuing series in my blog entitled "Activities for Anxious Speakers, Part x" (Vrooman, 2015c). There is a search box on the blog if you want to find the whole series.

Channel Your Nervous Energy

First, it is important to see your nervousness as not only inevitable, but as a valuable source of energy. My old theater/calculus (!) teacher in high school, Joe Parrish, used to say that if you weren't nervous, your performance would be dead. And I think this is true. My fears about the beginning of the semester make me care and make me a better teacher. At a simple level, we know that passionate energy is one of the keys to good delivery, and nervousness is the most reliable source of that energy.

At a deeper level, your nervousness is about the audience. You are worried about their reaction to you, their eyes on you, their judgment. But isn't that exactly what Bateson and Burke and Gadamer would say it should all be about, a connection with the audience as people? Your nervousness is your willingness to open up to that experience.

And that experience *has* to be scary, or it is not authentic. Peter Kenny (1982), writing about what he considered the abysmal state of speaking skills in the fields of science and engineering, suggests that the problem is that we flee from our nervousness instead of embracing the "intense awareness" (p. 37) that is the gift our nervousness provides:

> As you sit awaiting your turn to speak you can feel your heart beating faster than normal. Your stomach quivers with 'butterflies'. Your mouth may feel dry, or, alternatively may be producing an excess of saliva. The room feels warm: you may be breaking out in a sweat. You have a repeated desire to swallow. All these symptoms are

> perfectly normal. Your body is preparing itself to deal with an important event demanding your full concentration and capabilities. This is what is happening and this is what you must tell yourself is happening. Accept the feelings as a natural process; let them happen. (p. 34)

This is your body giving you the energy you need to go into battle. Do not waste it!

The real problem for those of us who get nervous is the way we deal with that anxiety. We close down. We read our speeches word-for-word. We read the slides off our Power Points with our backs to the room. We kill all of those potential places we can connect with the audience, those places that scare us. Instead of giving them the opportunity to reject us, we reject them first, like an awkward teen drama. This leads to a terrible speech experience for all. And it cements our nervousness because of those bad experiences, and our new certainty, each time, that we really suck at public speaking.

Kenny (1982) describes this kind of failed confidence game of reading or memorizing word-for-word as superficially "fluent" but "isolating," "oblivious," and "boring" (p. 73). As an engineer, he doesn't comment on it when he calls this kind of thing "insulated," but I think there is a useful electrical metaphor there. An insulated wire is a safe wire. You cannot be shocked when you touch it. But that means it also cannot transmit any electricity. But if you are a public speaker that's why you are here!

So how do we stay in communion with our nervous energy? For each of us, channeling that energy will look different. Here are a few examples of ways I've seen it done successfully:

- A faculty member who had to present an idea for discussion at a faculty meeting (notoriously contentious places) began with, "Ooh, it's just as scary up here as I thought." She made repeated, good-humored references, in response to aggressive questioning, to her nervousness: "See, that's why I wanted someone else on the committee to do this instead of me." And when she finished, a "Phew, I did it. -----'s turn next time!"
- A professor of mine, Fred Corey, used to take a deep breath before each public presentation, an ostentatious inhalation with bobbing shoulders. Then he would exhale, open his eyes, smile, and begin. He told us that while he did that he imagined his breath expanding into the room and taking with it this store of his nervous energy that he then transferred to his audience.
- Many students begin with humor or a dramatic story, not just to get the attention of the audience, but to dissipate their own nervousness. One, in particular, began an informative speech about the birth process of cattle by pulling on an over-the-elbow glove that she wears when she, in her words, "has to reach up in there and turn the head," while demonstrating the movement with her arm. The audience laughed, and she used the most embarrassing thing she had to talk about first so that she could take off the glove, laugh with them, and offer it to someone in the front row, who declined.

CHAPTER 2

Forget Performance

Second, it is important to think about speaking as a communication task, not a performance task. Michael Motley (1997) innovated this approach in his work with the extremely, clinically nervous speaker. Focus on the information, the idea goes, and teaching it to an audience who might need to learn it, not a performance that involves them looking at you, like a trained seal, reading or reciting things from memory. In a communication situation, you can't mess up. You could trip over the podium and everyone would remember what you were saying for the rest of their lives.

In other words, make what you are doing a conversation between actual people, not a show in front of a faceless crowd. Do not look over their heads, as someone once told you. Do not imagine them in their underwear. Focus on them, specifically, and who they really are. See if they are getting the point. Stop and explain it again or argue in a different way if they don't. I never let students stop when they get into a difficulty and ask me, "Can I start over?" Of course not. Your audience just saw all of that. There is no do-over they didn't already see. Don't pretend they are not there. You don't get another take.

At least once a semester I will have a student blank, stop talking and then find himself/herself unable to continue. It's like an evil magic spell had been cast. Usually this student won't flee from the room, although that has happened. Usually this student will just stand there, getting red-faced, unable to continue. Every time I help them fix it. I call the student by name until she/he looks up at me. And then I don't tell them they are doing fine or that everything is going to be okay, because we all know that would be a lie. I remind them of what they had just been talking about and ask them a question about it. Half of the time the student asks if they can sit down and stop. I tell them no and ask again about their content. Eventually, with enough questions, they answer, even if just out of annoyance with me. After answering me, they can continue. Sometimes they need a few more questions from me to prod them along the way, but everyone in my classes always finishes.

Since the first edition of this book was published, though, this has not happened once. I require this book for classes I teach where students give speeches. And no one has needed to stop. I interpret that as evidence that this chapter helps. This may be a *post hoc* fallacy, to look ahead to Chapter 14, but it is possible that this chapter already cured you of the possibility that such a stop-in-the-middle might happen to you. Come on. Believe it. ☺

Formerly "America's #1 Business Speaker," "Sell the Sizzle" guru Elmer Wheeler (1957) began his career in the spotlight with heavy nerves. His secret was: "Never let anything get between you and the other person. The closer you are to people, the less fear you'll have, and the more courage you'll gain" (p. 40). In a living room with friends he was comfortable, but from behind a podium or conference table, he wasn't.

What all this says is that even the most paralyzing nervousness will fail to the insistent pressure of another human being who wants the information. Find someone in the audience who will provide that for you if the worst happens. Just talk to that one person for a minute until you can pull it together. Or take a breath, stop, and ask someone where you were before you lost your way. Better still, focus, in all of your practice, and throughout your speech, on getting the ideas across to a real set of people in the room with you, and you will make it.

Don't let them remain a faceless zombie horde. Make

that human connection.

Conclusion

I'm not saying you will enjoy speaking. It really is okay that you never will. You can hate speaking, your speech, this book, me, the world, stupid zombie references, and your $%*&*#@?#$!! Power Point. And it will be fine if you hate all of those things in every speech for the rest of your life.

But you can still get it done.

Every few weeks on Twitter, something like this shows up and gets heavily retweeted.

> Kids with broken legs don't have to do PE, but kids with anxiety have to take speech class. There's something wrong here.

I hate this (Vrooman, 2014a). I have two arguments with it. First, it oversimplifies anxiety into this unchangeable thing which can never get better and just sits there encased in plaster, unmoving, while you drag it around. Second, it gives anxious and depressed speakers this feeling that they are an oppressed minority in a sea of happy extroverts. Here is the amateurish cartoon I created to demonstrate this:

OMG!! Nervous!!!!

LOLZ! Speaking!! W00t!!!

But, really, McCroskey's numbers tell us something totally different. The world really looks like this:

Hey, speaking is rad! Trust me! I blog! Just practicevisualizebreathe and #WIN!!!

Let's all hate this together! Yay us!!!

We are all over here in a clump of people who don't love this. But it's okay. We're all cool over here. Let's sing our collective songs of failure and, as Dory says in *Finding Nemo*, just keep swimming (Stanton & Unkrich, 2003).

And after listening to over 3000 students give over 25,000 speeches, I am pretty sure that you, in all your nerves

CHAPTER 2

and hatred and dark Sith-y emotions (That's a *Star Wars* reference; don't judge) over there on the right in that cartoon, you will have a bigger impact on your audiences than the 5% who give speeches without a whisper of nervousness. I've seen it over and over again.

If the secret to speaking success, according to Chapter 1, is making that human connection, well, you've already got something in common with 95% of the people out there. Use it.

THE ZOMBIE GUIDE TO PUBLIC SPEAKING

CHAPTER 3

Chapter 3: Depression

Let's see: Failure. Anxiety. Depression. I think this book is going well so far, don't you?

I have never seen a public speaking book with a chapter on this subject. None of my *MOPSBOTS* even talks about the issue at all! Although there are thousands of studies on anxiety and public speaking, there are only a few about depression and other mood issues and how they interact with the fears and feelings of failure that many of us associate with giving a speech.

You might feel like skipping this chapter because this doesn't apply to you. You're not depressed, have never been depressed, etc. You might even feel self-righteous about what you think: "Happiness is a choice! Why can't people see that?" Get through the first four paragraphs before you give up on this. I'll bet there's some stuff in here that feels familiar. Some depression is long-term and biologically based, yes, but we can all experience the negative self-talk that is at the core of many kinds of depression in smaller and more fleeting ways, especially when confronted with the stress that speech-giving can provoke, especially in the professional world, where you will rarely give a speech for which your entire competence and reputation are not on the line.

I have taught a lot of students who struggled with depression. Although you can perform well in many tasks while depressed, public speaking seems to be an area where it can come unglued for folks who are managing it in other areas of life.

The *DSM* tells us that in any 6-12 month period, 2-5% of adolescents are depressed (American Psychiatric Association, 2013), that equates to 20% who experience a depressive episode at least once during high school

(Gillham & Reivich, 2004). It's 7% for adults. Depression is also difficult to figure out. The last time I was depressed, I didn't "know it" for months. I was just distant and angry and everything pissed me off. So we might not even know it is happening. We just know that if we have to give one more damn speech to that stupid room full of stupid people, we're gonna start flipping tables. For some people depression is a long-term challenge, and for others it comes and goes. Some, like Allie Brosh (2013), end up curled up in the corner while they tell themselves things like, "Do you want to play a game? The game is called Stand In A Corner And Look Stupid. Ready? YOU WIN" (p. 109-110), for a time, but feel like a blank and emotionally void computer at other times. It has different and shifting forms and demands.

This chapter is not about providing a solution to help improve your depression. How could a book chapter do that? I encourage you to seek help if you need it. I have seen many students who thought they would always be "that way" better able to manage after some kind of professional help.

This chapter is designed as a supplement to that. It is about finding enough of a push through the immobility at the heart of many depressive episodes to allow for the completion of a task we can't avoid, a tactic *Prozac Nation*'s Wurtzel (2002) managed to practice, occasionally, as a college student. Ideally, we'd find ways to get better. Ideally, getting better would be, well, *faster*. But in a non-ideal world, sometimes we just need to find ways to get things done.

It is not easy to figure out how to do that. The things we do to help speakers with their anxiety are not necessarily helpful for speakers with depression. This is a problem. Even though there are connections between anxiety and depression, and you may very well have both, the experience of how anxiety interacts with public speaking is very different than how depression interacts with it.

The structures of anxiety and depression are different. Witt, Roberts and Behnke (2008) found that this is how the two things differ and graphed it thus:

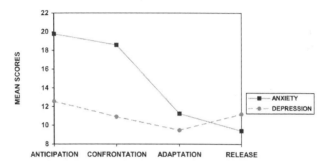

Figure 1. Patterns of Anxiety and Depression at Public Speaking Milestones

The heights (y-axis levels) of the lines represent the amount of, say, "badness" you feel. The "confrontation" moment is when you start the speech. Anxious speakers (the solid line) feel better from the moment they start, and at "release," which is when they finish, they feel even better. Finally done! Whew! However, depressed speakers (the dotted line), who never felt quite as bad as the anxious speakers did, have a bump up in "bad feelings" after the speech is over that anxious speakers do not. Witt, Roberts and Behnke interpret this moment as "Just as I expected – I knew I couldn't do it" (p. 226).

Perhaps that continues to build across time. If you imagine a sequence of speeches over the course of a semester or your first year on a job and continue that graph to the right, we could imagine that the anxious speaker's bad self-talk line likely has a high point that just gets lower and lower on the y-axis in the "anticipation" phase until it is mostly manageable over time. That's how I feel about my speeches after 30 years of practice. It's still there, but I can deal with it. Research has long shown that almost any form of practice helps to reduce anxiety levels. In fact, that finding is so clear that they haven't done that much work on the issue since the early 80s (Black & Martin, 1980; Glaser, 1981).

We can imagine that for a depressed speaker, the "release" level of bad feeling, which is almost back up to where it was for "anticipation," quickly returns to the top. I imagine the chart expanding to the left, say a week or two before the speech. The anxious speaker is likely not all that amped up yet, but the depressed speaker might be. There may be a steady state of negative self-talk interrupted by a few moments of actual speech-giving which distract.

I posted a draft of this chapter to social media for feedback. One student had this to say about the graph and my interpretations of it:

> I connect with a lot of this, but the graph doesn't quite resonate with me because although I'm very anxious, depression has always been higher than anxiety for me (a "more bad" experience? not sure how to phrase that in terms of the axes). Even so, like other high anxiety scorers, I still feel much better after I've completed a task like speaking or writing, for a short period of time, and then, whether I've processed the thing as having gone well or badly, I get the blank computer feeling. Thinking the thing went okay only changes the feeling "I suck" to "I will always feel sucky even if I don't suck." So my graph would be a lot more up and down, and my

CHAPTER 3

> experience of depression isn't dependent upon negative self-talk. The really cool thing, though, is that I hadn't yet explicitly processed some of that. So it's helpful data whether or not it's 100% describing a student's experience.
>
> Also, I don't know if this is true for anyone else, but my experience working on group speeches/papers has always been completely different. Working with people drastically changes things for me and might also be worth exploring as a suggestion for students that are struggling.

So maybe your own individual graph is unique, as well, like a fingerprint? Thinking about its details can help.

Another early reader of this chapter, who has struggled with depression herself, commented: "Perhaps more dreading, leading to procrastination, leading to feelings of failure, and, more than likely, actual failure due to the lack of prep. Depression and procrastination go hand-in-hand, I've long felt." Yet another reader expanded on this idea:

> I just wonder if maybe you could add a little to the procrastination topic? Mostly to incorporate the whole "I can't get out of bed" part of depression, those episodes are the worst and sometimes all you can do are just make a simple checklist and try to celebrate doing the most basic of things. It isn't procrastination it's just...shit hitting the shitter...like the best example for what I mean is the worst speech I ever gave in my entire college career just getting the bare minimum done was all I could do because on a personal level my friends and family were more concerned with "have you

> eaten, taken your medication, showered etc." that doing a speech over vampires was practically impossible. As you know I failed spectacularly on that one, but I did it, and the main thing is that sometimes you will fail spectacularly but that doesn't define you because you at least did it. I don't know if any of that made sense, but adding something like that about little goals and little victories is another thing that could help students.

Others had similar comments. The procrastination connection really struck a chord with people. For me, my depressions are kind of a secret to myself until I start procrastinating at levels that are orders of magnitude more than my usual. It really is the first marker for me. I also think I've seen all of this in my students.

A study by Cocker and associates (2014) on the impact of depression in the workplace suggests keeping people at work and engaged (even with a lowered workload) is better for the person and the company than time off work. Depression might get easier if you make yourself stay engaged? Okay, but many people experience depression, at least when tasks (like speeches) are approaching as "an unexplained and prolonged lack of motivation" (Gardner, 2003, p. 30). If this happens to you, you might already have had the feeling that here's yet another thing you are doing wrong. You notice the lack of motivation and procrastination and then use that as further fuel for negative self-talk.

For many depressed students in my teaching experience, something like a speech seems to weigh as a

CHAPTER 3

larger and larger task as it approaches[1]. It seems more and more insurmountable and so, well, why bother working on it? Or, as Klibert and associates (2014) put it: "I'm a failure" and "I cannot escape my fate" (p. 75). Assuming that there is not an option in school or profession to NOT give that particular speech, we are in a particular dilemma whereby the kind of thinking that would lead to a more positive outcome is circumvented by a depressive state of mind which foils such thinking. The workload which must be reduced is subjective and changeable, but it seems to only grow the more you think about it. Perhaps this is a familiar feeling, reader? It does seem like the structure of catch-22 people who suffer with depression report in other elements of life. This cycle is so difficult to break that researchers in Sweden have found a generalized statistical link between lower GPAs and depression but admit that they can't tell

---

[1] I find that in my Senior Thesis class, where students work all semester on a project, is particularly conducive to this kind of thing. In many other classes I have fairly large assignments with a small amount of allotted work time, much less than they might get with another instructor. I find that 1) most students procrastinate anyway, so I'm not really taking much away from them, and 2) I've seen dozens of my students who struggle with depression excel at those quick assignments. There just isn't time for their negative self-talk to build to the semester-long project's epic levels. I'm not sure how this would help you, as this is more a message to managers and professors out there, but perhaps a way through would be to *own* your procrastination enthusiastically in some way? Plan for it. Set the right date and time to begin. You are smart enough to know how much time it will take. Write down the time you will begin work and leave yourself alone about it as much as you can! Then do something else. You are allowed. This book said you could! If it turns out that you were wrong and didn't leave enough time, and your performance is less-than-stellar, well, lesson learned. Adjust for next time. You are a performance system. We are not all Hondas that last forever or McLarens that go real fast. You might be my first car, my grandmother's 1978 Toyota Corona. You never knew when it would start. Kind of a pain. But it all ended up okay.

which is the cause and which is the effect (Jonsson et al., 2012). The likely answer is a knotty interaction that seems inescapable.

Obviously some people are helped, at times, by various forms of therapy and/or medication. But what about in the moment when you need to prepare this speech that is freaking you out and your current therapy and/or meds don't seem to be helping quite enough to get you over the hump? Here are a few options:

The ABCs

The Penn/ABC model has a lot of experimental support, and for a lot of people, it is a very effective tool in their therapeutic journey. But there are plenty of studies where it just doesn't work (for reviews of the research, see Gilham & Reivich, 2007; Nehmy, 2010). My advice is to try it. If it doesn't work, move on to something else (but it's not *you* failing if it doesn't work!).

This model, the Penn Resiliency Program (Gilham & Reivich, 2004), is based on Ellis' (1962) *ABC* model, which, if you've had some intervention for your depression before, you've likely seen. *A* is an activating event. Let's call it this speech you are going to give or just gave. *C* is the consequences. The *A* does not directly cause the *C*. There is a *B* that mediates or processes the *A*. The *B* is our thoughts and beliefs about the *A*. Those might be super-negative and seemingly indestructible, as we discussed in the previous section of this chapter. The first goal is to learn that you are not experiencing the "reality" you think you are. The second is to understand how negative and self-sabotaging those *B* thoughts can be. Here's an example of how this works:

> PRP participants learn the ABC model through the

use of three-panel cartoons, in which they are presented with an adversity and the emotional consequences, and they must fill in a thought bubble with a belief that fits the logic of ABC. For example, in one cartoon, the first frame depicts a student being handed back a test that shows many incorrect items. The third frame shows that he is feeling extremely sad. The adolescents are asked to identify what the boy might be saying to himself that is causing him to feel extremely sad (e.g., "I'm stupid" or "I'll never do well in this class," etc.). After working through a series of these cartoons, the students practice identifying their own self-talk in situations from their lives and then identifying the emotions and behaviors that their self-talk generates. (Gilham & Reivich, 2004, p. 154-5)

So will this work for you? Here is a zombie version of the three-panel strip to try out:

Another way to do this is to test the accuracy of your own B thoughts about your speeches. To do this, VIDEO RECORD YOURSELF. I know. *I know.* I can hear you groaning through the page. Either give a speech to your iPhone and then watch it, or have a friend record a speech you give for class or in a professional context. Watch it. Grade it. If you are in school, use the rubric your instructor will grade you on. Or make up a different one related to what seems to count as a good speech in your professional environment. Now grade yourself.

The next step, if you are in school, is easy. Compare this graded rubric to the one your teacher returns to you.

Stop it.

I heard that.

Your teacher is not going easy on you. It's not just because they "like" you if they graded you higher than you thought you deserved. Hey, wait a minute! If they are giving you inflated, fake grades because they think you are cool, well, then, why not just keep giving the darn speeches? This is school! Who said you have to like it?

If you invited a business colleague you trust to evaluate your speech for you, you might have the same conversation with yourself. Then find someone you *don't* like at work. I know, right? We *always* love all of our colleagues, so this will be a hard person to find.   :/

The scary part here is that although I am confident that if you are still reading this chapter willingly you will be harder on yourself than they are, what if you give yourself a C and they give you a D or F? Now you KNOW FOR SURE that you suck and everyone hates you, right? You can predict exactly what those *B*s in the 3-panel comic will sound like. But I will bet that the grades are not the same. For example, you might hate the way your stupid arm looks hanging stupidly at your stupid side like you are stupid. But they didn't say anything about it. Maybe you thought your topic was extra-stupid or your introduction was boring or you look like a freak. Maybe they, instead, wrote about how you forgot to cite your sources and how that background on your Power Point, which you thought looked so cool, was kind of distracting. It's okay if they have real criticism of you. It is okay for you to criticize yourself.

What is not okay is if you are not accurate.

Becoming a more accurate self-evaluator will help. It will help that line on the page 51 graph stop going up so high afterwards.

I Still Feel Like a Failure, Vrooman

Yeah, I get that. The thing about all of these therapies is that each person responds differently. Look at the list of all the things you might try on the *beyondblue* website (find the link in the Reference List at the end of this book under Jorm et al., 2009). ACT is different than CBT, which is different than MBCT. If you've had a lot of these therapies before and still feel like you, in the words of the Internet, "can't even," you should check it out and see if there's something new.

I have another suggestion for you that has worked for many of my students in the past: the "failure" theme of Chapter 1. If the audience isn't going to like it no matter what, then why put so much effort into it? The effort, in these cases, is often mental: the vast worrying over just the right opening line to use, the paralyzing indecision over what font to use on a Power Point with that particular audience, etc. Cutting back on that mental effort is important. The more the thoughts are directed outward, at a presumed audience who will hate you unless you unlock the secret to doing what they want (this is called *socially prescribed perfectionism*), the worse it gets:

> socially prescribed perfectionists are paralyzed by perceived failures, ultimately inhibiting access to important psychological resources (e.g., positive

> reappraisal) that promote the desire and ability to overcome adverse conditions. (Klibert et al., 2014, p. 79)

Perhaps *giving up* on the audience is a key to help unlock your potential here.

This reminds me of my students the first time they saw *Frozen* (Buck & Lee, 2013). We've all seen enough toddlers lip-syncing "Let It Go" for the film to have lost its power, but initially, Elsa's shift from "be the good girl you always have to be" to "I don't care what they're going to say" brought some of my students to tears. For one student, Elsa's power and this song perfectly encapsulated her struggles with depression and mental illness. Her version of "Let It Go" was to mutter "Fuck it! Fuck it! Fuck it!" privately before her speeches started. She had done sooooo much work. Her content was always great. However, the additional work of pleasing her perceived audience was simply too much. She had to . . . let it go.

Get the audience out of your head.

You might think they hate you. So what? Sawyer and associates (2010) did a giant study in Australia that, in my mind, supports this approach. They performed a huge anti-depression intervention that was associated with creating a better supportive environment at the schools. It didn't work. There are lots of reasons why this might have happened. But maybe one of them is that, in the end, your depression is yours. It doesn't matter if the people around you are supportive or not, sometimes. It doesn't help.

Maybe being surrounded by an audience you think hates you doesn't matter either? Really, if the whole audience gave you a standing ovation and cheered you on and had you autograph their speech outlines and took selfies with you they Instagrammed with #MicDrop

CHAPTER 3

#PublicSpeakingRockStar #WeAreAllWitnesses, wouldn't you think it was all crap anyway? Even if they just say, "Good job," afterwards, don't you really just think they are totally full of shit? If a good audience won't help, a bad audience doesn't hurt.

Give up on them.

Stop trying to please them.

They are ignorant and need to learn your information. What the hell do they know, anyway? I mean, literally, what do they know?

Realistically, they probably will like your speech, but it won't matter to you. Screw it. Assume they will hate you. Feed off of it.

I have occasional Twitter conversations with people who hate giving speeches. Here's a section of one such conversation I had:

> @MoreBrainz: "Plow through it. 's ok to hate every minute. Just get to the end."

> Person X: "I have to give it in front of a group that think they know the subject matter better than the lecturer they are dicks"
>
> @MoreBrainz: "Almost all audiences think that all the time. Don't you, usually? Give em 1 tiny new thing. That's all u can expect w/ any grp."

This person's speech turned out fine. Good enough that they immediately followed me on Twitter, so I can't be totally full of it. I gave permission to blow off the stressful audience, and it worked.

Ultimately, I have little faith in the power of practice and optimism for a person whose depression is interacting with their public speaking. Instead, I have seen that the realization that most speeches are failures, that audiences really are mostly bored by most things and that your speech is not a special failure, but yet another brick in the wall of the collective waste-of-time that is much of social life, really does help many in these situations. *We need to feel free to not try to hoist the unliftable weight of success.*

We, like zombies, are shuffling through an apocalypse of our own devising when we are depressed. We keep drawing the picture of that apocalypse anew as we talk to ourselves and imagine the outcomes. But if we're always, already going to lose, why not give one last doomed shuffle into the mall? Your audience is barricaded against you. They might even blow you away. But, really, did you have something better to do?

CHAPTER 3

Conclusion

I have outlined two almost opposite approaches finding a way to get through speeches when you aɪ depressed. It is likely neither of these will really work for you. That's fine. If they are opposite, there are probably bunches of things in between these options that would be better. Try something, and don't give up.

If it works, let me know. Maybe your idea will help somebody in the third edition of this book. At the very least, I'll put it on my blog, where it will help tens of people. ;)

GUIDE TO PUBLIC SPEAKING

CHAPTER 4

Chapter 4: Ditch Your Speech

Remember Chapter One, you cognitive miser? The message thus far is that we need to get our audiences to parallel process by making a personal connection with them that will help them make the leap from the simple, fun and exciting things we use to get their attention and motivate them to the more complex kinds of thoughts that will actually teach them something or change their minds about something important.

This is hard. Especially when we are nervous. But to manage our nervousness we need to make real connections to the audience as people and focus on how to get our information across, not on performing some good-looking show.

This is the first place we can begin to be optimistic. Those are the *same* things. What is good for you and your nerves is also good for achieving your interactional goal – personal connections.

We never do that, do we? Instead, our answer to the content question is to write out the whole speech and/or memorize it. Our answer to our nerves is to do the same thing. But that is the *opposite* of what we should do!

For Wheeler (1957), his best practice was to throw out the first three pages of his manuscript. He was sure an audience would see a thick speech and sneak out the side exits. The written-out speech manuscript gets between you and your audience. If you put it on note cards you can (and I've seen it done!) literally raise them up as a shield between you and them. Or, if you read word-for-word from sections of Power Point, you can turn your back. Kenny (1982) argues that reading or memorizing a speech destroys "the conviction of the moment," which is "what gives a speech life and holds the attention of an audience more than anything else" (p. 25). He wants your words to be "full of feeling" as you speak them, not the remembered feelings produced by reading or memorization.[1]

Kenny further argues that you cannot adapt to audience questions or comments very effectively if you are reading or performing a memorized speech. And isn't that how you would help them learn? Isn't lack of adaptability the classic mistake made in zombie movies? In *Zombi 2* (Fulci, 1979), the audience always groans at the long scene where the husband just stares at his now zombie wife as she approaches. It's not like this is the first zombie he's seen. When I showed this movie, the audience yelled at him here. Of course he gets munched. And what zombie movie doesn't end with a hastily choreographed escape from a formerly safe place? You've got to be flexible. As we're told in *Zombieland* (Fleischer, 2009), you've got to have cardio. You've got to keep moving to escape. Allow yourself that ability.

More than attention and questions, though, this kind of speaking is really about facilitating the learning of your content. Mills (1977), whose handbook was designed to teach engineering teachers and trainers how to do it more effectively, suggests that the norm is that trainees want to 1) take part in the lesson by turning it into a discussion, and, 2) find ways to re-sort your material into patterns that fit the way they know they learn best. How are we to do that if we race along with our blunt, pre-planned fully-scripted speech?

---

[1] Are you remembering that his book is a guide for engineers talking to other engineers? Careful of your stereotypes and snap judgments about the nature of the "real world".

CHAPTER 4

Extemporaneous Speaking

What we want is extemporaneous speaking, which is speaking off-the-cuff, or speaking which is largely improvised based on a set of brief notes.

You are really *there* doing the talking, not robotically reading a paper, and they are really there, feeling more compelled to listen since what they see in front of them is a real person. In many speaking classes, I have students get up every day and speak. The speeches are short and usually about simple things the students know the answers to easily (hometown, favorite movie, which is best: pie or cake?). The delivery is warm and interesting and engaging. But then when they have to give big, researched, graded speeches, out comes the manuscript and away goes the interesting person that we had all gotten to know.

Perhaps you have suffered through lectures like those of Professor Binns, the ghost teacher at Hogwarts, who died years ago but keeps coming back to read the same lectures decade after decade (Rowling, 1999). Which teachers have you liked best? Which teachers in your life taught you the most? No one who read their notes or Power Point word-for-word, I guarantee.

We know, intuitively, that avoiding this is the best way to speak, but knowing that is not the same as gathering the courage to do it.

In my experience, it seems that there are two separate but interlocking fears here.

The first is that sometimes we are just afraid of eye contact. We are afraid of looking at the audience. Reading the speech is a convenient excuse for avoiding that. If this is your fear, go back and reread Chapter 2.

The second is the fear that you will forget your place in the speech or forget what you are going to say. This is a more complex fear to deal with. But this fear chains you to the performance mentality that causes such problems with anxiety (again, reread Chapter 2, the final section). And, in fact, this is a kind of paradox, since you can *only* lose your place if you are reading word-for-word. If you are speaking from an outline, it is ridiculously easy to find where you are, since there is not much there.

We need to relearn how to outline, so that we have the confidence that when we need it to remind us what is next, we have faith in it.

None of this means you should "wing it" or not prepare. Outlining only works if you research and practice enough to feel confident.

Repurposing the Outline

Most of us have learned how to outline in two ways, both of which are counterproductive to public speaking. The first is the passive outline, as you take down notes when teachers teach. The second is the active outline, where you sketch out the basic form of your arguments before the first draft of a paper. But neither of these forms will help you at the podium. Let's call what we want a *working* or *coordinating* outline.

On the next page is a section of what it should look like:

CHAPTER 4

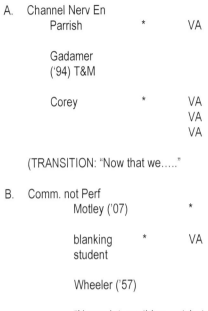

Make sure it is all big enough to see! This works on paper or an electronic device.

I like to use a table format. Here's how to understand each column:

The first two are the basic pieces of the speech. For a speech I might call "The 3 Biggest Challenges in Public Speaking," this is the first of those challenges, the first main point, with the two subpoints, the two ways to reduce anxiety. There are no definitions, no sentences. You should know enough about the meaning of "Communication Not Performance" that you don't have to write down an explanation (or worse, a dictionary.com definition!) that will distract you, get you lost in the outline, and make you want to start reading. If you don't know enough, go back and do more research/more practice.

I have added a reminder to do a transition between the points, as I sometimes forget them (more on those in Chapter 5), but I'm not going to write it all out because every word on the outline is a distraction tempting you to fail, so I will be conservative.

The third column is the supporting material. I have citations for sources (Cite everything! Verbally! Always! Use your outline to help you remember. [More on this later]). I only write out what information I might forget, like Gadamer's book title. I know my Joe Parrish story very well, so I don't have to write out anything. I just see "Parrish" and then I can look up and tell the story. I will be interesting when I do so. And if I stumble over a word, it won't matter. And it certainly will be better than a monotone reading of my memory to you word-for-word. I included the quote from Wheeler because I like the way he phrases it. Otherwise there is *no reason to quote!* Quotes force you to read and are generally not worth it. More on this will be covered in Part Three.

The fourth column is about time and audience adaptation. I put stars next to all the things I HAVE to cover to make my point. If it gets a star, it is worth telling. If it doesn't get a star, I can eliminate it from my speech if I am running short of time, or if it looks like my audience gets the point and I should move on without another example. It is best to make those decisions at home, and not in front of the room under stress. So make sure your outline has space for that kind of marking. I will also cross out any items before I speak if I get a chance to evaluate or get to know my audience. Does it seem like they need that detail?

CHAPTER 4

Maybe its importance to the overall speech is less than I thought last night. Maybe the previous speaker already made that point.

The last column is a column where I cue myself to remember things I might otherwise forget. In this case, the "VA" stands for "visual aid." I've listed when I transition between the Power Point slides so that I don't forget. You and I have seen many student speeches where, at the end of the speech, the student goes back through to show all the slides s/he forgot to use. Not good. Here, for example, I can see that I have quite a few slides to deal with for the Corey part, and this will help me remember that.

Additional information like the VA column may be needed depending on your goals and what you have a hard time remembering to do. I used to have a column with a red "LOOK UP!!!" every few points when I had a difficult time with eye contact. I still have a "SLOW DOWN!!!" column, as it is something I continually struggle with. There might be a column for figurative language or humor or other elements of delivery you need to remind yourself to work on, as well, for example, like the UUUUUMMMM therapy described at the end of Chapter 16. Kenny (1982) used smiley faces in the margins to indicate that it was time for a "light hearted comment" (p. 23).

My favorite is from a student outline this past semester. At the top of her outline she had this:

> TRY NOT TO LOOK AT ME MUCH
> LOOK AT YOUR AUDIENCE
> THEY LIKE YOU

THE ZOMBIE GUIDE TO PUBLIC SPEAKING

Practical Outlining

Let's take a look at some actual outlines used by some actual students.

Avoid outlines which are slide-by-slide Power Point guides, whether printed from the software or created by you, with what looks like 28 subpoints. Worse, don't use the actual projected slides as memory prompts while we look at your back. Energy, eye contact and connection with the audience suffers.

Here are some interesting examples where we can investigate with more specificity the question of how much to put on the outline.

For this example, compare the way these three points are outlined in this section of Samantha Lopez's work on a Jack the Ripper[2] speech:

I. Mary Pearcey
    a. Believed to be "Jill the Ripper"
    b. Lover's wife and baby
    c. "savage throat-cutting"
    d. Killing private and public
    e. Labeled the *mad midwife*
    f. Was hanged in 1889

II. Perelman
    a. Presumption
        i. Conviction of killing
    b. Justification
        i. Witness

---

[2] I will draw quite a few examples form student work on Jack the Ripper. You may be thinking, well, "Yuck!" That's fair. The students said that, too. These projects were designed to get students investigating argument for and against suspects in an unsolved crime. And this is just the most famous such crime, with lots of Internet theories to evaluate.

CHAPTER 4

    III. Fallacies
            a. False Cause
                    i. bogeyman
            b. Weak Analogy
                    i. DNA not enough results

The last two points need much less elaboration, since she knew exactly what, for example, those fallacies meant and the example she was using to apply them to. But for the details of Mary Pearcey, this was something she might forget to cover, so they are more heavily detailed than "bogeyman."

Another example, from Arthur Munoz, shows a similar thing:

    1) Kosminski
        a) Background
            i) Jew Leaving Russia
        b) 4 main suspects
            i) CITE: Metro Police
        c) Entire Dissertations linking the named and him
            i) CITE: *Kosminski and the Seaside Home* by Stewart P Evans
        d) Location, Religion, Bad child hood, mentally unstable, occupation

Note subpoint *b*. He will remember the names of the four suspects because he is well-prepared. But he knows he might forget to cite his source, so that shows up on the outline. Also take a look at subpoint *d*. He needs to make sure he gets to all five points, but he clearly knows what he will say when he gets to each one, so it remains simple.

Here's another good example on an outline, from Mason Allenger for a project analyzing the Black Power social movement:

THE ZOMBIE GUIDE TO PUBLIC SPEAKING

Introduction:
Attention Getter
-Startling truth, famous figures　　　　The American Economic Review

Preview
-What I'm doing, tools on pieces (Mag. feathers)　　　Vrooman Charts,
　　　　　　　　　　　　　　　　　　　　　　　　　ATH & P&SM

Credibility (history major, 98.9),
Thesis explanation (what, how, yes or no? good news)

Body:

Piece 1 (Black Power Address)　　　　　　　Americanrhetoric.com
Figures (Schemes epistrophe, euphemism),
Fallacies (Ad hominem, poisoning the well),
Perelman (Time, repetition)　　　　　　　　　　　　Vrooman Charts

Piece 2 (Boycotts)　　　　　　　　　　　　　　　　youtube.com

-Tragedy, language, clusters　　　　　　　　　　　　　　　ATH

Piece 3 (1968 Olys)　　　　　　　　　　　　　　　wikipedia.org

-Social movements
(Non verbal & symbolic acts, slogans,
relating to others, size)　　　　　　　　　　　　　　　　P&SM

Piece 4 (Baltimore)　　　　　　　　　　　　　newsweek.com
-Social Movements (Stages)　　　　　　　　　　　　　P&SM

Conclusion:
Thesis "Black power was a full-fledged social movement to get blacks rights by force, it didn't get those rights but it got the conversation going, and it is still going partly because of the movement."

Psych Closer/Clincher
-The conversation

CHAPTER 4

What really stands out here is how much he knows his material. The "98.9" is a joke he tells at the beginning. That's all he needs to cue it. All the bits in "Piece 1" are all very complicated bits of rhetorical analysis, but he knows what they are. He just needs to remember the order. Your audience can tell if you are this well-prepared.

And that's really the additional bonus of this kind of preparation. If you can't get by with this kind of minimal outline, you know you are not ready yet.

This kind of outline works best for helping you to achieve the kind of delivery that feels natural and that will connect you with an audience.

Why I Hate Notecards

Thinking about all these examples, you can also see that *notecards are a poor choice*. They simply don't have the space and information bandwidth to allow you to have all of this information and cueing in front of you all at once. Notecards make the speech a series of desperate moments, stripped of the surrounding ideas, with a stack of more to come. It's bad. And it tempts speakers to break away from their audience to mess with their cards.

In all this time teaching public speaking I have never once seen a speaker who was better with notecards than with an outline. It just doesn't happen.

The only other reason to consider notecards, aside from the fact that you might have been trained to use them in high school, is that you may have no podium and worry about holding your outline. Bring a folder to put your outline on or print the outline on cardstock.

THE ZOMBIE GUIDE TO PUBLIC SPEAKING

The outline is a full map. Notecards are tiny pieces of the directions that are as unadaptable as the Power Point printout. Just imagine you are on card 12 of a 30-card stack. Could you adapt to a bored audience who already understands the point you are belaboring? If someone flashes the time and you have 7 minutes left, do you remember what material to cut? And there are other examples of difficult to impossible adaptations in a notecard environment.

When I see a person stand up with notecards, I have a visceral sense that they don't care about us in the audience much. And I'm pretty sure that if there is a speaker in the room who is going to go staggeringly longer than their allotted time, it will be them.

You can do better.

To wrap this up, your goal is to create a speaking outline that will help you stay alive and adaptable, not stuck, physically or mentally, like zombie food. This is the only way that extemporaneous delivery can happen. And although we will cover other important elements of delivery in Chapter 16, this is the most important element of your delivery.

Part Two:
Reanimating the Bones

THE ZOMBIE GUIDE TO PUBLIC SPEAKING

CHAPTER 5

Chapter 5: Organization

If the dilemma outlined in the first chapters is accurate, then we need to think about all of the building blocks of speaking in public in a different way. Instead of doing the things we always have done, that Cicero taught, that speaking books teach, that your teacher told you to do, that you think will fly in the business world, etc., let's approach every element with care. Do you just want to "fit in" and do what everyone else tends to do? Just read *Dilbert* to see how effective that kind of thinking is.

In the French zombie film, *La Horde* (Dahan & Rocher, 2009), cops and drug dealers must stop trying to kill each other long enough to try to escape from a high rise building when the zombie apocalypse starts. The characters who survive for any length of time are able to creatively respond to this new dilemma of enemies who need to become friends. Habits are hard to break, especially when we used to think they were good.

Remember our dilemma: *We've got to balance motivation and ability by constantly providing things that are simple and things that are complex.* To do this we need to be adaptable.

Questions of structure and order, especially if we are extemporaneous speakers, are some of the most important decisions we will make.

In Max Brooks' (2003) *The Zombie Survival Guide*, there are 126 pages devoted to how to organize and maintain your living space, including a 9-point plan for how to defend a two-story home. And we all read that book. Most of my students have a plan for what they would do and where they would go when the zombies rise up.[1]

Really? We spend so much time thinking of fake organizational tasks. Do we not have the patience for it in real life?

Maybe so. In terms of our lives and our email inboxes and our cars and our speeches, we generally try the first idea that comes along. It is unsatisfying. But you can always try a new way of putting things in the glove box or the junk drawer. However, as with the need to fill the upstairs bathtub before the water shuts off during the end of days, with a speech, you only get one shot. Yet, it often feels like an afterthought, at best, in so many speeches I see.

Organizing your speech so that it becomes clear to the audience is one of the most important ways to achieve simplicity/ability. But there are a few key ways that you can push on issues of complexity and motivation here, as well. Sometimes mystery is good and makes us want to get to the end to find out whodunit. Sometimes mystery is just tiresome. It is important to figure out how to produce one of those effects and not the other.

To do this, we will first talk about connectives. Then we will make one detour into movie trailers and another into video games.

Connectives

Dolman (1922), in his handbook of speaking, tells the familiar story of students who are not listening well enough to get the information: "who can blame them for losing interest?" (p. 50). He describes "a constant leakage" in a

---

[1] I know at least two people who have worked out a plan for harvesting the glands of pigs so that they will be able to continue to provide their much-needed thyroid medicine during the zombie apocalypse.

CHAPTER 5

speech where "ideas are escaping" listeners all the time. In STEM fields, the audience seems to oscillate between the wandering brains, resigned to "the fact that they will gain nothing" (Kenny, 1982, p. 13) and the theoretically ideal committed-note-takers who descend into a "deadly process" whereby information goes from the speaker's notes to the audience's notebooks "without passing through the heads of either!" (Mills, 1977, p. 210).

As a graduate student, I taught speaking class using one of the *MOPSBOTS* that was really enamored of lists. I eventually learned that lecturing on six different kinds of organizational patterns (just look at the next section of this chapter) was pointless, but when I first started teaching, I was not yet prepared to adapt to my bored audiences (my first semester of teaching, classes started at 7:40am!). I remember overhearing a student in the second row leaning over to her neighbor and loudly whispering, "He just said six. My last number was three. How many do you have?" I think the seeds of this book were planted then.

Connectives are needed because of this lack of attention. In a world where even the most rapt of audiences is getting distracted, and where many hostile listeners and/or cognitive misers are actively thinking of something else, we have to provide them a road back into the speech when they get lost. Even the best of audience members will wander. *Your organizational strategy has to be based on the need to gain back the attention of wanderers, not to handhold people who are hanging on every word.* You need to organize for the real world, not a world where you are afraid too many organizational cues will bore your biggest fans.

Connectives consist of two things, which are vitally important, and which most *MOPSBOTS*, to their credit, will describe in similar ways.

First, you need to use *transitions* between ideas. A

transition is an entire sentence, not the word "next." It is a sentence which gives a short summary of the idea that came before and then gives a short preview of the idea that will come next. An example: "Now that we've talked about the color red, let's move on and consider the color blue." A full transition like this, especially when your delivery and/or visual aids emphasize it, is the perfect way to pull slackers back into your presentation.

Transitions should occur between:

- Your introduction and your first main point ("Now that we know where we're going, let's move on to the first point, cats."

- Every main point ("So that wraps up sushi. Let's get to our next raw fish dish, ceviche.")

- Your last main point and the conclusion. ("Planting native plants was our last step in water conservation. Now we can wrap it all up."

In addition, for longer speeches, transitions should happen between the subpoints as well.

In Chapter 7, we will deal with how you can visually cue these transitions.

Other things you can do to make them stand out for your audience are to add figurative language or humor (see Chapters 11 and 12) or to make them a part of an ongoing narrative. Think about the presentations or videos you watched in elementary school to teach things like water conservation. Somebody would turn to Ricky the Raindrop and say, "That's great, Ricky! I never knew you could save so much water just by taking shorter showers!" The Ricky would chime in, "That's right, Steve! And you can save

CHAPTER 5

even more water by watering your lawn only at night! Here, let me show you!" Super-cheesy, right? But I still remember it, so that's got to mean something.

The second thing you need for connectives are *internal previews and summaries*. In Chapter 6 we will discuss how to preview your main points in your introduction and summarize them in your conclusion. But internal previews and summaries are also needed for the subpoints within those points. Here's an example on a topic once very popular with my students:

> *Transition*
>
> "Now that we've talked about Xbox, let's start up the Playstation."
>
> *Main Point*
>
> "I think the Playstation 3 is the superior machine for many reasons. . . ."
>
> *Internal Preview*
>
> "It has better graphics, free online multiplayer, and is the only place you can play *God of War*."
>
> *1st Subpoint*
>
> "The better graphics come from the hardware . . ."

These two elements of connectives, transitions and internals, are the keys to the simplicity element. If you want the rest of your organizational scheme to provoke and be complex, and especially if you are designing a presentation that will have audience discussion and participation, even debate, anchoring the speech with these connectives is key.

Movie Trailers

There is a difference between good and bad movie trailers, right? Some give away the entire plot. Some are so vague as to be frustrating. But some, for example the trailer that helped *The Hunger Games* achieve a then record-breaking opening weekend for a nonsequel (Young, 2012), are very effective. It centers on the emotional impact of the main character's "I volunteer!" moment to save her sister and enter the Games. Then it shows you character and dialogue and some vague and uncertain scenes of forests and action. It closes with the tributes on their circles as the countdown begins. It works because it leaves just enough out so that you want to go see the film to get the answers.

Contrast that with the thousands of speeches I've seen (and likely a large number in your experience too), which all follow the same horrible, predictable pattern. The four main points are

I. Definitions, Both Obvious and Uninteresting!
II. A History Which Is Not Integrated Into The Rest Of The Speech!!
III. Pros / Problem / Cause
IV. Cons/ Solution / Effects

Group speeches are particularly likely to inflict this upon innocent audiences, as usually the groups have only two things to say but need to invent the first two points so that everyone in the group will get a chance to speak. The group members will bob to the surface for their part, read it desultorily, pass the baton to the next group member and then stand around looking just as bored as the audience. Braiiiiiinnnnnnnsssssss!!!!

The troubles with this are many, but we can boil it

down to two main issues.

First, for most speeches we don't need those first points. And if we did, why are they not integrated into the nature of the ideas in point III?

Second, since we hear this ALL THE TIME, it shoves our brains into cognitive miser mode. The recognizable organizational structure itself is a heuristic cue that this speaker doesn't care enough to have done good research, that this speaker is just trying to fill up time and isn't interested in what I learn from her/him, and that this speaker doesn't really have anything to offer us on this topic that we haven't already heard before. "Oh good," my miserly brain says to me as I snooze, "You just used *Webster's* to define what 'football' is. I can safely sleep, as you have nothing to teach me."

The traditional solution to this in the *MOPSBOTS* is to create lists of organizational structures that you can apply to your topic, like creative cookie cutters in interesting shapes. Here are some examples:

- *Hunt (1987):* topical, spatial, chronological, step, advantage-disadvantage
- *Wolvin, Berko & Wolvin* (1993): spatial, chronological, topical, causal, comparison-contrast, problem-solution
- *Brydon & Scott (1994):* time, spatial, categorical, problem-solution, refutational, causal, Monroe's Motivated Sequence
- *Grice & Skinner (1998):* topical, chronological, spatial, causal, pro-con, gimmick
- *Sprague & Stuart (2000):* chronological, spatial, cause-effect, problem-solution, topical
- *Lucas (2001):* chronological, spatial, causal, problem-solution, topical

- *Sellnow (2005):* chronological, narrative, causal, spatial, topical, compare-contrast
- *Fraleigh & Tuman (2009):* spatial, temporal, causal, comparison, problem-cause-solution, criteria-application, narrative, categorical

Of course, as you can see, most of those lists are depressingly similar, which means if you are speaking to an audience that's heard a lot of presentations, say in a school or business or church or, really ANYWHERE, they will quickly end up with the same level of ennui – "Another problem broken into parts. . . . I wonder if I get strong enough wifi in this room to check my email?"

The earliest I can find this sort of list is in a textbook by Mosher (1917), which has four such schemes:

- Cause and effect
- Chronological
- Space
- Predetermined Analysis[2]

If we add the unique elements from the list above, we also get:

- Comparison/Pro-Con
- Problem-Solution (Monroe's Motivated Sequence is a particular form of this, as well)
- Refutational
- Gimmick
- Narrative
- Criteria-Application

---

[2] Later books call this "Topical."

CHAPTER 5

Nothing here is especially revelatory, so Foss and Foss (2003) try to develop more creative schemes. What they add that is not already covered is:

- Circle
- Continuum
- Facilitation
- Metaphor
- Multiple Perspectives
- Spiral
- Thinking Thing Through/Elimination
- Web

Most of these are simply attempts to allow your topic the full complexity the *MOPSBOTS*' lists don't allow. In a circle or continuum or multiple perspectives speech, for example, you recognize that points of view on an issue don't neatly fit into simple categories.

Overall, it might be best to simply do what the old books that didn't love lists did. Winter (1913), Winans, (1920) and Stratton (1920) assume that organization will come from an analysis of how your content can be made to adapt to the situation and the audience. Shurter (1903) leaves off the question entirely, simply noting that "it is therefore assumed that you have something to say" (p. 9).

If these patterns inspire you to find new ways to connect your topic to your audience, then by all means use them. But the focus should always be on creating a dynamic connection with the people who are listening.

Develop a clear set of main points and subpoints. Never create a point out of habit or to fit a predetermined form. And always have a reason for everything. What is really worth everyone's time?

Remember, if we don't have a clear organizational

structure and connectives, audiences will tune out in confusion. But if we do have those things, they may easily get bored and see no reason to continue listening. What do we do?

I wish I had a clear answer to this. A possibility comes from the world of video games.

Link/Mario Picks Up The Key/Sword/Amulet/Rock

Look! Zombie Link!

CHAPTER 5

In various genres of video games, but especially in role-playing and adventure games, the character you are playing is supposed to find items along the way. They might be new swords or boots or armor or something you can immediately don to become better. But they also might be items which you are not allowed to use and have to shove into a backpack or satchel, like a bow you don't have the skill points to shoot yet. And they might be mysterious items that you are not sure you will ever need, but might just be something you'll have to have later to solve a puzzle or build something: a feather, a paper with mysterious writing, a rock, etc. In *Ready Player One* (Cline, 2011), a novel that is a love letter to 1980s arcade games, a character in a future MMORPG-style simulation game (like *World of Warcraft*) completes a task and gets a virtual quarter. He puts the quarter in his inventory and investigates it but can't figure out what it does. But you know what will eventually happen, don't you? As you read the next hundred pages, you keep wondering when that quarter will matter. Eventually it does.[3]

Clearly this happens so that the game won't quickly become repetitive. Also, it creates a system of rewards that video games excel at. But the common device of picking up a mysterious item and wondering whether you'll figure out what to do with it also serves to create exactly the kind of mystery we want our speeches to have but which they

---

[3] I'm not saying anything else. That's all you get. Already this is spoiler-y enough. If you want to find out what happens, read the book. If you are motivated to read it JUST to find out what happens, not because you are a Gen-X nerd who remembers when *Centipede* games actually were in the tables at pizza parlors, well then, the theory in this section is correct – mysterious Easter Eggs can motivate us to seek information.

usually lack. How can we integrate this?
Imagine this:

> I. The Dilemma of Organization
>   a. Connectives
>   b. Patterns of Main Points
> II. Magic Feathers
> III. A Few Solutions

You will do your duty with the connectives, and the basic form of this speech is a simple problem-solution structure, but if you leave the "Magic Feathers" bit somewhat mysterious, cueing it with something like, "Second, we are going to learn something about feathers. I promise it will become important . . .", that is a more complex moment for your audience than they might be expecting.

It promises something strange. They might simply reject this, because they are cognitive misers. But if you use the Magic Feathers bit to explain how we might think about the problem in a new way, in this case using lessons from video games to make better speeches, and then if you build that lesson into the solutions to follow, I think it will be helpful and valuable.

There are a few reasons for this. First, it becomes a heuristic cue that immediately signals that you've put more work/thought/effort into this than they might have expected. That is always a good impression. If nothing else, they will remember that about you. Second, it helps to short-circuit Evans' selective scrutiny and mental modeling, since the ambiguity of the point makes it hard to ignore your premises for their own. Third, it creates suspense. Maybe it is not as good as *The Hunger Games* preview, but it turns out that anything that makes an argument feel more like a narrative is a generally good thing, as we will discover in Chapter 9.

A good example of this occurred in a speech delivered in 2013 by April Estes. This is the only speech I've ever seen in my classes that got any sort of a standing ovation, so that's got to say something. Her speech was on whether or not Thomas Neill Cream was Jack the Ripper. She presented her organizational pattern as if he was, but every time she made a transition, the background of her Power Point, which she never looked at or acknowledged, switched to:

The audience, at first, was a bit confused. It seemed like it was a mistake or a contradiction, as her delivery and arguments expressed such confidence in his guilt, or so it seemed. The audience pointed and talked amongst themselves. She just let it go. Toward the end they were laughing every time. It was the perfect example of what a bit of mystery can do. Her final point shattered the illusion that she believed he was a suspect and she destroyed her previous arguments in less than a minute: Dr. Cream was in a prison across the Atlantic in Illinois during the Ripper murders. Her point was how gullible we can be, jumping to conclusions and drawing patterns where none really exist.

Another great example comes from a 2014 group speech by Derek Cantu, Hayden Chadwick, Kelly Dooly and Gabby Salazar on bigfoot. The preview for their speech showed these main points:

1. Description
2. History
3. Evidence
4. Sightings
5. Survival Tips

The last point was mostly a joke, but there was also some serious information in there about how bigfoot supposedly smells and hears and reacts to stimuli. And all along the way, I could not help but wonder what those survival tips would be. As they presented the sightings evidence in point four, for example, I was engaged with their material in a way that I would not have been without that joke. I was trying to think about bigfoot's top speech based on how far apart some footprints were, etc.

Now, those of you who are terminal skeptics will be thinking that if this book is used in your class and if everyone in your class does this strategy, it will start failing to work as everyone comes to expect it. Maybe. To do it well requires the research to make it not feel like a cheap gimmick. But everyone is doing the boring structures already anyway, so there's really nothing to lose. Plus, this kind of thing is hard, and you just might be sitting amongst slackers.

CHAPTER 5

THE ZOMBIE GUIDE TO PUBLIC SPEAKING

CHAPTER 6

Chapter 6: Introductions and Conclusions

We intuitively know how important these parts of the speech are. We know about first and last impressions from shampoo commercials. This is the famous "Curve of Attention." The idea, according to Mills (1977), is that

> Interest starts off high, though no matter how good an instructor may be [she]/he will rarely have the full attention of all the class. Interest drops. Fatigue and boredom set in and persist, until banished by the pleasant anticipation of the end of the period. (p. 19)

Although the numbers behind the various forms of this graph are quite dubious (see Chapter 8), it does correspond with, I think, our experiences in the classroom. If there is some truth to The Curve, we need to make the most of the moments at the beginning and the end. And we need to do this while keeping our basic dilemma between simplicity and complexity in mind.

Think about how long a good opening can get you to watch an otherwise uninteresting film. Romero's (1985) *Day of the Dead*, for example, is a difficult film to watch all the way through. There are some interesting zombie ideas in the film, including Bub the undead guy who learns to shoot a gun, but it is a film filled with unpleasant characters and uneven acting. The first time I watched it, I thought it was boring. The beginning, where you get a glimpse of all the exciting zombie action taking place outside of the bunker we spend most of the film inside of, has such promise. It can pull you in for 20 minutes or so before you go to the next film in the Netflix queue.

And think about how effective the end of the *Dawn of*

the Dead (Snyder, 2004) remake is. It seems the typical thing. They finally get to the island and the zombies come running out of the jungle. Then the heavy metal starts. Perfect. You knew they had no hope. You've seen that ending before. But the quick, loud edits and then the music make it all worth it. You might even want to see the movie again. I did. Don't judge me.

Beginnings and endings are the times when people are paying the most attention. Think of the term, "paying." Give them something for their money.

Introductions

For thousands of years, the idea of an introduction's function was clear, even if the source of that idea was not. Cicero (Stratton, 1920), Quintillian (Rener, 1989), and Augustine (Todorov, 1984), three of the most important classical rhetoricians, all saw its function as making the audience *benevolent*, *attentive* and *docile*. Perhaps it is sacrilegious to rhetoric to say these guys were wrong, but I've never met that audience, regardless of what I'm talking about. Have you? Even the audience at TEDx (which I was a part of when I wasn't speaking), where people *paid* to go to an event just to hear speeches, was afflicted with some wandering attention, especially after lunch.

I am certainly not the first to worry about this. Dermatologist Malcolm Morris (1901) began a lecture with these words:

> How can I hope to make you benevolent and attentive, coming before you, as I do, a man unknown to most of you, and with no special claim on your attention? And how can I expect to find you docile when doubtless you already know

all, and possibly more than all, I have to teach? (p. 413)

Even when I can't flatter my audience like Morris, many I see are *judgmental, distracted* and *restless*. I certainly am when I am in an audience.

But it is a mistake to try to fix that. Instead, we need to find a way to connect with those audiences as they are. Stratton (1920), for example, moves past Cicero to assert a more productive way of thinking about it. The only purpose of an introduction is "to bring the topic of the succeeding remarks clearly and arrestingly before an audience" (p. 73). This is our dilemma expressed as strategy. Stratton emphasizes that introductions need to be brief to accomplish this, but they also need to arouse interest and clarify the ideas.

Unfortunately, most introductions only seek to clarify. This is the "Hi, my name is [blank] and I'm here to talk about [blank]" introduction, a failure in every way. How about an acronym? We can call this the *HMNIBAIHTTAB* fail[1]. You can feel The Curve of Attention sagging, can't you? It's not the content that is bad. It's the order. Two key parts of all introductions would be to introduce a topic or thesis and to introduce yourself. An added element needed for clarity is the preview of the main points to follow in the speech, as most speaking or composition books would want.

But wait.

Did your attention wander while reading those last two sentences? Mine did, and I was writing them. We've got to begin by gaining attention. When you walk up to the

---

[1] I tend to pronounce this the "Homni Batab" fail.

podium, either we already know who you are and what your topic is or we don't. Either way, telling us your topic only feels like you are sealing our doom for the next twenty minutes.

Let's think about the situation where the audience doesn't know you. There is a kind of tension there, as they wonder what you will do or say. When we begin with our topic and our name (or worse, if we've had it up on a Power Point title slide the whole time while they were filing in), we immediately dissipate that helpful and suspenseful tension. Instead, choose to begin with something like Jenny Quackenbush did back in 1995, my first semester of teaching public speaking. She simply started with a story:

> In Hampton, Virginia, on December 13, 1993 . . . Officer Les Bollinger, at approximately 10:25 am, observed an individual smoking what appeared to be an illegal substance. When he approached the car, [the suspect] took off immediately. The chase lasted for approximately fifteen minutes, during which the guy was throwing drug paraphernalia out the window. They went through the city and got four miles down the interstate where it ended very abruptly with the help of additional police vehicles. The suspect was taken into the investigations department for questioning. While he was there he began to complain about his handcuffs being too tight, which is a common complaint. Most officers try to accommodate that. However, this time when Bollinger went to loosen his cuffs, the suspect ripped his hands free. Everybody went and jumped on in a big jumble. At the same time Officer Bollinger's arm got pinned. He couldn't guard his gun, so the suspect

CHAPTER 6

> was able to get his gun out of his holster. The suspect fired two shots before they were able to get the gun away from him. The shots hit Officer Bollinger and one other officer. However, fortunately neither one was a fatal shot due to the fact that they were both wearing bulletproof vests.

Even though this is not the most amazing story ever, it pulls you in. When she finally reveals her thesis, that all police should be required to wear bulletproof vests when on duty, followed by her name and qualifications as a criminal justice major, and her four main points, you are far more inclined to care. At least I was.

Part of the reason we dissipate the tension that allows for stories like that to work is that we are nervous. We don't like tension. We don't like the pressure of them caring about the mystery of what we have to say and what kind of speaker we are. So we kill that pressure by telling them as quickly as possible and destroying their attention in the process. We energetically choose to seek comfort over risk and say what we've heard others say before. Kenny (1982) notes something similar in the professional world:

> Do not thank the Chairman or the audience. Do not attempt to tell them that you are pleased to be there, and above all do not elaborate on your lack of skill as a public speaker. Audiences do not like speakers who apologise. They find it embarrassing. (p. 35)

When you fail to introduce your speech properly, especially with the *HMNIBAIHTTAB* beginning, we are, in effect, apologizing. We are announcing that we feel bad that they are looking at us and that we are taking up their time. So we lower their expectations and give them permission not to care. And, in so doing, we make a decision to actually waste the audience's time by refusing to create content that will engage them.

There are many ways of gaining attention, not just stories. The chapters in Part Three all outline ideas that can be productively used to gain attention:

1. narratives
2. statistics
3. humor
4. figurative language
5. visual aids

Two additional potential attention-getters are:

6. Interesting quotations from interesting people, as long as they serve a narrative (dramatic) or humorous function can work too.
7. Doing something weird or startling also can work, but do less of things like screaming at your audience as someone in the back of the room turns off the light (saw that in class once), and do more of Amy Cuddy (2012) having her audience freeze and examine their posture to see what it would tell them about their projections of power.[2]

Avoid some of the suggestions from the *MOPSBOTS*:

- *Complimenting your audience* (Hunt, 1987). "You

---

[2] Watch her talk. You'll see how well it works. Her conclusion (to skip ahead to the "Conclusion" part of this chapter), does exactly what Kenny (1982) suggests, also.

CHAPTER 6

guys look so smart and energetic today!"

(Vrooman tries heroically to not make a sour face).

- *Rhetorical question* (Hasling, 1998). "What is it about hot dogs that makes them so tasty?"

 (Vrooman begins to wonder if anyone ever listens to him. What is the point of teaching, when you think about it? The students don't listen. They don't think you know what you are talking about anyway. Spend all this time preparing and they just . . . .).

- *Promise something beneficial* (Grice & Skinner, 1998). "What I will tell you now about retirement planning will change your life."

 (Vrooman hopes the class will not lose faith in him if he weeps publicly).

- *Asking an audience-response question* (Hasling, 1998). "How many of you have ever driven a car?"

 (Vrooman dies a little inside. Perhaps zombification wouldn't be so bad after all).

Now, there may be times when you need to ask questions of the audience to be sure your material is going to serve their purposes, like when you have a complex process that you need to explain if some people in the room don't already know about it, but that is NOT the attention-getter. Similarly, you may have a need to compliment your audience ("The fact the you are here says something important about your willingness to begin finding solutions for your problems") or to thank or honor those present ("Board members, President Dorsey, faculty, staff, alumni, parents and, especially, the graduating class of 2015 . . ."), but these should take place AFTER the attention-getter. You know, when they are actually paying attention to your compliments?

So this means we have an introduction with a series of parts:

1. **Attention-getter**
2. **Thesis/topic**
3. **Introduce yourself and your credibility on the topic**
4. **Preview of your main points.**

The third part might need some additional clarification. You can omit the "My name is _____" in a room full of people you know, but even then you might need to explore why we should listen to you on the subject.

There are a few approaches to this. First, you can cite your professional/research qualifications. Second, you can describe your personal experience or expertise with the issue at hand. Of course, perhaps we, who are often in a position to listen to you, our teacher, manager or president, know all of that about you already. If there is nothing new in your experience or work that would help induce us to listen to you a bit more closely than usual, then some attention to why you are choosing, yet again, to bend our ears might be in order. In other words, we already think we know you, but have circumstances pushed us toward considering your expertise again?

The following examples demonstrate how these three

tasks can be performed, usually in conjunction with each other:

- I have spent the past summer volunteering with rescue dogs . . .
- "But there is something different about tonight; there is something special about tonight. What is different? What is special? I, Barbara Jordan, am a keynote speaker. A lot of years passed since 1832, and during that time it would have been most unusual for any national political party to ask a Barbara Jordan to deliver a keynote address. But tonight, here I am. And I feel that, notwithstanding the past, that my presence here is one additional bit of evidence that the American Dream need not forever be deferred." (Jordan, 1976)[3]
- I am a lifelong mountain climber and have read extensively on the subject of the business of Mt. Everest . . .
- "I farm hydroponically, in the middle of the city, in San Antonio, with the company I helped co-found, Local Sprout" (Hagney, 2014)
- Like you, I was upset when a Hogwarts invitation did not arrive by owl when I turned eleven . . .
- "If we are going to continue these shows, I just need to hear myself talk for a couple of

---

[3] This speech, at the Democratic National Convention in 1976, was the first keynote address by a woman and by an African American at a major political party convention.

minutes, so, uh, that's what I'm going to do here." (Letterman, 2011).[4]
- Now, I'm not a detective or anything, but I have watched a lot of Wishbone and Dexter.[5]
- "I gave a preliminary statement right after the ruling on Sunday, but watching the debate over the course of the last week, I thought it might be useful for me to expand on my thoughts a little bit" (Obama, 2013).[6]

There is no easy formula for establishing your credibility at the beginning of a presentation. It is always a question of addressing your link to the topic, audience and situation in a way that suggests you have something new, relevant or important to say.

To these four parts of the introduction we might add the WIIFM (What's in it for me?) that Fraleigh and Tuman (2009) suggest. Right after the credibility step, they suggest telling your audience what they will get from listening. It does work better here than as an attention-getter, but I'm not sure this is always necessary, and with some audiences and topics, it seems cheesy.

Conclusions

These are even trickier than introductions. Mosher (1917) explains the trouble with conclusions in language very similar to our simplicity-complexity dilemma. You can't just summarize and sit down. The audience will feel a bit confused and unenthused. But the temptation to go on

---

[4] This was David Letterman's first show after 9/11.
[5] I did not write down the exact wording of Brandon George's introduction in his true crime speech, but you get the gist.
[6] This was a speech about Treyvon Martin.

CHAPTER 6

and on in misguided attempts to inspire now that you are almost done and you feel the elation of your nerves relaxing should also be avoided. You might simply just confuse them as it gets hard to follow. I've seen this happen often.

You want to achieve what Stratton (1920) calls the *retrospective function* (the audience is reminded of what you've said) and the *anticipatory function* (you clarify what all this might mean for them going forward). Sprague and Stuart (2000) call these *logical* and *psychological* closures.

Unfortunately, although logical closure can be achieved with a summary, there are no easy routes to figuring out psychological closure. Carnegie (1955) thinks you have to get a *feeling* for it from experience. There are no "mechanical rules" (p. 231). That is probably true, but it is certainly unhelpful, so let's try to break it down further.

Jenny Quackenbush ended her bulletproof vest speech with this corker of a circular conclusion:

> I'd just like to end with an explanation of why this is such an important topic for me. If you recall my introduction . . . during the shooting on December 13, 1993? I was, unfortunately, the second officer involved in that shooting. I was shot in the back [she demonstrates where on a Kevlar vest she has put up on a board]. Fortunately Hampton Police has mandatory vest laws so I was wearing it. But, believe it or not, I thought a lot of these myths -- I believed them to be true. I may not have been wearing one, and may not be here today if the law was not enforced.

Psychological closure is where you make sure your arguments have what Perelman (1982) calls *presence*. In Chapter 14 we will explore that more fully, but for now, the idea is that you make your reasoning *really matter* to people. You find a way to hit them in the gut or to make their imaginations take flight, depending on how violent you like your metaphors. Those elements that we will explore in Part Three, as with attention-getters, serve well here. One of Perelman's examples of presence is "Caesar's bloody tunic," presented by Antony after the assassination (Perelman & Olbrechts-Tyteca, 1969, p. 35). This illustrates what they cite Bacon as arguing, that rhetoric should unite *reason* and the *imagination*.

Another example is the closing of Patrick Henry's famous speech before the American Revolution, which connects the logic of the speech to the reality outside of that room in an emotional fervor that rallies the country:

> Our brethren are already in the field! What stand we here idle? What is it that gentlemen wish? What would they have? Is life so dear, or peace so sweet, as to be purchased at the price of chains and slavery? Forbid it, Almighty God! I know not what course others may take; but as for me, give me liberty or give me death! (Peterson, 1954, p. 142)

Generally, what we are looking for in a conclusion, then, is that culmination of the logic of the speech married to some final emotional connection with the audience to give them a reason to remember or act.

If you can't imagine fomenting a revolution, here's the conclusion from Dave Grohl's (2014) speech during Nirvana's Rock and Roll Hall of Fame induction:

> Because I think that's the deal — you look up to your heroes and you shouldn't be intimidated by

> them; you should be inspired by them. Don't look up at the poster on your wall and think, "Fuck, I can never do that." Look at the poster on your wall and think, "Fuck, I'm going to do that!"

Not bad, eh?

A conclusion's closure is so important that if you need to have a question-and-answer period at the end of your presentation, you should make sure you include it BEFORE the conclusion. It is the last main point in your speech, and so it got previewed at the beginning ("Today, we are going to talk about three kinds of zombies. First, slow ones. Second, fast ones. Third, extra-fast wall-climbing ones. After that we'll have a little Q&A before I wrap it all up."). Then, when the Q&A is over, you begin your conclusion so that the audience can reconnect with you. Judy Shepard (2013), for example, who speaks about hate crimes and her son Matthew Shepard's murder, delivered a lecture at Texas Lutheran University where she did this very effectively. Given the nature of her topic, it is inevitable that some of the questions would be highly problematic and perhaps even derail her message. The opportunity to come back with a further summary and story after an awkward moment or two is key. She decided, at a certain point, that she was only going to take two more questions, did so, and then made a transition back into her material and gave her conclusion. It was extremely effective.

But we need to add two more parts to this model of summary (simplicity) and closure (complexity). Lucas (2001) points out the importance of signaling to the audience that you are approaching a conclusion. Often this is achieved with the final transition (see Chapter 5). For Lucas it can be as simple as "In conclusion." These words can lead to an immediate uptick in attention. Even if we love your speech (which is probably a rare response) we are still most excited by the idea that you are going to be finished[7]. When we hear that you are wrapping it up, we also get a tiny spurt of panic, especially if somewhere or sometime we might be held responsible for remembering anything you've said (a test, perhaps, or a response to your question of "How did I do?"). We know this is our chance to prove we listened.

Growing up, our pastor in church used to say "finally" a lot. It was frustrating, because it always felt like he might be done, but no, that was just the final part of the first main point. So we'd stop noticing, the mind would wander and then he'd say "Amen." But then how were we going to prove we'd listened to the sermon in confirmation class that Wednesday? Thinking about it now, maybe it was all a plot on his part. Well played, Pastor Hirsch.

We also need a moment after the psychological closure that Sprague and Stuart (2000) call the *clincher*. You cannot simply peter out with a "That's it," or, worse, walk back to your seat because no one knows you've finished, only to get clapped for as you slink into your chair. With word choice and elements of delivery like energy and pause, you need to communicate to your audience that you are finished:

> To get it right you have to be intensely aware that this is the ending. You must say it as if you will never speak to these people and you want above all else that they will remember these final words

---

[7] Really. I was (am) a nerd. I loved school. A great lecture from a professor? Ermagherd! But good ideas always provoked me to ask questions. Some profs didn't do questions mid-lecture. For these, I would pounce on them after class with my questions. See? Even your biggest fans are looking forward to the end, sometimes.

CHAPTER 6

to their dying days. (Kenny, 1982, p. 37)

If you think Kenny is laying it on thick here, give his ideas a shot just to be sure. He is writing to a reader who is likely giving boring technical speeches all the time, not social movement agitators. Whatever your topic, find a lever or a door into caring. I was thinking of Kenny's idea when I concluded my TEDx speech (Vrooman, 2014b). How'd I do?

My colleague, Tracey Rhodes, uses the metaphor of "pixie dust" here. You are spreading just a little bit of magic into the room before you go.

The conclusion is the first time in the speech you and the audience have agreed fully. You are both happy the speech is done. Make sure you take a moment to allow for the applause.

To sum up, your conclusion looks like:

1. **Summary**
2. **Psychological closure**
3. **Clincher**

None of this is a Works Cited at the end. Chapter 8 will detail further why you should be using and citing sources with more depth and strategy than simply plopping up a Works Cited at the finish. In terms of the impact of your conclusion, though, I can think of few last moments less effective than the "and here's my references" I get from students who haven't read this far into the book. The end-of-speech Reference List is an artifact of some teacher's choice to convert a paper into a Power Point somewhere back in time. Whether it was to seem hip and with-it or whether it was to help students embrace new technology, this assignment, in unthinkingly carrying over artifacts from paper to speaking with technology, made a large error. Since this kind of assignment seems to have spread like, well, zombies, over the past twenty years and is slowly infecting the professional world, as well, it's time to call for a halt. The end-of-speech Works Cited is downright hostile to your audience. It demonstrates a profound lack of understanding of how they listen, what they need from you and when, and what works best as your concluding thoughts. And if it is likely that someone needs your references for the original reason they were included at the ends of papers, so that could look them up on their own, aren't there a number of better ways of achieving this than making them quickly write down a cite on a slide you zip past?[8]

I guess that is what really irks me about the references slide at the end. It is a lie. You are lying when you do it. No one is going to want to or be able to write it all down. If they cared about more details or a critical question about a source, they needed that citation when you first used it. If they are really engaged, they want to look it up right now on their phones and ask you about it during the Q&A. But instead of engaging those few people, the people who are actually LISTENING to you, you throw up a Works Cited at the end and pretend.

Regardless of the fate of The Curve of Attention in Chapter 8, most of us would agree that the beginnings and ending of speeches are the times when your audience is ignoring you the least. So give them something to pay attention to. In keeping with our zombie theme, as Frost ("Rumpled," 1961) suggests, "rumple their brains fondly."

---

[8] Handing out a hardcopy Works Cited, announcing that the Reference List is on your blog, sharing the link and announcing that you tweeted the link just now, as well, etc.

CHAPTER 6

That means giving their brains a few more w

CHAPTER 7

Chapter 7: Visual Aid Architecture

Is there anything more responsible for the living death of audiences than this? Think of the dilemma of the film *Zombie Honeymoon* (Gebroe, 2005)[1]. The new husband is bitten and must spend quite a bit of time trying to not become a zombie. He tries to remember what it means to be human so he can stay with the love of his life just a little bit longer. Now imagine that she tried to help him stay human. She tried to help remind him of what mattered. Of all the hundreds of things you could do or say to him, where would a Power Point presentation be on the list? The "What It Means to Be Human" slideshow with 47 bullet points?[2]

If something really did matter, if something really was in jeopardy, would this be your tool of choice? In a zombie apocalypse, would the lack of Power Point to coordinate survivor meetings be what you missed most about electricity?

It is difficult, in a world of ever-expanding Power Points, Apple Keynotes and Prezis, to think of the tasks of organizing a speech without thinking in terms of a slidedeck. Unfortunately, in the words of Witt's (2009) title: *Real Leaders Don't Do Powerpoint*. His point is that if you are supposed to be leading, you are supposed to be inspiring, creating vision and connection. Power Point is usually a mindless slog through detail. But does it have to be? Can we rescue it from what its harshest critic, Tufte (2004) calls its overriding organizational feeling of being "one damn thing after another?"

---

[1] Yes, I have seen a movie called *Zombie Honeymoon*. I taught in in Zombies class. Yes, I have taught a class called that.
[2] "Wait, honey! Don't bite me yet! You haven't gotten to slide 36! It has swooshing sound effects as the bullet point swoops in in a circular animation. It will remind you that human life is precious!"

We allow this architecture to determine our content to a depressingly ineffective extent. Craig and Amernic (2006) cite an example about a professor who dropped a great book from his course because he couldn't figure out how to put it in Power Point form. They further cite a series of studies indicating that the overly structured lecture form Power Point represents is a bankrupt method of teaching. Adams (2006) details many student responses to various kinds of Power Point lectures and provides the following account:

> In my class yesterday, I asked a question and the professor said that she'd be covering that a few slides ahead. But then several slides later I remember thinking, hey, she's forgotten my question. I felt annoyed and wanted to say something, but then I couldn't remember exactly what I was wondering about. The moment had passed. (p. 403-4)

This is painful for a person who cares about students and audiences. *The moment had passed.* Was there really anything more important in that next slide full of bullets to write off this member of the audience entirely, simply because it is easier to let a Power Point do the work for you?

Bad, boring, bloated slidedecks make me think of Lyons' (1931) pre-computer lament about speakers who care little for their audience but seek only to "relieve themselves" upon the crowd. He calls them "unloaders" (p. 376).[3]

In this chapter we will learn how to better design visual aid architecture and how to create useful organizational

---

[3] If you read his essay closely, it seems like he really does mean what I think he means.

schemes in visual form. Chapter 13 will deal with individual slide design.

Strategic Ambiguity

Look up images or video of the late Steve Jobs giving presentations. The visual aids behind him are never of this format:

> # Title of Slide!!!!!
> *Subtitle/section in case you are lost!!!!*
> - Some stuff!!
> - And more stuff!!
>   - With additional stuff I hope goes here!
>   - ....but I'm not sure about logical levels, so....
>   With additional stuff I hope goes here!
>   but I'm not sure about logical levels, so....
> - Is it time for a definition yet?
>   Because Wikipedia....

Jobs would usually have a dark black background with some images or diagrams that would pop up as needed.[4] This is in contrast to what you often see in classrooms and boardrooms around the country. This is a basic level of strategic decision-making that many of us are not doing.

If everything is clearly detailed on the Power Point, you do not need the person in the front of the room. If everything is

---

[4] Search YouTube for his introduction of the iPhone in 2007 for an excellent example.

clearly detailed on the Power Point, the person in the front of the room is not a leader.

Nervous speakers might prefer that. But if you are trying to reach your audience, if you are trying to teach or inspire or lead, the way we always do Power Point is a failure. *If I can send you my Power Point via email and you can understand it without me, why are you speaking?* Why should I even show up to be in the class or audience in that case? Because it is required? Can you feel yourself losing them? Why not just write up an outline in easier-to-read format and distribute it to people? And then make class or the meeting into a time where good discussions occur, where important questions are asked, where something with high impact happens. My old philosophy professor, Dr. Shanahan, used to do just that. He'd print out a prewritten page of notes and give a copy to everyone in the class at the start. Then we'd discuss the issues. Then we'd LEARN. He just cut out the boring lecture middleman.

Is it because we think that's what people want and need? Well, how much have you learned in your lifetime of Power Point lectures? Environmental science professor Agoramoorthy (2012) suggests that the darkened rooms simply allow an audience to fall asleep more easily. Research indicates that slidedecks of this kind have no additive value on learning (Hardin, 2007; Jandaghi & Matin, 2009; Ricer, Filak, & Short, 2005)[5]. One researcher found that a lecture-only condition led to better learning than the lecture plus Power Point condition (Amare, 2006).

---

[5] Levasseur and Sawyer (2006) analyze dozens more such studies. Most conclude that visual aids add nothing to student learning outcomes or test scores. The few studies that indicate positive learning from visual aids are scathingly critiqued in their article as having significant methodological shortcomings.

CHAPTER 7

Why is this? You know why. When confronted with so much Power Point, you let your cognitive miser out to play. You can just write down the stuff on the Power Point and stop using your braiiiiiinnnnnnsssssss. We are so committed to being cognitive misers that Amare found that students *liked* the Power Point lectures better and thought they learned more from them, even when that was not the case. Lest we blame "lazy" students for this, Levasseur and Sawyer (2006) find the same basic phenomenon in their analysis of dozens of studies. An interesting example of this is a study that found church-goers not learning more from Power-Pointed sermons (Buchko, Buchko, & Meyer, 2013). There really are no such studies of how people in meetings in the professional world recall or understand information in business presentations, which is depressingly significant. For Farkas (2006), this is part of the problem: hasty meetings with unclear purpose run by undertrained presenters making Power Points according to templates. These are the products of corporate or organizational cultures which are dysfunctional when it comes to communication and employee time. There are often no clear learning objectives you could test employees on.

Tufte (2003), in an analysis of the Power Point slides used by NASA to decide whether or not to try to land the space shuttle *Columbia*, makes a convincing case that the Power Point format is partially responsible for the deaths of those astronauts. The visual aids actually helped people make bad decisions.

Do we keep using the same tired slidedecks because the bulleted horror show is what looks "professional" or is "expected in the _____ world"? Was Steve Jobs not the most influential CEO in the country for a while? Are the thousands of TED Talks with minimalist slides watched for entertainment (Speeches! For fun!! Who would have thought?) irrelevant to the world?

Here's how to have an impact: turn it off. Blank slides. I like to have my Power Points white text on black background so that when I insert a blank slide it does not mean blinding whiteness or a color shift. In my experience in a world with under-performing projectors and suboptimal lighting conditions, black or dark backgrounds provide the highest visibility in the space. Kenny (1982), in his study of legibility in the slide and overhead projector world, suggested that black backgrounds, although atypical for the time, were always easier to see. Highway signs seem to be designed this way for similar reasons.[6]

When the slide goes black, many in the listening audience turn to look at you, which is how you connect with them, as Bateson wants, and how you lead them, as Witt wants. The non-listening audience will not, which tells you exactly how much work you have if you are teaching. Train your audience. Make them look at you. Make them listen. Mary Civiello, a communication consultant for large businesses, suggests the same thing. Use blank slides. Never start your Power Point before you make a personal connection with them first (Civiello & Matthews, 2008; LeRoux & Corwin, 2007). Kenny (1982) suggested bringing a large paper to cover the overhead projector in the pre-Power Point days. It seemed obvious to him that you had to turn the visual aids off now and then to make your point (but you didn't want to distractingly turn the machine off and on). Why is it not obvious to us, when the technology

---

[6] This is a topic rife with seemingly fake statistics and will be dealt with more fully in Chapter 8. The most accurate story seems to be the one told on the Federal Highway Administration's website (Weingroff, 2013) that they simply tested various sign color combinations on roadways and 58% of drivers preferred white-on-green.

allows for a much easier solution than his simple kludge of a big sheet of paper?

We need to use blank the slides often for a variety of reasons.

First, the audience's emotional dependence on the slide show is not to be underestimated. All of us recall that "AAAwwwwwww" moan from the students when the teacher turned off the filmstrip (baby boom), VCR (GenX) or DVD (Millennial). It is an immediate, almost primal wail of disappointment. It's not that educational filmstrips were all that entertaining (although the *Signal 30* film (Wayman, 1959), filled with bloody bodies pulled from car wrecks, was horrifying when we saw it in Driver's Ed class), but they are perhaps more engaging than mediocre teaching or at least require less effort. Adams (2006) relates the experience of a student who not only was not listening to the professor before the Power Point "fired up," but was actively annoyed, "impatient" for the "real information" to begin (p. 399). I have seen plenty of students who are simply lost when the slides stop moving in a traditional Power Point lecture, when an idea takes longer to explore and the presenter talks "too long." As Clark (1983) suggested in response to video-based learning 30 years ago, students choose media that "inadvertently" teach them less (p. 455). But I'm not sure how inadvertent this really is. The pictures are like a comforting security blanket. But how comfortable do you want that audience to be? Aren't you asking them to think and change?

Second, although there is good evidence that many people prioritize the processing of visual information and that images affect us more deeply than, say, audio information, there is a tension. Levasseur & Sawyer's (2006) research suggests that catering to an audience's precocious ability with images can overwhelm their ability to process any other information. Some simply cannot hear you when there are images. This is a problem. Even if you wanted to put all relevant information on the slides and stand there silently, is this the human connection Bateson would want or the leadership Witt desires?

The third reason is exactly that Bateson/Witt question. We need to connect and inspire, not encourage tuning out. A former student tried my advice in a presentation for another class where the traditional mode of Power Point was typically practiced. When she inserted the blank slide, her professor, who had not looked at her since 30 seconds into the introduction, looked at her again. He actually interrupted her and said, "What happened to your Power Point? I was reading that." She told me that what she wanted to say at that moment was, "Exactly. But now you're listening to *me* for once." But offending your professor is usually not the best way to get an A.

Managing Focus

Your job, when designing a visual aid system, is to maximize attention to what matters. What matters is you. But sometimes we need a slidedeck to manage additional content. What counts as that content will be outlined in Chapter 13, but it is unlikely to be an entire speech, sentence-by-sentence, translated into bulleted form on a set of 78 slides.

The next section of this chapter will describe how to use Power Point for a better organizational scheme than what we typically see, but I wanted to take a second to talk more about this question of focus and some additional critical elements.

Here's a theory: *Everything on a slide distracts from everything else on a slide.*

CHAPTER 7

Perhaps you don't believe this, in spite of studies that demonstrate that it is true, especially with slides (Levasseur & Sawyer, 2006). Perhaps you make sure you pick a nice background with swooshy things or diamonds or rainbow colors. Perhaps you add lots of clip art images of books and computers and silhouette figures pushing pencils or scratching their heads. Perhaps all the things in the bulleted list enter with different sets of strange animation effects, maybe accompanied by a sound, like a boing or crashing glass or a honk.

Krug's (2000) book on how to design webpages is called *Don't Make Me Think*, and one of his central arguments is that to make a webpage useful, you have to make it simple enough so that people can find what they need or do the task they came to the site for. He compares most messy websites to distracting cocktail parties. His maxim on simplicity is "assume that *everything* is visual noise until proven otherwise" (p. 39). And since your audience in a speech can't click on anything to figure it out, it is worse for them. They are mouse-less captives to our lazy designs. A nice rule-of-thumb is to think about your audience members, each with a mouse. How long do you suffer through a website that isn't communicating before you move on? How long would they really give your Power Point if they could click it away?

The issue is not just clip art and backgrounds. Those are easy to eliminate. What about pieces of our content we don't need? The majority of any slide is what Krug would call *navigation*, to continue the web metaphor. Titles, subtitles, additional words added to bullet points to clarify how they are different from other bullet points, etc. The amount of actual content nested in there, especially given how big a font you have to put it all in so the cool kids in the back of the class can read it, is sadly often small.

THE ZOMBIE GUIDE TO PUBLIC SPEAKING

The biggest offenders are titles and subtitles. At every second of every speech, do I need to be thinking primarily (it is in bigger type and at the top of the page, after all) of what main point and subpoint we are in the middle of? No? And is it possible that I can't fully think about the content of that subsection while I am being pulled to read the title of the larger section of the speech we are in at every second?

Before Power Point, it was easily technically feasible to put titles on the tops of things like overhead transparencies, posters, flip-charts, etc. *But until Power Point suggested that we do so, no one thought that was a good idea* (see Fluharty & Ross, 1981; Kenny, 1982; Mills, 1977; Winans, 1920). According to Gaskins (2012), one of the key creators of Power Point, some of the decisions that led to the typical Power Point format are not exactly logically compelling. Gaskins thought things should be centered at the top of the slide because he liked that. Gaskins and co-designer Austin created title/layout background structures that could be replicated throughout the slideshow based on how that reminded them of headers and footers on a book page. These are not good reasons to continue with the official Power Point style. As with the Works Cited as a final slide strategy critiqued in the previous chapter, the more we rely on paper and book metaphors to understand electronic communication, the more we are in danger of bad communication.

Gaskins does suggest that they designed features based on his extensive collection of overheads from speeches around the world. He points out that the vast majority of those had titles and bulleted lists, which does seem like a good reason to continue this practice – it's what everyone did and does. But he also admits that he feels like the slides in his collection were like this because of the "poor tools" used at the time, including the basic difficulty, which he describes in detail, of overheads being made by individuals or groups working with paper who would then give the notes to a secretary to type into an overhead creation program. Hmmm. How much of the titling is a function of making sure all the people in that process knew they were on the same page (literally)? Again, this not a compelling reason to continue that practice. In sum, Gaskins and Austin designed Power Point, not with what was good for the audience or persuasion in mind, but, first, based on a series paper and books metaphors which persist in the program. Second, they based Power Point on what was close enough to existing practice that it would sell. Hard to blame them. I don't. I blame us for perpetuating a now antique style.

Take a look at this slide:

Zombie Art
black and white

- Here's a picture my son drew for the book.
- I guess I should put text over here since the PowerPoint default template says so.
- Look me me college-ing!!

Why not just show us the picture in the full frame? I mean, if you want us to look at the picture, GET OUT OF THE WAY! AND TAKE YOUR LITTLE TEXT, TOO! The same problem would be there if you were doing what I now name The Stock Photo Side-by-Side Layout Fail. You've seen this one a thousand times. To supplement the text, which uses, say, the word "fight," the slide designer grabs images from the Internet that might relate, perhaps one of those ridiculous stock photo setups, like people yelling at technology, that look totally fake.[7] How does this help us understand the idea? It doesn't:

Inspiring Slide! About!! Our!!! Services!!!!

- We will FIGHT for your organization! (Get it? Fight? Like she totally is boxing, right?
- So keep paying us for our services!
- Because we are fighters!
- LOOK AT THE PICTURE INSTEAD OF CRITICALLY ASSESSING OUR VALUE!!

Everything distracts from everything else. When I see slides like this I usually think the designer lacks competence. But on bad days I think they are hiding

---

[7] I am not critiquing the *entire* art and practice of stock photography. In fact, in Chapter 13 I suggest some useful stock photo resources. The trouble is that not all stock photos are good. A bigger issue is that not all stock photos are helpful for the particular message you want to convey even if they seem to be about the same subject. When you add bulleted sentences next to it, well, yuck.

something from me. They are designing this way on purpose. They are not just not-communicating, they are ANTI-communicating!

Reflect, if you please. Do you like reading the rulebook and learning how to play new games? Do you prefer to read the instructions for how to use the TV or just plug it in and push buttons? You are not alone. There is a reason that video games no longer ship with vast manuals you have to read to figure out how to play. Now you can play tutorials as you go, because you are only able and motivated to (remember the HSM and ELM again) learn how to use the gravity gun when the game actually gives you a gravity gun, right?

Tell me something when I need to know it, and only then. When you are done with it, make it go away. This is, to use a contemporary business metaphor, *just-in-time delivery*.

Winans understood this about charts and human attention back in 1920, when it was much harder to accomplish than it is today. But how many times have I had to look at the picture of the hungry child in the charity speech for so long that I began to wonder why his eyebrows were of different shapes as my attention wandered?

If I don't need to know exactly where every slide fits into the big picture at every time, then most slides don't need titles. How does the audience follow it all? Good question . . .

Organizers

Keeping these lessons in mind, and remembering what we learned about connectives in Chapter 4, this should give us a new vision for how to organize things. *Connectives instead of titles.*

I begin my hypothetical speech on this chapter with the

following preview:

> **Strategic Ambiguity**
>
> **Managing Focus**
>
> **Organizers**
>
> **There Is No Spoon**
>
> **Professionalism**

When I fully preview everything, and I make my transition to the first point, I show that by having that slide fade into this one:

> **Strategic Ambiguity**

When I am finished with this section, I bring back up

the entire preview slide to remind us of where we are; then I fade into the Managing Focus slide. Then comes the material I use to explore the Managing Focus question in that presentation.

And so on. Put the items in an invisible table and then just make the font color on the unused items the same color as the background on subsequent slides so that you can keep things in the same place on each slide, and so that you can revise your content at a later date if needed.

This kind of thing, because it stands out so much from your other title-less slides that happen in-between, actually makes it easier for people to follow the presentation. Every word matters, unlike the norm. This makes each one easier to remember. And the fade to a new slide, which looks as if the list of all the points is disappearing into one, is a great marker for the verbal transition you are making at that exact moment.

This style also allows to easier re-entry into the presentation for sleepers, slackers, and folks who stepped outside to answer their phone, get a drink, visit the restroom or generally take a short break from your speech. Typical title- and subtitle-heavy designs simply don't sufficiently cue audiences to the organization of the presentation. If I miss a few slides, it is difficult to make it back. The organizer style outlined here, though, provides constant avenues of re-engagement.

You can have additional nests of items as you need to explore subpoints. Here's an example I use in my Film Studies class:

THE ZOMBIE GUIDE TO PUBLIC SPEAKING

Composition & Framing	Lighting	Photography
		aspect ratio
		lens
		image quality
		exposure

You can see here that this is the internal preview for the subpoints in the third main point of the lecture, "Photography." Eventually, everything but "aspect ratio" will fade out as I transition into that point.

If you've used a decent number of the image-based slides we will learn about in Chapter 13, you can even begin to associate smaller versions of those images with the organizers in your summaries and transitions. Then, by the end of the speech, you can use those thumbnail images to add to the organizers. Imagine, for the slide above, for example, a small version of the image comparing telephoto and wide-angle lenses popping up next to "lens" or instead of "lens". In my editing lecture, after I associate one style of editing with D.W. Griffith and another with Sergei Eisenstein, I can use smaller versions of their pictures to represent those subpoints on the organizer slides.

In my TEDx Talk (Vrooman, 2014b), that is how I organized the subpoints:

CHAPTER 7

I described the main points while showing versions of this slide as:

1. Shoes
2. Selfies
3. Star-lord[8]

That translated into what we would eventually discover about those points:

1. How we customize objects in our daily lives
2. Social media sharing as audience customization
3. What we can learn from social media shares

Different audiences and different occasions will need different approaches to this question. But none of those answers is to simply title every slide and have, in essence, 45 main points.

To pull it all together, then, your task is to create a Power Point that will guide those audience members who

---

[8] This was my version of the "magic feathers" idea from Chapter 5.

are paying attention without overwhelming them with minutia, provide a window for audience members who are not paying attention to relocate themselves into the presentation, and to wrest control of the speech away from a technology which wants to supplant you.

There is No Spoon

Perhaps you recognize this quote from the *The Matrix* (Wachowski & Wachowski, 1999). A boy teaches our protagonist about manipulating their virtual world. Knowing it doesn't exist is the key first step. The same is true for you, creating a much more low-tech and less immersive virtual audiovisual world for your audience than the Matrix: there is no slide.

If we think of a presentation with visual aids as a collection of individual slides, we are making a mistake. What matters are your communication objectives. Those are your only "objects." When we think instead of slides as objects, we misplace our focus and effort, and we can no longer bend the spoon. We care more about our slides than our ideas.

They sure seem like objects. I know. Even if you use something like Prezi, that tries to build an overarching presentation metaphor as a swooping through an information space, in the end, you are designing slide-by-slide, whatever software you use.

We are even given a set of slide-design rules over the years that reinforce this bias, like the old-school 6 by 6 or 7 by 7 rules are that you should use no more than 6 or 7 words per bullet line and no more than 6 or 7 bullet points per slide (see Mackiewicz, 2008). These were well-intentioned enough, I suppose, but you can imagine how people sat down to their computer and what they made with these rules in mind: static, boring, still text-heavy but now abstract-language and jargon-heavy slides. The newest rule sweeping the blogosphere is Guy Kawasaki's (2005) 10/20/30: no more than 10 slides, 20 minutes, and use 30-point font. His defense of his rule illustrates the fundamental problem with seeing slides in this way. He asserts the 10 part of the rule is needed because "a normal human being cannot comprehend more than ten concepts in a meeting." But why should concepts and slides be equal?[9]

Although Doumont (2005) argues that each slide should contain only one idea so that it can be understood easily, Godin (2001) argues that a good idea will take many slides to get across. He demonstrates that in his TED Talks (2003, 2006, 2009), which use visual aids in creative and funny ways. Farkas (2006) suggests that unless we do serious thinking about the scope and complexity of an idea, we should avoid the one slide=one idea rule entirely. Even more intriguing, Djonev and Van Leeuwen (2013) demonstrate the ways some ideas simply come out wrong when squeezed into traditional Power Point layout slides.

If we begin with the idea more clearly, where does that take us? How do I get a concept across the best way? Kenny (1982) suggested that more complex ideas should be taught using multiple slides which build "complex diagrams in stages" (p. 61), a pretty difficult task in the days of overhead transparencies, requiring "hinges, "opaque material" and "sliding or rotating layers." What is our excuse for not doing this when technology has made it so easy to do so?

You can see examples of this using numerical data in Chapter 10 and in my TEDx Talk (Vrooman, 2014b, see the

---

[9] Maybe if we used as many slides as we needed to explain a concept, people could learn more in these meetings?

sequence beginning at 7:00). Other great examples of this are TED Talks by David McCandless (2010, see the sequences at minute 3:00 and 6:15 for examples) and Rob Reid (2012, see the sequence beginning at 1:10).

You have also likely seen this done with images before in the news media, documentaries or sports coverage: an image is shown and then something is circled or highlighted. Or perhaps an arrow is drawn. Maybe the rest of the image is greyed or blacked out. Maybe another picture from another time or place is added on top, for just a second, for comparison. I'll bet you see this kind of thing every day, just not in thoughtlessly constructed visual aids.

Concepts work that way, too. Here is a recreation of Spencer Stephens' final slide in a long sequence of explanation and history for his Senior Thesis presentation on Batman and changing pop culture masculinity:

Masculinity in Media		
Western Hero	Civilized Hero	Negotiating Hero
1930s-1950s	1960s-1970s	1980s-1990s
	Adam West (1966-1968)	Frank Miller (1986)
1930s-1950s	1960s-1970s	1980s-1990s
Batman Masculinity		

This is fairly complex. He is presenting two histories which interact with each other to set the stage for his analysis of the newest Batman movies. To present this, he broke it down into pieces and took his audience through the history with examples. His first slide in this sequence was like this:

CHAPTER 7

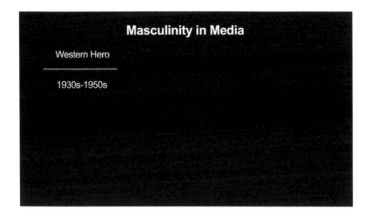

Then he added an image of John Wayne on a movie poster. He continued in that manner through a sequence of 16 slides. It helped us all follow his logic.

Sometimes even simpler ideas require this kind of pacing and spacing. Direct our focus in pieces, or as a narrative. Let the idea decide how to deal with questions of space and time, not your technological habits.

You will need to add formatting the layout and background of your slidedeck to your checklist of things to do when beginning one, which should already include:

- Figuring out how to manage the organizers and visual consistency for a group presentation *before* people start working on their individual portions of the work.
- Formatting for either 4x3 or 16x9 format, depending on what the screen and projector are set up for in the environment you will speak in.[10]

---

[10] You don't know that? Visit the site. Call someone onsite who can tell you. Aspect ratio issues are critical in making sure your slides look their best.

THE ZOMBIE GUIDE TO PUBLIC SPEAKING

- Figuring out how to embed the fonts in your presentation so everything doesn't change when you open it on a strange computer.[11]
- Finding out whether or not you really need to use your organization's slidedeck template, which often comes with distracting title bars, or, at the very least, little logos in the bottom corner.[12] These generally distract from your message, but often we just use them out of habit. Use only if required.
- Finding a way to minimize the distractions of any required template. If the template has just a logo on the bottom left or right, for example, situate organizers on the other side of the space to draw attention to them. And choose colors which contrast with the template colors. If the template has a lot of material across the top, be extra careful about putting information too close to the top of the slide. And, especially if the template has some sort of background pattern that will interrupt your ability to use those magic rectangles suggested a

---

[11] Google this for the software you use. In the current version of Power Point, this is in the following menus: File>Options>Save.

[12] I know. Maybe someone in marketing or PR wants everyone to use these templates for "branding consistency." Okay. That is useful, up to a point. But is the corporate logo needed on all 450 slides shown at the weekend retreat? Should we really have our mission statement about valuing people across the top banner when the Power Point explaining why no one is getting raises this year is presented? Don't we all know who we work for? And in terms of external communication, do you want that logo highlighted for *everything*? Firings, apologies, etc.? When we brand too much, it becomes a ubiquitous message we no longer see. If you have a choice, make sure you brand when and where it will have the most impact.

few paragraphs from now, be sure to create the equivalent of a blank slide while keeping the template in place. Perhaps something like a chalkboard visual metaphor in the center of the slide which you explain as a space you will be doing something in at various parts of the speech, like building diagrams, etc.:[13]

Then, when you bring that recognizable chalkboard iconography back up, it will serve as a weak form of a blank slide.
- Instead of using the prepopulated background and layout styles that come with your software,

---

[13] This kind of thing has serious limitations, but the imposition of a template has saddled you with limitations. Your task is to work creatively with them as best you can.

choose everything. Make the layout blank so you can decide, on that canvas, where you want things to appear and how. And choose a simple background, both to avoid distracting from your other content and to allow for simple multi-slide tricks that are harder to achieve when the complex background removes the two key tools in the multi-slide toolbox from your arsenal: font color and the giant box.

For Spencer's Batman presentation, for example, the simplest solution was to design the final, most complex slide first. You can see how it looks, how it fits, and whether, upon sober reflection, it makes sense. Then you copy the slide and start taking things away. You can delete words, but sometimes that messes up your placements, especially if you use invisible tables (the designer's best friend) to keep everything orderly. Making them the same color as the background allows them to disappear while still leaving them in existence for future edits. Or covering everything with a box or other shape the exact color as the background is a wonderful kludge that can quickly cover pieces of a picture or misaligned images or make elements of a graph disappear as needed, as in Chapter 13.

There is no spoon. There are no slides. Focus on the real question and make choices.

Professionalism

Many of you who resist this chapter will use the ideograph "the real world" to resist these ideas. According to McGee (1980), an ideograph is a slogan-like abstraction that we use strategically and politically to make people

CHAPTER 7

agree with us. Examples are things like "love," "liberty," "patriotism," "justice," and "America." None of these things have definitions that are fixed and agreed-upon by all. What exactly is "justice" for a murderer, for example? Death or life in prison? Begin the debate with your political opponents . . .

Ideographs are used to manipulate.

Allow me to suggest that we manipulate ourselves by using our conceptions of "the real world." What we usually mean is stuff we've seen before or habits that we were taught by people connected with professional fields we'd like to enter. But what if Godin (2001) is right that those experiences were lazy and wrong? What if the Power Points you often see are not the result of professionals doing their best, but of people just trying to get by with a technology they don't fully understand, doing communicative tasks without ever really thinking of their audience?

You've all been to websites that were frustrating to use and seemed to hide the only information you went to the site for, right? As Krug (2000) points out, most websites are badly constructed and never really tested fully (if at all!) for usability. Yet it costs a lot of money and time to launch a website, and the impact a bad web presence can have on an organization is deep and probably not calculable. Thus, if so many organizations are throwing up lazy and ineffective websites, which costs them money, what are the chances that all the Power Points at all their meetings are well-designed?

You have experienced thousands of Power Points in the world of education. How many of those daily slide shows were carefully constructed by educators who understood what impacts their technological choices were having on their students? How many were, in fact, provided by textbook companies whose goal is to tie instructors so closely to the chapters and content of the book that it makes it difficult for educators to ever switch textbooks?[14]

I commonly have students who reject these ideas by arguing that, in their field, where there is more "highly technical" information required for their Power Points, I am teaching a Power Point style that lacks relevance. Chapter 13 will address how to deal with the questions of content on slides when information specificity is required. In that chapter we will discuss the physics lectures of Nobel laureate Richard Feynman. Certainly his lectures on quantum mechanics count as technical.

This chapter is about what goes in between the moments of information, so I find this ideographic objection to be curious, but also illuminating. Are these students rejecting all the research that supports the claims of this chapter because they are uncomfortable being perceived as making an effort at communicating? Would my methods reveal that they care about their audience and that they are trying to reach them? Does this bring along fears of rejection? Isn't this the kind of retreat from

---

[14] As a graduate student, I attended a required meeting with the author of the *MOPSBOT* we were adopting for all our classes. The author joked that our school had adopted the book because of what he called "the thud factor" as he dropped piles of stuff for teachers that came with the book. There was a teacher's guidebook, a CD/DVD with sample speeches to show students and a test bank (questions for your texts) with an answer key. There was also a giant notebook of color overhead transparencies (which have, of course, now been turned into Power Points) we could use to teach the classes. It might seem like these were pedagogical gifts, but really they were marketing. They were handcuffs designed to make it hard to change texts. Now, the books also come with pre-crafted online courseware, as well. The interactive Power Points run on the publisher's server so you and the students have to keep buying access. How much of your education has been constructed as marketing to buy your teachers' allegiance?

CHAPTER 7

communication that Chapters 1 and 2 were about?

No one likes to hear that the way they've been giving speeches (taught to them by someone they liked, probably) is ineffective. We'd all like to believe that we have been doing a good job. We'd all like to believe that the dominant impression we left on people as a result of all those presentations was positive. But this is not a book about what you want your life to have been. Let it go. This is a book about making your practices better.

I'd encourage all of you to think hard about what "professionalism" really is and what simply parades around as if it were.

In the end, for me, "professionalism" is concrete and specific. *Do not waste other people's time*. By that standard, I would say a lot of what calls itself "real world" is simply not.

In closing, I have additional, relatively unrelated, notes on questions of professionalism and the real world that are important to keep in mind. If a professional communicator's job is to communicate without wasting time, the least she/he can do is be ready. In your classes and in the rest of the world, know that nothing on your Power Point matters if we have to wait for it, if we have to wait for you to get the right cable hooked up and press F5, if we have to wait for you to load it from your thumbdrive or email, if we have to wait for the hotel to deliver the projector to the conference room. This is the ultimate test of professionalism. If you can't respect my time enough to be ready, I lose my respect for you. If you aren't sufficiently expert in your topic to go on without slides, you are not, in fact, a professional at all.

My old public speaking course director, Clark Olson, shocked all of us new grad student teachers by telling us that a real professor doesn't need notes. If you have to look at something, you are not expert enough, and he would lose a bit (or a lot) of respect for you. That might be a bit much, but applying this to Power Point is revealing. Ask yourself for every presentation if you can go on without it. It will happen some day: a projector bulb failure, a computer virus, a blackout. If you can't give the presentation, you tell the Clark Olsons in your audience (and believe me, he is everywhere) that you are an amateur.

When you watch Mitch Hagney (2014) speak at TEDxSanAntonio, he seems calm, cool, and collected. They've even edited his Power Point slides into his presentation. But live, none of his slides worked. Here he was, at TED, with more than 600 people in the audience, and his slides weren't working! But you cannot tell. He just sails through, knowing that his goal is to take this one chance and connect his important message with the audience. Although we later found out that his wireless presenter had run out of batteries, he was so good live that I assumed, in his audience, that he'd simply decided to bail on his slides and do it old school. That's how good he was at carrying it off.

In the end, if you have an mp3 player or a tablet computer of any kind in your possession, your "real world" was created for you by Steve Jobs, who violated the way we do Power Point in the "real world." Remember Apple's slogan, "Think Different"? Most of his major speeches are still on YouTube. Watch them. You'll see.

PART THREE

Part Three:
Resuscitating the Flesh

THE ZOMBIE GUIDE TO PUBLIC SPEAKING

CHAPTER 8

Chapter 8: The Uses and Abuses of Sources

We know that people are complex. We know that "speakers who would move audiences must play on many strings" (Peterson, 1954, p. xxviii). Aristotle asks for pathos as well as logos. Peterson worries that speakers tend to do only one or the other, and Stiff (1986), writing about the ELM and HSM, suggests that the more variety of supporting material used, the harder it is for audiences to resist you. Naistadt (2005), in addressing contemporary speakers in a business context, thinks of both hard data and narratives as the evidence a speaker should use, and she spends much time trying to teach speakers to use those narratives, assuming that they will default to numbers, incorrectly, in a business context.

We need to ask ourselves what we are using evidence for. How does it work? What should we choose to motivate our audience? Richard Feynman, whose early 1960s lectures at Caltech revolutionized the teaching of physics, made this note to himself on sabbatical in Brazil in 1952: "First you figure out why you want the students to learn the subject and what you want them to know, and the method will result more or less by common sense" (quoted in Goodstein & Neugebauer, 1995, p. xx). Start with the *goal*.

Think, for a second, about the need to not only inform people about what they should do to prepare for disease pandemics and hurricanes and other disasters, but the need to convince them to change their behaviors and prepare for something which seems to be a far-off or unlikely fear. The Centers for Disease Control and Prevention have created a whole set of zombie preparedness information (http://www.cdc.gov/phpr/ zombies.htm) because that is what will get enough attention to affect people's behavior. Preparing for zombies is actually a decent way to prepare for earthquakes, except you won't need a katana in an earthquake.

Instead of this kind of thinking, which has communication in mind, so many students want to give a bunch of dictionary definitions at the beginning of every speech. As Statler and Waldorf, the old men from the Muppets, say in *The Muppet Christmas Carol* (Henson, 1992) when confronted with Fozzie's traditional speech: "And it's tradition for us to take a little nap!"

The worst offender in the corpse of typical student speechmaking is the quotation. Oh, my students love a quotation. When you read something and pull out a quote, it feels like you are doing work. Many of us learn how to write with the idea that paragraphs have topic sentences and then quotes that are *related* to that topic, and then additional sentences of elaboration we create around those quotes. If so, we are bad writers. Writing and speaking are about making arguments. Is that quotation really that important? This is what my colleague, Margaret Gonzales, a professor of composition, calls "drive-by quoting." You drop a quote in and then speed on without engaging.

A few years ago, a particular student gave a speech comparing the Xbox 360 and the Playstation 3. He would read direct quotes from electronic gadget review websites. These were really simple quotes like "The Xbox 360 has a deeper catalog of interesting games, plus really good unique-to-the-platform titles like *Halo*." Then, he'd look up at his drowsy audience, and "explain" the quote to us, like this: "So what this is saying is that the Xbox is better because it has more games and really interesting games, like *Halo*."

That kind of work is dead. It really feels like work, but it is making zero difference in the minds of the cognitive misers in the audience. We need to make it all come alive again.

CHAPTER 8

When I see or read people doing this, students, bloggers, TED speakers, pastors, meeting presenters, etc., it reminds me quite intensely of the "stragglers" in Whitehead's (2011) zombie novel, *Zone One*. Some zombies, the "skels" are the cannibal monsters we've come to expect from zombie movies, but the "stragglers" have just had their brains zapped by the zombie virus, and they go through the sad motions of their lives, seemingly forever: "Their lives had been an interminable loop of repeated gestures; now their existences were winnowed to this discrete and eternal moment" (p. 50), forever holding a fry basket in the dark and deserted fast-food joint or forever pushing buttons on the dead copy machine. When I see people wasting their audience's time with this kind of drive-by thinking, drive-by quoting style, a small part of me imagines them as "stragglers," swaying up at the podium, holding a wireless presenter, gesturing at a broken computer, giving the same speech to a dead audience forever. It doesn't matter what they say. They are just completing an assignment, a task, the next thing. Forever.

Drive-By Quoters

When I work with high school students or first-semester first-year students I see this kind of thing the most. High school students are being taught to write papers by finding three or four quotes and then "elaborating" on them in their five-paragraph essays, as in this guide to the AP History test:

Body Paragraph (5 sentences)
    1. Topic Sentence (subtopic 2 from Intro)
    2. Evidence 1 with significance/explanation
    3. Analysis (relate to thesis)

4. Evidence 2 with significance/explanation
5. Analysis (relate to thesis) ("The Five," n.d.)

Here is our problem. You are encouraged to simply drop evidence in and then do this *significance-explanation-analysis* dance. In speeches I hear this as:

> Vince Lombardi once said "Perfection is not attainable. But if we chase perfection we can catch excellence." *[evidence]*. He would know. His team won the first two Superbowls *[significance]*. That means, for those of you who don't know anything about football, that he was really successful *[explanation]*. So, um, you know, this just shows why we should always work hard, as I've said *[analysis]*.

None of this is good *significance-explanation-analysis*, but it goes through enough of the motions to pass the exam, it seems:

> To score at least a 3, students would be wise to make use of pertinent references from the text. Encourage them to use specific quotations to back up their assertions. However, remind them that they must explain their quotes clearly and demonstrate how they are relevant to the question. (Shelnut, 2015)

Really? This is the low level of analytic achievement we are looking for to pass a test for college credits? I grade these papers and speeches for a living, so I already know the answer, sadly. Yes, all we seem to expect is that they "explain" and then show relevance. Relevance? Is this why

CHAPTER 8

I get things like this, which we might add on at the end of the Lombardi bit from before?

> All of this is why Pinterest is good. Because even though you might not make everything you pin like you were perfect, you just might make some excellent things! #NailedIt

Sigh.

This becomes a horrible cycle. I see students with a desperate, almost homicidal glint in their eyes when I critique them on this style. "But this is research! There's no other way to do anything! Everyone knows that! I got a 5 on the AP test!! Why do you hate me?"

The next section will detail this pathological research process for a (stereo?)typical student. The section to follow that shows how these habits stick around after graduation and mar our discourse long after college.

The Horrible Cycle

Let's explore the inner workings of this process.

When students start to explore topic they, as a recent student described her process for me, "look for quotes." This process is kind of like the indiscriminate hunger of a zombie wandering across a post-suburban wasteland.

Say the assignment is to give a presentation or write a paper on why we should use figurative language in speeches. Student X will often begin by Googling "Why should we use figurative language." I guess that's better than Googling "figurative language," which would give us an even larger blizzard of stuff. Here's what we might do with the Google results I found by doing this search today.

First, "Tanya," whose profile picture is a pair of

puppies, says: "Authors use figurative language to make their stories more vivid and interesting" ("Why Do," 2015). If I'm a student trying not to have to find more sources than I have to, I will cite this as the overall website host, because I think *Yahoo!Answers* sounds more credible.[1] So, based on this mysterious Tanya's expertise, I have my first uninteresting quote. I will probably read it word-for-word, too. Why? Because it sounds like a thing if I read the quote. But if I paraphrase it, well, then it just sounds like what it is, an unsubstantiated statement with no persuasive value.

The second thing I see in my Google parade looks good,[2] but when I click on it, it's about short stories. Bummer. But I did all this work to skim the big blue headings,[3] so I'd better get something out of it. So, um, the last bit says "Figurative language can elevate ordinary, everyday language" (Layfield, 2015). Sweet! One more quote. And the author totally has a Master's degree, so she's like an expert. A little Google search for a definition and I can say elevate means "to raise to a higher intellectual or spiritual level" ("Elevate," 2015). Boom! #CrushIt

I need two more sources if there is a five-source minimum, so let's see what's next. eHow.com, that's what's next! A giant quote that will burn many seconds and get me closer to the 6-minute minimum for this speech:

> Language that draws you in does so by prodding your imagination so that your brain needs to

---

[1] Does it really, though? Does it?   no.
[2] By "good," I mean that I'm totes tired of school right now #boring, so I'm going to do this fast enough so I can get a few more cat videos in before I have to get on Instagram #yolo.
[3] Literally, it was like 20 seconds of my life I will never get back. No way I'm wasting that, Vrooman. #literally #hashtag

> know more. Ancient storytellers needed all the rhetorical tools they could get to keep people listening, and they found the best ones by exaggerating and stretching words to get the most extreme meaning possible. (Anderson, nd)

Almost done! Ancient storytellers, bro.

But Vrooman is kind of a jerk and wants us to get peer-reviewed articles, whatever those are. So let me add "peer reviewed article" on the end of the Google search and try again. This takes longer, but I long ago figured out that Google adds a name and a date and a "Cited by x – Related articles" under things that might be peer-reviewed,[4] so I find one that has a sentence I can understand. I only get a small piece of a larger article in a snapshot view on questia.com, but I find a phrase I can quote, so I will just say *The Philological Quarterly* "emphasizes the enormous difference language can make" and not look for the whole article, because yuck.[5]

This student now pulls together a speech where they do the surface-level *significance-explanation-analysis* dance. And, of course, all of the arguments are all of the weakest type, really close to being fallacious: the argument by authority. The best arguments by authority persuade

---

[4] You don't think I learned that, Vrooman? I tried it one day because there's no way I'm going to use a library database like you told us to. #snoozeworthy

[5] If we actually do find the article, it talks about how figurative language is used in a particular piece of literature to reveal tensions in social and class level, the way those interact with gender, and the way those are encoded in language (Migiel, 1998). Pretty much nothing to do with our topic. So, yeah, this is why this kind of "academic" research is inaccurate and unethical. I'd like to stop seeing it every semester.

when they can defend the qualifications of the authority in question on the issue specifically at hand. Rarely do we go to that kind of trouble in this sort of work. Often students say things like "And I have a quote here on that . . ." as if the act of quoting some exact wording that exists somewhere on the Internet counts as persuasive. These are incredibly weak arguments by authority which rest on the warrant (see Chapter 14) that "Words I find on the Internet are true."

We can get better and point out that *The Philological Quarterly* is an academic journal, in which case that warrant turns out to be "Words I find in peer-reviewed journals are true."

Neither of those warrants are true or persuasive. Further, none of this says much about the relevance of these quotations to the issue at hand, the way figurative language affects audiences in a public speaking context. Doesn't it seem immediately obvious that Martin Luther King's figurative language-heavy "I Have a Dream" speech might be using it differently and for a different purpose than the metaphors in a poem?

Drive-by quoting leads to a stack of lazy authority arguments, which leads to an audience that is mentally checked out.

Zombie Statistics

We never really learn. If you graduated long ago and are reading this chapter thus far with an avuncular shake of the head at "Those silly students, heh, heh, heh," this section of the chapter addresses our ongoing failure to grasp these issues as a larger society. The three examples of fake, undead information in this section are not only all over the Internet, but I'll bet you've heard them trumpeted

CHAPTER 8

as fact in your workplace, as well, perhaps even with the same graphics.[6] These things are information viruses, like the Rage virus in *28 Days Later* (Boyle, 2002). Brendan Gleeson's character gets a bit of fluid in his eyes, and it's zombie time. These stats get in your eyes, and, boom: zombie researcher.

We drive-by cite our whole lives. We don't really do deep research. The Internet has made it easier than ever to just troll for something that looks like what we want.[7] What we need instead is a rigorous citation practice where we engage with what we find and trace it back as far as we can. For example …

The Curve of Attention

This thing has been trotted out for years. We believe it because it makes sense. I even suggested it might have some merit in Chapter 6. The audience pays the most attention to us at the beginning, gets sleepy and then wakes up at the end. Here's Sam's version of it:

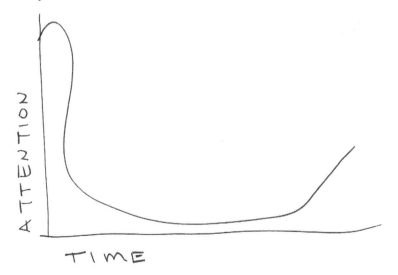

Each version has a slightly different shape to The Curve. The reason is that there is no actual data to back this up.

I first saw this while writing the teacher's manual (Vrooman & Egan, 2009) for Fraleigh & Tuman (2009), where the authors suggest that it is based on a "Study by TCC Consulting (San Francisco, Calif.), undertaken between 1987 and 1997" (p. N-4). Emails to the authors about this data never got a response. I found The Curve again in Kenny (1982), who suggests it is a result of studies conducted on students. The y axis of his graph is labelled as "Percentage of class paying attention" (p. 13), but he then describes some uncited experiments about how much students can *recall* after lectures of different lengths, which is a different sort of y axis entirely.[8] He cites Mills (1977) as the source of The Curve and the research behind it, but when I finally tracked down a copy of Mills' book, his Curve, exactly the same as Kenny's, is based not on data, but on "an analogy between the learning process and the process of digestion" (p. 18).

A digestion analogy. Really?

What he suggests about this analogy makes intuitive sense, which is why people keep reproducing it, but what we have is something that has become "fact" for us only because it got turned into a graph. And Mills is reasonably clear that this is just a thought-experiment and analogy: "the shape of the curve in the hands of a good instructor can be modified almost at will" (p. 19).

---

[8] I was going to reprint the graph for you, but it turns out that reprinting one graph from a book 30 years out of print would cost me more than $150. Since I'm trying to keep this book as inexpensive as possible, that wasn't going to happen. Welcome to the ins and outs of self-publishing! You can, if you'd like, go to Google Books and search "Peter Kenny attention curve" and see the famous graph for yourself, though.

CHAPTER 8

I later found McGrath's (2015) citation that The Curve is based on Bligh's (2000) book, first published in 1971. Bligh bases almost all this on Lloyd's (1968) work, creating a series of diagrams based on what Lloyd "hypothesizes" and "confirms" (Bligh, 2000, p. 49). The trouble is that Lloyd's two-page article is based on his own observations of student restlessness in his classes, hardly sufficient rigor to "confirm" a hypothesis and graph the data.[9]

Yet, by now The Curve is used as if it were a *classic study*, you know, with *data* behind it. Red Magma (2009) tosses their version into a Slideshare which sells their elearning consulting. They use it as the *central data point* for why lectures are an inefficient method of learning. Sharpe (2012) suggests The Curve is an "amalgam of all sorts of things from physiological responses to recall about part of the session." She cites additional "numerous studies" on our 10-15 minute attention spans in "passive tasks" like lecture. This is a commonly reported statistic that, according to Wilson and Korn (2007) has no real supporting evidence besides personal experience and anecdotes.

The fun of all of this is that writers keep changing the shape of The Curve for their own purposes while still asserting that it is based on data. Fraleigh and Tuman's (2009) Curve jumps up a bit higher at the conclusion than the 50%-ish in Mills' (1977). Niemantsverdreit (n.d.) has a curve that goes to 100% attention really quickly at the introduction and then never seems to get up to 50% again.[10] McGrath (2015) has another like it. Sharpe's remains really flat at the end, popping up to what we might imagine is about 20% at best. In contrast to these attention skeptics, MichCommunication (2012) gives us a graph that looks like

---

[9] Wilson and Korn (2007) demonstrate the problems with Bligh's entire approach in their article.

[10] Sam and I decided that our Curve goes to eleven. #ListenToTheSustain

a bowl, with the conclusion optimistically popping up to what looks like is even over 100%! Reimold and Reimold (2003) have a graph that pops up to the 100% at the end, but really sharply. Like the one I commissioned for this chapter, it looks to be drawn by hand.[11]

If I see you presenting this Curve of Attention as a fact you will lose just about all of your credibility with me. This graph is reproduced because visual aids seem "truthy." It is what happens when people do simple searches to find something they want to say and need simple support. Everyone just needs to do better research, especially in professional contexts. The Internet makes it easier to find zombie statistics, but it makes it easier to debunk them, as well.

The Corrupted Cone

This might be the king of all zombie data. You have probably seen a version of this slide, which has no creator who claims credit for its blurry glory:

---

[11] If you Google "Attention Curve" you will see these versions and many others. You will also see some distressing examples of The Curve being adapted to other contexts, especially for Internet content audiences. The virus spreads...

CHAPTER 8

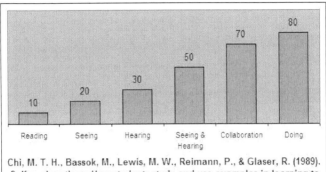

Chi, M. T. H., Bassok, M., Lewis, M. W., Reimann, P., & Glaser, R. (1989). Self-explanations: How students study and use examples in learning to solve problems. *Cognitive Science, 13*, 145-182.

You can find 3D multicolored versions of this graph, as well.

Thalheimer (2006) shows this graph to audiences and most raise their hands when he asks if they've seen it. So you probably have, too. But he's debunked this data in a variety of ways, including a call to the lead researcher, Michelele Chi, who has no idea where it or its data are from.

Thalheimer traces these numbers back to corruptions of Edgar Dale's "Cone of Experience," his take on learning which was never based on research. Here's one person's adaptation of it:

THE ZOMBIE GUIDE TO PUBLIC SPEAKING

EDGAR DALE'S CONE OF EXPERIENCE
(Graphic Remake by Royce A. Calingal)

- VERBAL SYMBOLS
- VISUAL SYMBOLS
- RECORDINGS, AUDIO
- STILL PICTURES
- MOTION PICTURES
- ATTEND EXHIBITS AND SITES
- FIELD TRIPS
- DEMONSTRATIONS
- DRAMATIZED EXPERIENCES
- CONTRIVED EXPERIENCES
- DIRECT PURPOSEFUL EXPERIENCES

Sometimes the levels are curved. In both versions, it *looks* like it is a proportional diagram. But it is not. Dale himself cautioned against using it this way, but the persistence of this fake information continues in terribly robust fashion (Thalheimer, 2015). A recent article on inc.com (Jay, 2015) reproduces this quote, shared on thousands of pages across the Internet:

> Based on a study by Edgar Dale, we remember:
> 10 percent of what we read
> 20 percent of what we hear
> 30 percent of what we see
> 50 percent of what we see and hear
> 70 percent of what we discuss with others
> 80 percent of what we personally experience
> 95 percent of what we teach others.

Now it is "a study by Edgar Dale" eh? Apparently just making things up while we lazily cite is just fine? Others cite the research of William Glasser on this stuff. Sure. Why not? Who else can we pin it on?

CHAPTER 8

Betrus (2014) traces this back to a snippet from a journal in 1913, which is simply quoting some sort of old aphorism which the writer links to the new (at the time) Montessori method of teaching. Although Montessori (1912) writes of mixing different kinds of stimuli in her educational method, no version of this formula exists in her work.

My students have shown me this graph and cited these numbers many times before. But even more common is one that was originally produced by someone writing a guide for OSHA employees who were giving presentations out in the field (Construction Safety, 1996). You've seen it, I'm sure. Its yellow bars suggest we retain: 10% of oral information, 35% of visual alone and 65% of both together.

There are no citations for where these statistics came from, and in the past few years the document has been removed from the osha.gov website, so no one is standing by this material's accuracy. Bloggers use this stuff with abandon, especially the "83% of human learning occurs visually" bit that follows the yellow bar graph in the original document. They cite OSHA or the Department of Labor, and it all just sounds *super credible*, right? Government studies! Something going on there about worker health and productivity! But these are just the poorly cited ideas created by an unknown author whose internal public speaking how-to ended up on the Internet in the early days of Mozilla.

I searched for research studies published in the twenty years before this OSHA document to see if I could find what data the author was using, but I could not. I did find that two researchers who were pretty sure that visuals were easier remembered than verbal-only information were surprised that their two studies showed no difference or only a small difference between those two conditions (Gehring & Togglia, 1988). So, you know, the yellow bar graph is probably wrong. And the blue bar graph is definitely wrong. But, hey, there are bars. And numbers. #Nailed It

Why Are Highway Signs Dark Green?

My experience in a variety of classrooms with different qualities of projectors, screens and lighting controls is that dark/black backgrounds with light/white text are easier to read than white backgrounds with black text. Others disagree. It would be nice to find a research-based answer to this.

When you search for this, you end up with this pair of sentences, which is swiped word-for-word and splashed, unattributed, *all over* the Internet:

> In fact, according to a study by the Outdoor Advertising Institute, reverse messages are up to 40 percent more visible. That is the reason that Departments of Transportation use white type against dark green or dark brown backgrounds on their highway signs.

There are numerous problems with this. The first is that there is no such thing as the Outdoor Advertising Institute. There are some organizations which sound kind of similar, like Institute of Outdoor Advertising, Inc., which merged into the Outdoor Advertising Association of America in 1994 (History of OOH, n.d.), but nothing that is exactly the cited organization . This should give us pause. But apparently it doesn't.

This pair of sentences gained web traction in 2004 when Fleming posted them to a blog. They are originally from an article by Fleming and Hunt (1996). Maybe this

CHAPTER 8

Outdoor Advertising Institute existed in the 1990s, at the time of the Fleming and Hunt article? Searches to that effect turned up the name, most notably in the obituary of advertising executive/golf enthusiast Cornelius C. "Neal" Weed, Jr. (Bebow, 2005), who is cited as an officer in said organization. Perhaps it really existed? Or perhaps this is all just a Pynchon novel?[12]

If the IOA and the theoretical OAI are the same thing, whatever report this is based on, if any, seems a bit lost in the pre-digital murk. The Duke OAAA papers archive contains some IOA documents, but the IOA is described as the "marketing arm" of the OAAA, which should make us wonder about the accuracy of the information. The OAAA itself was the subject of a blistering report commissioned by the state of Maryland, which concluded that the OAAA's study, which showed that electronic billboards (you know, the ones that change) were not any more distracting than conventional, unchanging billboards, was quite badly done and should not impact policy (Wachtel, 2007). Wachtel suggests that "objective, independent research" should be done instead of, if we read between his lines, this biased report form an industry advocacy group.

Based on the few things digitized in Duke's Rubenstein Library (n.d.) collection of OAAA (and some IOA) papers, the reports that exist tend toward the "do-s and don't's" style, which give numerical suggestions for type size, etc., but little or no supporting evidence aside from something like the "above recommendations are result of tests by Traffic Audit Bureau, Inc" ("Outdoor," 1950, p. 51). There is a depressingly eerie familiarity about

---

[12] This is a joke for those of you feeling too highbrow for my hashtag jokes. #yourewelcome

this rabbit hole citation style.[13]

You might say, "Hey, Vrooman, you may be the only person who ever tried to look all this up. Doesn't that mean that it is okay? People are probably persuaded, so why not?" I don't think it means that. I think people just stopped listening/reading and have some vague sense that maybe dark backgrounds work for a good reason. And that's it. It probably doesn't impact them much when they are instructed to use a black-on-white PowerPoint template by their boss or teacher (or simply don't know how to turn their backgrounds dark). Quite simply, the trail of lazily cited research has not only not durably persuaded anyone, but it has given us a swamp that makes people want to give up on the issue entirely. Great job, Internet! You've made people flock toward ignorance!

The Federal Highway Administration website (Weingroff, 2013) has the real story, in case you'd like to know. In 1958 a section of highway in Maryland was set up as a visibility test. Hundreds of motorists chose between white on either green, blue or black backgrounds. 58% chose the green, 27% chose blue, and 15% chose black, so they used green (Ingraham, 1958).

Perhaps this does mean that the white-on-green is very readable, as this was a pretty good field test. Of course, there were no black on light color signs as part of that test, so this doesn't really help us make that comparison. See there? Better research did tell us something. It is not what I wanted to find when I started all of this, a slam-dunk study that proves black backgrounds are the best, but I am confident that you and I, sole reader who is not desperately skimming this

---

[13] #Pynchon

CHAPTER 8

chapter by this point, will be the smartest people in the room on this subject when it comes up (which it will, at least for me). And that will mean something.

There is lots more zombie data out there in different areas. These, in this chapter, just happen to be about visual aids because it is a subject I am constantly researching. But I would guess that every interest area has a similar collection of this stuff. And I'm sure someone important in your field knows it's fake. Let's assume that person is in your audience.

Zombie data works according to Evans' (1989) *mental model* theory. I have an idea I think is true. I find some data that works for it. I don't research it that deeply because I already agree with it, so, yay numbers! I present you fake data with a chart. Since it seems intuitively reasonable, you accept it because you are not listening to my reasoning now anyway.

But here's how this stuff works now that people like Wil Thalheimer and me are ruining the gravy train of zombie data for everyone: You present what we now know is fake information. I conclude you are not credible and will no longer listen to you. The end. Not fair? Are you sure? If you present this data I know for a fact that I know more about this subject than you. What can I possibly learn from you and your sloppy research skills?

This is the legacy of drive-by quoting, zombie data and an abuse of authority arguments. My final caution is this: I don't fail students who present this kind of data (and I see it a lot).[14] I do deduct points from their argument and

---

[14] Or I did before I added this chapter to the second edition. I hope I will see it less now. Of course, after this, my additional conclusion when I see zombie data is that you only pretended to read my book. Hmmm.

supporting material grades. But they still (usually) pass the speech and the class. In a professional setting, where you may be presenting to your colleagues for years or your speech ends up on YouTube forever, the potential negative outcomes are much larger.

Do better work.

A Final Caution about Citations

Before we move on, I've got to clarify the single most important part of making this stuff work for you: citations. *Cite! Every!! Source!!!* Do it immediately, out loud, right when you use it. To do less is plagiarism. In addition, citing sources gives you and your arguments credibility you can't get in other ways. Cite this book, for example, by giving whatever credentials I might have as a speaker that will impress your audience with my expertise. You can sort them in the "About the author" section at the end of this book. TEDx? Professor? Consultant? Different audiences will care about different things. Or maybe you can cite the date, assuming that the book is still recent when you are picking up this copy. That can be important to an audience on current event topics that are a bit more time-sensitive than the nature of public speaking. I might cite Wil Thalheimer as a Ph.D. Okay, but not great. A Ph.D. who has spent the past 15 years studying the nature of audience recall, visual aids and the persistence of fake information about both of those subjects? That's a better citation. You are not using MLA or APA of Chicago style. What you say to the audience is what they need to hear.

If you aren't inclined to cite your sources already, starting to do so will feel weird and awkward. Get over it. Honesty usually feels weird and awkward when you try it for the first time.

CHAPTER 8

Do not wait until the end and throw up a Works Cited, like someone once assigned you to do.[15] Remember, I want to know if your statistics are from a biased source or your story was made up *the second* you use them, not at the end, as an accumulation of the dead bodies of your drive-by quotes. By the end, you've lost me entirely and I no longer care to listen.

There is real data and real research out there. There are things in the world besides quotes and elaborations. Find some.

---

[15] Remember that we covered this in a previous chapter? Pop quiz: which one?

THE ZOMBIE GUIDE TO PUBLIC SPEAKING

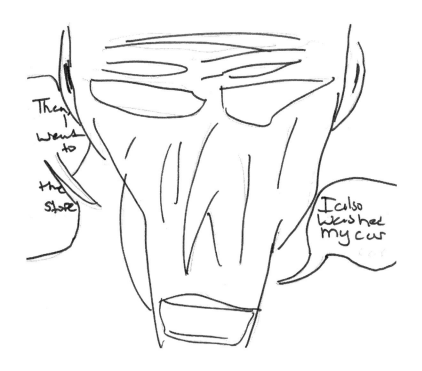

CHAPTER 9

Chapter 9: Narrative

Stories entertain. It's why we choose them in television, movies, books, whatever. And you know when a story is good. The trouble is that it is hard to say why. The idea, the essence, just speaks to us in a way that is powerful and deep. If you haven't seen the 7-minute zombie film *Cargo* (Howling & Ramke, 2013), go find it at https://www.youtube.com/watch?v=gryenlQKTbE), watch it, and tell me that a good story doesn't have power beyond what we can easily explain. Go on. Really. I'll wait.

***Cargo* (2013)**
Directed by Ben Howling & Yolanda Ramke
Produced by Ben Howling, Yolanda Ramke, Marcus Newman & Daniel Foeldes (Dreaming Tree Productions). Production still provided courtesy of the filmmakers.

THE ZOMBIE GUIDE TO PUBLIC SPEAKING

There. You see? Good film. It's okay if you cried. Really.

The importance of using this tool, narrative, in speaking cannot be underestimated. The best speakers have always been storytellers. Yet most *MOPSBOTS* seem, in the service of lists and specificity, to try to imagine that stories are only one kind of supporting material amongst equals. They all have the same list of six kinds of support:

- Narrative
- Statistics
- Definition
- Example/Explanation
- Comparison/Contrast
- Testimony/Quotation

We'll leave statistics for the next chapter, but the rest of these can be dispensed with.

But doesn't a quotation gain meaning when some kind of character identity is attached to the source (a journalist on the scene, Ben Franklin, Louis C.K.)? Isn't that how we avoid the kinds of trivial authority arguments the previous chapter warned about? For example, the following quotation, "the place of God in my soul is blank" is a kind of question waiting for a narrative answer. That answer leads to more questions in the complex story of belief and doubt in the life of the quote's author, Mother Teresa. Through most of her life of service to the poor, she suffered intense doubts about God (Crabtree, 2007). There is a story behind that quote. Your audience wants you to tell it.

Isn't a comparison just a story form of argument with two events? Let's say I was comparing the way the zombies eat brains in *Warm Bodies* (Marion, 2012) and in *I, Zombie* (Roberson & Allred, 2011). R in *Warm Bodies* eats brains in order to feel human, to connect with the emotional reality

CHAPTER 9

of humanity and, ultimately, to be able to feel a kind of vicarious relationship with his love, Julie, through her dead boyfriend's memories. Gwen in *I, Zombie* eats brains in order to avoid losing her own memories and intelligence. In one case, brains are for the emotional part of being human, and in the other, the intellectual. I have now told two stories and imply a third story, the nature of the human mind and memory and the place of intellect and emotion in all of our lives. I can add another comparison to each book's adaptation to film or television, and then the story would deepen further.

Isn't a definition or explanation just a description of how something fits into a larger story, like the history of a particular word's use in our culture or given a certain context? The inclusion of "twerking" into the *Oxford English Dictionary* in 2015 is interesting, for example, because the changing nature of the "approved" English language is always an interesting tale of changing culture and technology. But in this case, it is even more interesting because forms of the verb "twerk" have been around for 170 years (Martin, 2015)!

Isn't an example just a really really short story? An ineffective one, at that. If I want to argue that this book will help you a lot because my student David got a lot out of it, FOR EXAMPLE . . . . well, don't you feel like something is missing in order to make that compelling? Of course. To persuade you with that I need detail.

Foss and Foss (2003), who list two dozen types of supporting material to increase the diversity of speeches, are really just listing more types of story, including dreams, emotions, exaggeration, myths, prayers, proverbs, rituals, sensory images, songs and understatement.

Certainly there are other aspects to each of these types of evidence, but think of a criminal trial and what you present to the jury. Isn't all of this just part of weaving that larger story or guilt or innocence? This is not just for juries, either. Chestek (2010) demonstrates that the longer one is a lawyer or a judge, the more one ignores technical legal reasoning and prefers narrative.

Phelan (2010) points out, in an article on how to teach with stories, that everything really is kind of a story: "narrative is somebody telling somebody else on some occasion and for some purpose or purposes that something happened" (p. 219). There. A definition. With a particular set of phrasing that I thought was valuable. So I used it in quotation form. Did you notice? Did I add enough narrative to make it persuade you?

If you care about it at all, it is as part of a story. Perhaps it is a story of a person, James Phelan, trying to become a better teacher by using narrative. Does that story work better with more heroic detail? Would it be improved if I described the story he tells in his memoir (1991) about being so tired as a new faculty member that he fell asleep while meeting with a student? How about if I tell you he is pretty sure the student didn't notice?

Or perhaps it is my story: Vrooman simplifying all evidence down to stories (Me as hero gives way to you, cognitive miser, as hero, since you knew it all along!). Look, a list of 6 things boiled down to 2! We both win!!

Bruner (1990) spends a career arguing that when we process information, we do not calculate like a computer. Instead, we use stories to connect "the exceptional and the ordinary" (p. 47). In other words, we build stories to fit those exceptions (new information) into our ordinary, everyday world of what we think we already know. Argument asks us to connect some kind of universal larger idea with a specific fact of some kind. Fisher (1984) has long argued that we cannot do that and turn to stories instead.

CHAPTER 9

Given what Bruner tells us about story, and given our cognitive miserly tendency to stick with what we already know (our everyday world) instead of the new universal, we tend to continue to reduce argument to stories as we process ideas. McClure (2009) sees this in the evolution versus creationism debate, for example.

Others besides Bruner have argued that everything turns into a story. Schank and Ableson (1977) in the field of psychology argue that we process information by turning it into scripts we play a part in. Hazel (2008) uses brain science to support all of this. Roam (2014) has turned his arguments that all truths can only be told in story form and that stories increase clarity, include more people in our persuasive effect and make ideas harder to forget into a consulting business that has worked with organizations from the U.S. Navy to Google.

One of the most interesting lines of research on story has been the work of Melanie Green. She focuses on the idea that stories transport us to other worlds. Because we put aside facts to do so, we are more likely to believe a message even when put in a situation that should make us more critical or skeptical of the facts (Green, Garst, Brock & Chung, 2006). To critique the story's argument would destroy the pleasure of the story experience, which my students in Popular Culture class tell me all the time when I point out racism in *The Lion King*. We generalize from stories. This means that, in her study on cancer and communication, Green (2006) found that we use health stories with nontypical outcomes to generalize to everyone. So we do unhealthy things because it worked for some other person we heard about. The story doesn't even necessarily have to be realistic or about an experience you have familiarity with (Green, 2004).

Thus, storytelling is an excellent way to achieve

persuasion from the perspective of the ELM and HSM (Green, Garst & Brock, 2004). Stories give us heuristics of entertainment to keep us listening. But they also induce us to keep processing the information, but in a less critical way. Appel and Richter (2007) have found that the persuasive impact of these stories increases over time. They revisited their research subject two weeks after the first measurement and found the increase! Other researchers have found a similar "sleeper effect"[1] (Kazoleas, 1993). Escalas (2004, 2007) has studied this phenomenon in marketing and branding contexts and has shown how stories often distract us from weak arguments that would otherwise make us more hesitant about a product. Polyorat, Alden and Kim (2007) found that stories seem to sell telephones and sunglasses better than factual ads.

How to

Stories work, but the world is full of them. How do you make them work the best?

Details

Rowland (1989), in an argument with Fisher, points to how incomplete the kinds of stories in public argumentative discourse seem to be. He looks at examples in political rhetoric, like televangelist Pat Robertson. This points to something important as we try to figure out how

---

[1] A "sleeper effect" is something which gets more effective over time, as if it goes to sleep and then wakes up later. See Hovland and Weiss (1951). The sleeping metaphor is interesting, as it seems to suggest that we let our defenses down for a while as it sleeps. And then, when it comes to mind again, we are no longer quite as resistant to it.

to use stories effectively. If Fisher is right that the world is a universe of stories, Rowland is also right that they are mostly fragmented and incomplete. To stand out, we need to tell more complete tales.

Busselle and Bilandzic (2008) point out that if a story has insufficient detail, we will generally provide the missing context by relying on our own experiences and bodies of previous stories. This is similar to the phenomenon noted by Evans in Chapter 1, where we resist arguments by ignoring your reasons and adding our own.

So to make your story stand out, it need details. To avoid counter-story persuasion it needs details.

First, it needs emotional detail. Appel and Richter (2010) have found that the more emotional detail in the story, the more it creates a need, in the listener, to want to continue to process ideas in narrative form, not argument form.

Second, it needs moral detail. Carroll (2001), in reviewing the theory of how entertainment narrative creates suspense, concludes that surprise is less important than creating a meaningful moral dilemma. He claims to still feel the thrill of suspense watching *King Kong* for the fiftieth time. Good suspense stories put us in emotional turmoil. Bogdonovich summarizes an interview with suspense film director Alfred Hitchcock and argues that, for Hitchcock, suspense is when you want something to happen that is bad (the bomb goes off, the monsters win, etc.) because it would be thrilling, but you also want the good outcome (the bomb is defused, the heroes win, etc.) because you are a moral person and usually root for the protagonists (Cork & Van Eyssen, 2008). That dilemma is where entertainment comes from. Given that you are making speeches, not movies, telling stories with moral suspense is even more important in making an impact because, let's be honest, movies are usually cooler than speeches.

Jenny Quackenbush's story in Chapter 6 had both of these kinds of details, emotional and moral.

Have a Point

If you've been convinced that most of what you are doing is some form of story and you need to add the details, it may easily turn out that you have too much. Just ask a 7th grader about Minecraft and you know the kind of detail overload I mean. So how do you prune it down and choose the best narratives or details for your purpose? Wheeler's (1957) ideas on how to tell a good story are to keep them short, speak from your own experiences, and treat it all like a conversation. In an old book on how to have conversations, Carroll (1941) says that the test for whether to tell that anecdote in a conversation is four-fold:

- Is it relevant?
- Is it interesting?
- Has it been heard before?
- Will it "help the conversation along or thrust it into a maze?" (p. 95)

Perhaps this old-fashioned book still has something to offer. The story should do or mean something important. In the words of Steve Martin's exasperated character in *Planes, Trains & Automobiles*: "When you're telling these little stories, here's a good idea. Have a point! It makes it so much more interesting for the listener!" (Hughes, 1987).

The most successful narrative in the history of public speaking is in Russell Conwell's "Acres of Diamonds" speech, delivered over 6,000 times (Carter, 2012). In this speech, which he gave all across America a hundred years

CHAPTER 9

ago, he tells the story of a man whose imagination is seized by the desire for diamonds. So he leaves his rock-strewn farm behind and searches for years, until, finally, he fatally throws himself into the sea in despair. Later, his successor on the farm discovers that all those rocks were diamonds all along. Conwell's (2012) message, that wealth can be found and made where you are, was resoundingly desired by American audiences at the time, and his story was the perfect encapsulation of that message.

There are as many ways of giving stories "a point" as there are stories, perhaps. We all learned at least one model for narrative analysis in high school to prep for some test (probably the one that looks like a mountain with "rising action," etc. in it). But there are others, and I'm with Foss and Foss (2003) that we should expand our models for what makes a good story with new and creative structures. Find your idea and build your story's structure for it.

As an example, Roam (2014) talks about how boring football could be without the big story that everything from the clock to the announcers are trying to tell. Imagine just reading the box scores with no story to go with it. It would be "These people move this ball this far for this long and count how many times they do it. Yay (p. 56). Instead, televised NFL broadcasts have more airtime devoted to storytelling than actual playing time, which is really just about eleven minutes (Biderman, 2010).

If your message is like a set of football scores, which stories are you going to tell to make Dan Roam care? The aging veteran with his last shot? The quarterback who's struggled with confidence for the last three weeks? The storied franchise that might finally come up short? The defensive back who works with underprivileged kids, etc. Find your point.

THE ZOMBIE GUIDE TO PUBLIC SPEAKING

Get Personal

Wheeler's (1957) advice to pull stories from your own experience is good. He suggests it helps to bring humor into the presentation, because it is easiest and safest to make fun of yourself. Naistadt (2005), who boils down all speaking in the business world as I do, to stories and statistics, suggests mining your experiences for

- Your daily routine
- Lessons learned
- General observations

Stratton's (1920) generation felt this material had "a vividness, a reality, a conviction" (p. 123) that persuades, and the same is true today. You will find similar advice in the books written by communication consultants with experience in the business world. I'm not sure why so many of my students think "Business" is some country full of numbers and facts. Perhaps it's because they've not really been there before? Business speaking actually looks like Jobs (2005) telling people "No big deal. Just three stories," or Blakely (2012) telling a long story about the history of Chinese naval exploration in a speech about aerospace. I'm sure you can find examples of speeches without stories in the business world, as well, but there is a reason why there is a market for books like Roam's (2014), where he suggests that "Just because our boss asks for a boring report, doesn't mean we have to give it to her" (p. 81)

Think of the power of Jenny Quackenbush, who might have been dead, standing in front of you, asking you to support mandatory vest laws. In Chapter 11, there are many examples of humorous stories taken from the lives of the people who experienced them. I cannot express how

CHAPTER 9

powerful it is to listen to Tig Notaro's (2012) standup routine where she talks about being just diagnosed with cancer and losing her mother. You have to listen to it. And when you do, you might wonder what it is you have been doing, exactly, with all your speeches up until now.

THE ZOMBIE GUIDE TO PUBLIC SPEAKING

CHAPTER 10

Chapter 10: Numbers

In *World War Z* (Forster, 2013), zombies are a statistical force as much as they are a narrative one. As opposed to the focus of the first modern zombie movie, *Night of the Living Dead* (Romero, 1968), where the small, intimate stories of a dysfunctional family eating each other and the doom of an African American hero in a racist society are told, zombie films have progressively increased the scope, scale and budget of the zombie hordes. Building on the fractured and incomplete form of Brooks' (2007) book, the *World War Z* film's signature visual artifact is the way the zombies clump together and swarm like insects as they scale walls or topple buses. We are moved, sometimes by sheer number.

Think of this set of numbers, used by Prochnow (1942) to convince his readers that they owe their audience for their time:

> When one addresses an audience of one hundred people for thirty minutes, that is the equivalent of taking 3,000 minutes of one person's time. That means fifty hours, or more than six days of eight hours each. It would be little short of criminal deliberately to waste one person's time for six working days. (p. 2)

Statistics, like narratives, work in both channels of persuasion for the ELM and HSM, parallel processing. Not only do numbers get processed by the brain, but they also have an immediate credibility and expertise-enhancing heuristic effect (Kopfman, Smith, Yun, & Hodges, 1998). The Kopfman study actually concludes that numerical evidence is more persuasive than narrative evidence. Hornikx (2008) reviews the debates in the academic literature on this, which had gone back and forth on whether narratives or numbers are more persuasive, and he concludes that both are very important, but that numbers have the edge for people who expect that they will. In other words, for people who value numerical evidence, there is nothing better.

The question is how many of these people there are and how well numbers work to persuade them on big controversial issues. Kahan and Braman (2003) analyze twelve years of survey data on the gun control debate and find that people's opinions on the issue are largely created by a mixture of psycho-philosophical orientations and cultural background. Numerical data on crime rates and innocent deaths, which are the dominant way we talk about the issue, have almost zero impact on most of the people who hear or read about it.

On a more personal note, Alexander (2012) writes about how the exact same sets of facts and figures on the criminal justice system, prison, and race, at one point in her career, meant something simple. She scoffed at a flyer proclaiming the prison system the "new Jim Crow." But after working with the ACLU, her perspective changed and she interpreted that same data differently. She now agreed with the flyer. It was not the numbers alone that did that work.

Perhaps numbers, unlike narratives, tend to fit into our existing worldview a bit easier? Maybe (remember Evans from Chapter 1) we think we already know what the numbers mean and complete the argument before a presenter can? The trouble is how to push our audience past their habits with this kind of data.

To some extent, we all process numbers as a heuristic machine for producing credibility, which makes us feel like they are useful but still feeds into that persuasion gap, as we end up not doing the central/systematic processing we'd need to do to potentially change our minds. Seife (2010) points to how numbers create this aura of "proofiness" (p. 4). His examples include Senator Joe McCarthy's ability to induce anticommunist furor by simply naming "205" communists. The number was a lie, but the number alone seemed proof for some. Another of Seife's examples is the way we all tend to believe the correct body temperature should be 98.6. That decimal specificity is part of why we believe it, even though the story about how Carl Wunderlich came to this conclusion is sketchy, at best. This statistics=truth heuristic happens a lot (Ajzen, 1977), but this is weak, peripheral persuasion that doesn't last or hold up to any scrutiny or counter-argument.

So we need to have a good mixture to appeal to all audiences. I tend to tell people that if you only have stories, you will be interesting but not believed. If you only have numbers, they will believe you for the minute until they fall asleep. And there are some people who love both together, as the trend toward humorous infographics of things like rap music or of kills in *The Walking Dead* (see, for example, Johnson & Barr, 2012) demonstrate.

The more challenging issue here is one of form and style, though. ELM and HSM research tells us that when people are processing centrally, just as we'd like, thinking about our ideas, they are more easily able to generate counterarguments. When they take the time to think, they notice the flaws in our arguments more easily. Some studies of the use of numerical data in persuasion have shown just this effect, for example, Hoeken and Hustinx (2009).

To sum up, there are some people who cannot be moved except with this "hard" data. But they will be frowningly skeptical the entire time. Don't we all know people like this? It turns out that research says they are pretty common. So we need to develop a strategy.

How To

Avoid Misuse

To start with, we have to avoid misusing numbers. A key here is making sure you do your *due diligence* with your numbers and find out if they are true or if they are zombie data.

For example, in researching material for this book, I came across the "we use six metaphors a minute" in Geary's (2009) TED Talk. This turns out to be an easy statistic to research. The *first* step is Google. Simply Googling "six metaphors a minute" gave me a skeptical blog post by Rees (2014) as the second item on the list. She hyperlinked to a detailed analysis of the history of that data by Tosey, Sullivan and Meyer (2013). The statistic is not exactly zombie data, but I don't think it is accurate. So I would not use it.[1]

---

[1] I am thinking of two different sets of skeptical reader responses here.

Student readers might now be asking themselves whether their professor really wants them to do this. No professor has ever cared enough about that before, so…..

When I grade student speeches, I have a laptop and phone with me. I often look up their numbers as they use them. The "Corrupted Cone" section of Chapter 8 was written in response to yet another student using that yellow-barred OSHA graph. Maybe your professor is not tired of zombie data, like I am. Maybe.

CHAPTER 10

The statistics/graphs from Chapter 8 were a bit harder to track down, though, so here are the additional tools I used for each and which you might deploy to double-check your numerical data.

The *second* step is definitely to scroll through more Google results. Adding terms like "fake," "true, "source," and "where" to the "six metaphors a minute" search helps to find what you are looking for: someone like Thalheimer who has already done this work.[2] If no one has done this work for you, the way Thalheimer had done for the "corrupted cone" research in Chapter 8, you have to do a bit more.

The *third* step is to use Google's "Search tools" box, which appears on the top right next to things like "Images" and "Shopping" on the results page. You can set date limits to track down when something first appeared on the Internet, which helps track the source. I used this on the

---

Professional readers may likely think something similar about their audiences. After all, Geary (2009) did it in his TED Talk, so what's the big deal? All it takes is one audience member who knows you are using zombie data and you can do serious and perhaps unfixable damage to your credibility. Everyone was upset when anchor/reporter Brian Williams told false stories on the air, so he lost his job (Steel & Somaiya, 2015). But, given that research has shown us that some people prefer statistical data over narratives, wouldn't we expect that their response to fake data would be equally as intense as their reactions to his fake stories? I have been in numerous professional settings where people present zombie data. There are still some people whose opinion I have a hard time taking seriously because of this. It's not that I'm the Mr. Darcy of data ("My good opinion once lost is lost forever" [Austen, 1813]), but in a professional context, your job is accuracy. Not only are you not doing your job, but you are also profligately wasting your audience's time.

[2] In many cases, adding "snopes" helps, as well. Snopes.com is an urban legend analysis website, and it often covers popular zombie data, like men thinking about sex every seven seconds (Mikkelson, 2013) or humans using only ten percent of our brains (Radford, 2015).

highway signs sentences with the 40% ghost statistic. Everything started showing up after a particular blog post did, which was clearly the source.[3]

A *fourth* step might be needed if that doesn't get you what you need to make a judgment. This is one of my favorite tools, the Wayback Machine at https://archive.org/web/. You copy a web address and it will show you when a website was created, as well as taking you through its significant changes. I used this tool on the highway sign research from Chapter 8. When I finally found what looked like the real story, the Tallamy test, I found it on the US DOT website and on another state transportation website. Someone was copying someone else. The copyright dates on the bottom of the pages made it look like the federal page was the copier. That conclusion made me nervous. I needed to be sure that was correct before I published the book. The Wayback Machine showed me that Weingroff (2013), the author of the DOT website, originally wrote those sentences. Six months later the other website added them to the end of a paragraph that was originally a lot shorter. What does that do for me, aside from saving me from publishing an untruth?

It enables the *fifth* step. Contact the source. You'd be surprised at how many people will respond to email. Richard Weingroff responded to me within 9 hours.[4] He sent me .pdfs of all of his supporting information. I had less luck in emailing people on The Curve of Attention. But that lack of response told me something, as well, about the

---

[3] Of course this works with books and articles, too. I assume you know to trace back ideas from Reference Lists and footnotes to the source material and look at that. If you don't, there is another class that I teach…

[4] That's fast for responding to a stranger out of the blue. But that is an eternity if you are trying to cram all of this work in the night before. Hint, hint.

validity of that data. It didn't necessarily mean it was untrue (people are busy and have spam filters in their email), but it made me suspicious, and it allowed me to use the great journalistic trick of writing something like "Emails to ____ on this issue were not returned".

The *sixth* step, if needed, is to seek help in interpreting numbers. Tosey, Sullivan and Meyer (2013) take us through a nice analysis of where that "Six metaphors a minute" comes from and how it was compiled. Their analysis is rigorous and well-explained. Sometimes, though, when you finally find the source, it is a study and the data are hard to interpret. How do you know whether the research design or sampling procedure is good or bad? How do you know whether the effect sizes or significance levels or a particular statistical test are appropriate? If you don't remember enough from the classes that taught you that, call/email someone you know who can help you with it. Maybe your roommate is a psych major. Maybe your Mom is a research chemist. Maybe you are strolling through Emma Frey Hall and see a math professor's door open for office hours...

All these steps might be the work of minutes, but they might also take much more time than that. I think any other approach to data is unethical. Spreading untruth and wasting audience time are key issues for me. You might not share those ethics. In that case, from a self-interest perspective, yes, you will get away with not doing this work most of the time. But who will be in the audience and what do you want to be at stake the one time that you don't?

Avoid Simple Mistakes

The *MOPSBOTS* have a decent set of guidelines on how to use statistics:

- Round off statistics
- Use units of measure familiar to your audience (Grice & Skinner, 1998)
- Don't compare absolute numbers ($200,000) with percentages (6%) (Hasling, 1998)
- Avoid misleading statistics (Sprague & Stuart, 2000)
- Remember that statistics are biased (Sellnow, 2005)
- Establish context (meaning for/impact on your listeners) (Fraleigh & Tuman, 2009)

I would add a few things.

First, immediately give all relevant details as to your statistics' credibility. Decide on the degree of relevance based on the composition of your audience. An audience of specialists will want to know about study methodology, sampling procedure, etc., in their field. An audience on a politically fraught issue will be ready to discount your "damn lies and statistics" quickly if you don't defend and contextualize them. Other audiences will glaze over with too much detail. Read the room.

Second, understand what you are saying. Rattling off numbers you don't understand is a quick way to get you in trouble. As an example, the "a woman is raped every _____ minutes in America" number is often used by my students who speak on sexual assault. The trouble is that these terrible events do not evenly space themselves out in the year. This is simple division of the number of rapes in a year divided by the number of minutes in a year. So to end your speech with that old saw that while you were talking, four women were raped, is to shock and appall the few people who've never heard that kind of number used before and to

CHAPTER 10

disrupt the credibility of your entire speech on a very important issue for those who know where the numbers come from. Because of the way these numbers are calculated, they change based on new reports of crime statistics and the nature of the categories involved: every two minutes a sexual assault is the common statistic (RAINN, 2009), but that gets interpreted as a rape every two minutes by concerned but unqualified advocates (Paralumun, n.d.), when those numbers are different depending on how those two things are defined.

Third, make your statistics work for your audience. The rape statistic is an attempt to take big numbers and boil them down into digestible bits for the audience. I'm not sure they succeed, but the importance of the attempt is clear. Teach us. Help us understand. Here's a classic example of how to do that from Carnegie (1955). Instead of "The Vatican has 15,000 rooms," he suggests "The Vatican has so many rooms that one might occupy a different one every day for forty years without having lived in them all" (p. 279). I'd suggest telling us both.

THE ZOMBIE GUIDE TO PUBLIC SPEAKING

CHAPTER 11

Chapter 11: Humor

Burke (1984) argues that something he calls *perspective by incongruity* can crack verbal atoms by taking a word and "wrench[ing] it loose" from its existing context and placing it in another (p. 308). This is what humor and irony do (Bostdorff, 1987); they pull things into other contexts and open our minds to different ways of thinking (Foss & Foss, 2003). Summerfelt, Lippman and Hyman (2010) found a clear effect of humor's incongruity on memory.

Olbrechts-Tyteca, whose collaboration with Perelman on a vast project of argument will be introduced in Chapter 14, sees comedy as vital for rhetoric (persuasion), not just because of the emotional benefit in connecting with an audience, but because real argument ends up structured like comedy (Frank & Bolduc, 2011). This does not mean that humor always works. But I think that it opens people to ideas by shifting past their existing forms of defense as we experience "the surprised joy" (Sheldon, 1956, p. 20) in seeing the familiar anew. It is that surprise which, like Monty Python's Spanish Inquisition, is our chief weapon.

If I were to just make a film telling you that your daily activity was self-centered, clueless, pointless and depressing, you probably would not line up to see that. But if I make *Shaun of the Dead* (Wright, 2004) and show you Shaun's tired trudge to the corner store in the morning before and after the zombie apocalypse, which shows how like zombies we already are, the incongruity produces humor. It also produces an argumentative effect.

There is good evidence in social scientific studies that humor does that: Humor reduces people's ability and motivation to generate counter-arguments to your ideas (Polk, Young, & Holbert, 2009; Skalski, Tamborini, Glazer & Smith, 2009). Part of this is simply because of the increased cognitive difficulty humor gives to people processing messages, but that difficulty is a good thing: "the audience must supply meaning to get the joke" (Phillips-Anderson, 2007, p. 53). In language similar to Burke's, Young (2008) theorizes that it puts "two incompatible scripts or frameworks together" (p. 121). Young's study and Goel and Dolan's (2001) use of fMRI brain imaging both suggest that humor is also composed of multiple separate processes which have the effect of creating positive emotional connection.

This can result in increased recall or persuasion in a series of studies in various contexts: business ethics training (Lyttle, 2001), medical education (Narula, Chaudhary, Agarwal, & Narula, 2011), the law (Hobbs, 2007), and politics (Bippus, 2007). Its importance in the worlds of business (Ailes & Kraushar, 1988; Brings, 1954; Prochnow, 1942; Wheeler, 1957) and advertising (Djafarova, 2008; Junker, 2013; Sheldon, 1956) have long been understood.

What I find fascinating about different humor studies, though, is that that the positive emotional connection is so key. It reminds me of Bateson. And I think humor is even better than stories for finding that connection with audiences. Archakis and Tsakona (2005)'s research supports our everyday belief that humor binds people together and creates groups. Young (2008) found that, although humor reduces counter-arguments, it did not create long term persuasion. But she had her participants read a series of jokes. When Wanzer, Frymier and Irwin (2010) studied humor's impact in a teacher-student environment, where things like self-deprecating humor were used by the teacher to connect with students, increased concept processing and information recall were the results. A "sleeper effect," where the persuasion grows over time, as Appel and Richter (2007) found for narratives,

CHAPTER 11

can also be true for humor under these conditions (Nabi, Moyer-Guse, & Byrne, 2007).

Let's take a specific example. What if I wanted to review differential calculus for you (something I'm sure you're not excited about)? How about if I spend some time analyzing a joke about a speeder and a cop, like Richard Feynman (Feynman, Leighton, & Sands, 1963) did (p. *8*-3)? The example helps to explain, yes, but the humor is what allows us to get over our math demons and try to understand it all one more time.

Yet many of us feel some anxiety about using humor. We are not sure if we are *good at it* and if it is *appropriate*. The how-to section below will address the first concern.

The second concern is one of whether or not to use humor in all cases. The answer is yes. This is addressed by Feinberg (1994) in a piece written as AIDS slowly claimed his life. He argues that humor is indispensable when writing about AIDS. I would expand that to all controversial topics. This doesn't mean telling jokes about the horrific tragedies we are called upon to speak about. But Feinberg argues that humor is a key part of everyday life. I would further argue that in the everyday lives of people who experience tragedy, ironies and bits of humor float by, before and after the worst of it. If you do not know their stories, their bits of humor, I would say that is a red flag that you have not done enough research and have no business speaking on the tragic topic you have chosen for yourself.

For Feinberg, the keys are that humor allows you enough distance to process. He points to his hatred of the child with the brain tumor while reading the maudlin *Death Be Not Proud* in high school. Perhaps people need to respond to horrors with some distance that irony provides? If so, if you don't provide it, the audience will.

I remember a day in high school when we watched a

series of presentations (speeches and video) on the Holocaust. In my memory it was all day, but perhaps it was not. It was just really long and unrelenting for my teenage self. We attended by class (all sophomores at once, etc.), and as we trudged back to our regular schoolday at the end, we passed groups of students from the next year coming to take our places in the audience. Jokes about heading to the gas chamber were made and laughed at. *If you don't provide it, the audience will.* And they will likely do it in exactly the way you'd prefer they didn't.

Ace (1992) writes about finding laughs in the humorless text of *Final Exit*. In fact, Ace and Thorne, who edited the confrontational AIDS humor magazine, *Diseased Pariah News*, commonly wrote about the horribly humorous things they found in their everyday lives. For me, the tragedy of so many dying of AIDS is deepened, not trivialized, by stories like the one Thorne (1992) tells about the magazine's first editor's death:

> [T]he blinds were drawn and everyone was so quiet. The answer was obvious to me: Tommy was asleep, and everyone was taking care not to disturb him, since he'd been having trouble resting lately. I tiptoed around the dividing curtain and was horrified. "Tom," I said to myself, "Your color looks terrible. How did you get so jaundiced overnight?" I still hadn't caught on, but Tom R. mercifully prevented me from committing a horrible faux pas in front of the family by apologizing for not calling me, and telling me that Tom had just croaked (He would have wanted me to use that word, honest!). (p. 3)

This also supports Feinberg's (1994) other contention

CHAPTER 11

on humor, that it allows the audience to be "softened for the kill" (p. 86). As he narrates his own upcoming death toward the end of his book, Feinberg does this often. On one page, I find:

> What will I do when I experience my first life-threatening symptoms? Will I lie to my doctor and stuff my pockets with rocks to camouflage my weight loss? . . . . What will happen when I can no longer metabolize chocolate? Is Godiva available in IV drips? (p. 187)

In her last book before she died, Nora Ephron (2006) wrote about getting old, fearing death, and all sorts of regrets. She hated her neck, which hung there in flaps and made her look old. She was glad that age had brought knowledge of "what matters in life. But guess what? It's my neck" (p. 8). She finally found a place that sold jeans that fit her and was stunned to see Nancy Reagan there: "That's how old I am: Nancy Reagan and I shop in the same store" (p. 130). Knowing that Nancy Reagan outlived Nora Ephron makes that joke hurt so much more.

Thomas Frentz (2006) writes of his wife and academic partner, Janice Hocker Rushing's, death, and of his journey to bury her ashes. There are tragic details, like the red car he buys after she's gone that she always wanted but wouldn't allow herself to have. Then there's the remote rural cemetery where, bereft of enough supplies, he ends up digging her grave himself with a pocket knife and his bare hands. There are also darkly humorous details, like his fear that he might leave his dog orphaned when, on the way to bury Janice's ashes, he's hit by a Tyson chicken truck, his "jugular pierced by a wayward beak" (p. 199). My understanding of his pain is deepened with the final humorous detail: his having forgotten to bring her ashes up the hill, and the burial service to start in minutes.

Finally, there is no better example of the power of humor to work on tragedy than Tig Notaro's (2012) monologue about having just been diagnosed with cancer and losing her mother. "God, after all of these like, ice-pick stabbing feelings, I *better* have cancer," she says. The hilarious WRONGness of that has such resonance for anyone who's ever gone through such procedures. Notaro's story about the hospital's how-was-your-care questionnaire she got in her Mom's mail after the funeral is also priceless:

> Number two: "Was the area around your room quiet at night?" Or could you hear the twelve hours of your daughter alone at your bedside sobbing, and telling you things she wished she was brave enough to tell you when you were conscious? Number four: "Suggestions for improvements." Such as, should we stop sending questionnaires to dead people?

The story is so taxing for her she forgets number three, but the humor allows it to tax the audience in perhaps unexpectedly deep ways.

How To

Obviously my *first* suggestion is to do enough research into the lives and stories of the people whose issues you are speaking about to find these bits of humor. Or else, speak about something you know more securely.

The *second* suggestion comes from educational research, which suggests that self-disparaging humor is particularly effective for teachers (Wanzer, Frymier, &

CHAPTER 11

Irwin, 2010). Wheeler (1957) suggests something similar in his community and business speaking experience.

Given how important occasional humor is for attention, memory, and processing of information, we need to find ways to keep it up, but searching for jokes may not always be a good idea. Jokes, in fact, are really easy to mess up and should be avoided if you are not good at telling them (Sprague & Stuart, 1996). In addition, they are the most likely form of humor to be inappropriate.

Sprague and Stuart (1996) suggest some alternate ways to find humor, and most of these serve the purpose of the dual-processing perspective by incongruity that is closely aligned to humor's real impact on audiences. Their ideas will serve as suggestions *three* through *seven*.

Strategy *three* is *exaggeration*. Prochnow (1942) gives a few examples that count as taking an idea beyond logical limits:

> Soph.: But I don't think I deserve a zero.
> Prof.: Neither do I, but it's the lowest mark I'm allowed to give. (p. 90)

And:

> "These rock formations," explained the guide, "were piled up here by the glaciers."
> "But where are the glaciers?" asked a curious old lady.
> "They've gone back, Madam, to get more rocks," said the guide. (p. (180)

Strategy *four* is *understatement*, which Sprague and Stuart (1996) do just fine with:

THE ZOMBIE GUIDE TO PUBLIC SPEAKING

> The rains had turned the road into an estuary, so I left my car at the front of the hill and walked up. John's house was still standing, but the mudslide had filled it as if it were a Jell-O mold. The front door was jammed shut. I squeezed through the broken bay window and found John trying to dig his way to the closet door. When he saw me he put down his shovel and shook my hand, saying, "some weather we're having." (p. 278).

Strategy *five*, *irony*, has many different forms in literary theory (remember "dramatic irony"?) and in rhetoric (bet you've never heard of "antiphrasis"), but for us, the idea is to put the unexpected together to see what happens. Prochnow (1942) again:

> "You look positively beautiful tonight"
> "Oh, you flatterer!"
>> "No, it's true. I had to look twice before I recognized you." (p. 68)

Simpler forms of irony are easy to create in the moment, especially linked with self-deprecating humor. For example, in my TEDx Talk, one of my visual aids malfunctioned (Vrooman, 2014b). You can still see a tiny artifact of this error in the final video, but they edited most of this moment out (magic!). The biggest laugh I got from the room that day was from my response to the errors (also edited out), when I said, "I teach public speaking, not that you could tell from this." Very simple irony to highlight my mistakes in a self-deprecating way is not only effective, but it will get you through a difficult moment.

Strategy *six* is *anticlimax*, when a series of events ends with a letdown. Prochnow (1942) quotes philosopher Will

CHAPTER 11

Durant:

> Friedrich Nietzsche walked out of a hospital. He had been rejected from military service. He had weak ribs. He had poor eyes. He was flat-footed. He was a professor. (p. 38)

Seven is *wordplay*, or puns. These are not hard to find:

> Prochnow (1942): "All the Constitution guarantees is the pursuit of happiness. You have to catch up with it yourself. (p. 193)

> Bryant, Comisky, & Zillmann (1979): "It seems Shakespeare felt an unusual chill and asked a friend to check the seat of his trousers. Upon close inspection, the colleague reported, 'No holes, Bard.'" (p. 112)

> Or, as the promotional poster for *Zombieland* said: "This place is so dead."

Don't be tempted to reject puns. They are quick and common if you are Googling for humor. Lomax and Moosavi (2002) even published an article that is basically a list of puns teachers of statistics can use in class.[1] Research supports this robust connection between punning and memory (Summerfelt, Lippman, & Hyman, 2008).

Although seen as "the lowest form of wit for centuries" (Sheldon, 1956, p. 13), Hartsock (1929), almost a hundred years ago, suggested that we groan and bemoan a good pun because we are Puritans at heart. A pun is "the most

---

[1] I would like to thank (or blame) my student, Lori Wiese, for bringing this article to my attention.

pleasurable and consequently the most sinful" of all the "intellectual indiscretions" (p. 227). A more recent study (Rose, Spalek, & Rahman, 2015), which force-fed participants puns or jokes while looking at fMRI's of their brains, suggests that we actually don't find puns all that funny compared to jokes, but that puns create a fairly robust mode of "ambiguity processing," which sounds an awful lot like WATTage to me, if you remember ELM processing from Chapter 1. An alternative to Harstsock suggests that punning makes us feel vulnerable, which is in keeping with recent research:

> Puns are childlike. There is no rational reason we stop skipping or punning. Adults won't do it, but from a fitness perspective, skipping is much harder for the body to accomplish. It uses more muscle groups and more energy. Just like puns. Rarely do you walk into a pun. You have to be looking for it. They make you feel young.[2]

Transgressive, childlike ambiguity. Could you ask for something better from your audience?

I find this fascinating, and I think it applies to all forms of humor in public discourse. We love it with a childish joy but then feel bad for loving it, as if some kind of high seriousness is being missed. We feel immediately guilty for losing our boredom in the crowd, but we also desperately love the silliness like we used to love *Scooby-Doo*. If, for no other reason than this, find a way to incorporate some humor, just to put your audience on the horns of that dilemma. It is, as Burke suggests, exactly where you need them to be in order to change their ideas.

---

[2] Michelle Johnson, personal communication.

CHAPTER 11

I'd like to add two more strategies to our growing list.

Eighth is to *embrace the awkward*. In a post-*The Office* world, awkwardness is a key part of contemporary comedy. The great thing about public speaking is that, once your nerves and the chances for hitting the wrong button on a wireless presenter are added to the mix, the likelihood of awkward things happening at least once during a speech is reasonably high. I know you are afraid of this happening, but just as with my joke at the visual aid mistake at TEDx, if you own the moment, it will all work out better.

For example, instead of just sitting up there, silent, the world crushing your soul to atoms when you lose your place on your outline or forget the thing you didn't write out on the outline and were sure you would remember, be honest. We are looking at you. When you pause for 20 seconds, we are still here. In the room. With you. So many people will just pretend it didn't happen and go on, in a rush, when they figure out where they are in their content. But this creates an immediate disconnect with your audience, because you are asking us to lie and pretend we weren't there. I mean, if you want me to pretend I'm not in the room, I have a phone right next to me, blinking a notification light so. . . Instead, give us something like: "I lost my place. I'm going to stare awkwardly at my paper here for about 12 seconds. Talk amongst yourselves." This will always get a laugh. And it is a laugh you and the audience need.

Or, if you are all of the sudden overcome by a wave of crippling anxiety and can't look up, fight! Try: "I'm getting a little freaked out up here. Some guy in the back has 'scary thinking face.' I need a second. . . . . . . .Okay, I think I can start up again, but only if everyone says 'sandwich' all at once. Ready? Three, two, one . . ."

I know. You don't think you can do that. You'd be

surprised what you will be able to do, even under high anxiety conditions, if you set the tone for the awkward early on, before things get rough. Make a mistake on purpose with your presenter and a dummy slide near the beginning and hit the audience with a planned joke about it. Use random awkwardness to get you in that zone. One of my students, Liz Bosse, liked to throw images like this one up on screen every once in a while:

She's just say, "SHAAAAHHHHHHHK" and move on. It was funny, but even better, it created a relaxed space in the room. She didn't have any real problems in her speech that day, but if she'd had one, she could have easily said, "I lost my place. Darn. I wish I had a SHAAAHHHHKK image to put up here while I figure this out."

In closing, the *ninth* kind of humor is what I will call *intellectual suspension.*[3] In this type, one or more of the

---

[3] I understand that might be the least funny name ever. #irony

previous types of humor[4] are used, but in a joke that is purposefully unclear. You can imagine the speaker, crouched, looking at the audience with an expectant face, maybe a "come on" kind of gesture, as well. The idea is to tell a joke that is so obscure as to be almost un-gettable. But when a moment is taken to indicate that the joke is suspended in this way, the audience is invited to solve it as a puzzle. The humor achieved is then earned as a prize by the audience. They can even boo and reject the joke (and the joker), but the joke has served its informative or persuasive purpose. Here's my favorite example. It is a joke that illustrates the statistical concept of central tendency:

> Following a flaming snowmobile crash, one statistician asked the other if he was OK. The second said, "Well, my hair's on fire and my toes are frostbitten, but overall I feel pretty good." (Lomax & Moosavi, 2002, p. 118)

---

[4] Or other types you happen to know about. There are, indeed, typologies of humor out there (see Berger, 1999; Buijzen & Valkenberg, 2004).

THE ZOMBIE GUIDE TO PUBLIC SPEAKING

CHAPTER 12

Chapter 12: Figurative Language

The title of *The Walking Dead* is, you can learn from breathless posts on social media sites over and over again, is not a reference to the zombies, but to the survivors. We like it when things are "deep" like that. My favorite of Kim Addonizio's (2000) poems, "Night of the Living, Night of the Dead," begins with:

> When the dead rise in movies they're hideous
> and slow. They stagger uphill toward the farmhouse
> like drunks headed home from the bar.
> Maybe they only want to lie down inside
> while some room spins around them, maybe that's why
> they bang on the windows while the living
> hammer up boards and count out shotgun shells.

Does the basic metaphor of zombies as drunks wanting to lie down make you think about them in a new way? If you read the entire poem, you will have pity on the undead. And although that might ruin zombie movies for you just a little bit, isn't it amazing that just a few words can do that sort of thing?

"A nation's army is only the clenched fist of its factories and farms" (p. 57). That's Glenn Franks quoted in Prochnow (1942). It's hard to argue that such a thing is not effective. But it is important to understand why this stuff works because, let's be honest, using figurative language in an extemporaneous speech is really hard to do. Plus, in a world where we handle our nervousness by slacking, by losing energy and reading our Power Point, by disengaging with the cool-kid attitude that animated the back of the bus in junior high, figurative language is nerdy.

It works in a couple of ways. *First*, almost all kinds of

figurative language add difficulty and texture to language, slowing down processing, interrupting the moment. Assuming that you haven't lost your audience's motivation to process by using enough humor and narrative, this results in deeper processing of an idea, especially when the figurative language is coupled with that humor or narrative (Henderson, 2006; Phillips, 1997; Torronen, 2000).

Second, figurative language is defined much the way perspective by incongruity is. It is speaking of something in terms of another thing. It is this meshing of perspectives that inspires Gordon (1996) to write an entire book using the metaphor of ghosts and haunting to do sociology.

Pattie Sellers says that "Careers are a jungle gym, not a ladder" (quoted in Sandberg & Scovell, 2013, p. 53). Doesn't that prompt you to think about the nature of career? Sandberg uses that metaphor as an organizing principle for a chapter in her book precisely because she thinks the ladder idea is too limiting and makes people too often feel like failures or make poor decisions in developing their careers. Can changing one metaphor have such an impact?

This effect is so specific that different kinds of figurative language affect thought in structurally different ways, according to persuasion research. I can, to some extent, engineer effects on:

- the argument implicit in the figurative device (Bosman, 1987; Kozy, 1970; McCabe, 1988),
- the relationship between the speaker and the kinds of metaphors used in connection with their backgrounds (Bowers & Osborn, 1966),
- the relationship between multiple kinds of figures of speech used together (Mothersbaugh, Huhmann, & Franke, 2002).

CHAPTER 12

Third, there is just something pleasurable in what one translation of Quintilian calls "artfully varied" speech (Corbett, 1971, p. 460). When done well, people's positive feelings toward a speaker or product are increased (McQuarrie & Mick, 1996). Think of figurative language-heavy speakers like Abraham Lincoln, John F. Kennedy, Martin Luther King, Jr., Barbara Jordan, and Ronald Reagan.

Corbett (1971) quotes Aristotle on figures of speech as being "one of the best ways to strike that happy balance between 'the obvious and the obscure'" (p. 459). This is what the ELM asks us to do, as well.

Although it is a visual aid, a good example of the potential effect of this alteration in processing is the use of the white shawl on the heads of the Madres of the Plaza de Mayo in Argentina. Protesting the disappearance and probable murder of their children, the Madres all wore a characteristic white shawl on their heads in their protests. More than a feminine head-covering, though, these shawls were "a gauze shawl, a diaper" (Bouvard, 1994, p. 74), something that might seem shameful or ridiculous to hear on the head. Although some of the Madres were brutalized and killed, the surprisingly low level of repression given the demonstrated brutality of the "Dirty War" regime was, perhaps, in part because of acts like this, which turned conventional thinking on its head. In another example, when they were arrested or their protests, they would sometimes pay their arrest bill for next week, when they presumed they'd again be arrested. The power of incongruity is immense.

Although there are studies that show that metaphoric or figurative language is ineffective, this is always a question of whether audiences understood the language (Bosman & Hagendoorn, 1991). For example, one study found that kids did not understand the connection of a rainbow with a box of crayons in an ad (Pawlowski, Badzinski & Mithcell, 1998). When audiences were given figurative language they understood, it helped, especially in advertising studies (Leigh, 1994; Morgan & Reichert, 1999). As with narrative and humor, Sopory (2008) found a sleeper effect with figurative language. Even for tropes that don't seem to work initially, over time, the positive attitude shifts increase.

Travels with Feynman

Before I get to the "How to" section, I need to take a detour.

While testing this book on my classes, I found that students from the sciences and from the more technical aspects of business were often heavily resistant to the ideas in this chapter. They could not seem to reconcile the "hardness" or their discipline with the "softness" of these ideas. Some even used those words. The irony of this gets me every time, since they were resisting the use of metaphor by relying on a tired old metaphor they'd been insufficiently thoughtful about.

I turned to Feynman, whose very funny book, *Surely You're Joking, Mr. Feynman* (Feynman, Leighton & Hutchings, 1986), I was relying upon to get me through the stresses of that Spring's finals week. His style struck me. "Here's a scientist! A great one! Look how he writes!" is how I remember my thoughts at that time. By the time I checked out his *Lectures on Physics* from the Texas Lutheran library, I was hooked. Here was a scientist reinventing the way his discipline talked about science *in order to teach it better, to get audiences to listen more effectively*. He did it in a particular way. You can get a taste of that by looking up

CHAPTER 12

some of his lectures or interviews on YouTube.

For Feynman (Feynman, Leighton & Sands, 1963), figurative language, along with humor, is part of the key to his attempt to recreate the way physics was taught. Here are a few examples from his very first lecture, where he is discussing various magnifications of a drop of water: "Now the drop of water extends about fifteen miles across . . . it looks something like a crowd at a football game as seen from a great distance" (p. *1*-2). In the original audio of the lecture, he first tells the class "now the drop of water extends from here to Los Angeles, about fifteen miles" (Feynman, 2007). The book version, which was edited for an international audience who wouldn't necessarily learn from that reference to the distance between LA and Pasadena, leaves that out. At every level, the idea is to use language to push the audience to think in new ways, to open their minds to a new perspective. Feynman's use of figurative language, specifically, is often just as simple as personifying "not quite satisfied" carbon monoxide molecules (p. *1*-7), but it is enough.

Freddi (2011), whose chapter on Feynman came via interlibrary loan a few weeks later, was just the jolt I needed. Here was another Feynman fan! She listed and analyzed many of the analogies in his lectures. Some of her concluding words are a lesson to all who struggle with this chapter: "[Feynman's approach] is aimed at developing imagination and emotion in the audience, dimensions that are indeed indispensible for understanding science" (p. 221).

Feynman (Feynman, Leighton & Hutchings, 1986) repeatedly rails against fact- and definition-based education. He is sure he can just take a biology class and catch up to everyone in that different field because they "had wasted all their time memorizing stuff" (p. 59). He describes, in detail, the failures of Brazil's and California's science textbooks, which are overcrowded with definitions and not experimental results.[1] His own approach is quite different. Freddi's (2011) favorite example is his use of cartoon character Dennis the Menace to explain the conservation of energy.

As Fahnestock (2011) argues, language choices encode argument and ways of generating agreement with your audience, as we can see especially in her analysis of scientific discourse (2002). If you fail to use figurative language, you are closing off key avenues for achieving those goals.

I'll give Feynman (Feynman, Leighton & Hutchings, 1986) the last word: "I couldn't see how anyone could be educated by this self-propagating system in which people pass exams, and teach others to pass exams, but nobody knows anything" (p. 197).

How To

At a basic level, the difficulty here is that if we are speaking extemporaneously, figures of speech either have to be memorized or read. They rarely come spontaneously unless a person has deep practice with them. Here are a few suggestions for how to incorporate them.

First, use short quotes from poetry or poetic speakers like Kennedy or King in appropriate places. There are lots of poetry archives on the Internet. A few even let you search by subject, which is perfect for a public speaker:

---

[1] My son tells me this is still, unfortunately, the norm in pre-college science classes, at least in his experience.

CHAPTER 12

- poetryfoundation.org
- allpoetry.com
- poetryarchive.org
- poemhunter.com

Second, use a consistent pattern of figurative language in your transitions, which will likely need to be a part of your speech that is more heavily practiced so that you don't forget them. A different set of language in those moments will help those sentences stand out from the rest of the speech, which is exactly what you want your organizational cues to do.

THE ZOMBIE GUIDE TO PUBLIC SPEAKING

For example, if I was giving a speech entitled "Swim or Die: Lessons on Social Media from Sharks,"[2] I might use the following transition between my two main points, 1) New and Surprising Trends and 2) Potential Dangers: "Sharks are tricky. They have, in Rad Smith's words, 'astonishing skin, smooth as a headstone.' So to keep swimming, we will move from our discussion of the wonderful and the astonishing to the shadow of that headstone, the dangers of these new and deep waters of social media." The point is to use the complex (and perhaps cheesy) figurative language to get your audience to notice the transition. I found this poem (Smith, 2000), by the way, searching for "shark" using the websites listed on the previous page.

Third, related to that, think about organizing your main points or subpoints according to a larger figurative quote or sentence. That is your preview, and you revisit it with each section of the speech, peeling off another part of it to address that section. For example, Prochnow (1942) puts "He stuck to it about as long as a drug store cowboy on a broncho"[3] (p. 260) in his list of similes. I might use that in my introduction for a speech on what it takes to be a successful professional rodeo competitor. That would be my preview, and I'd tell the audience I'd take that phrase in reverse order. Point I is the bronco, where I'd talk about all the issues with the animals and adapting to them. Point II is the drug store cowboy, where I'd talk about the training and practice and attitude needed to be successful. Point III is sticking to it, where I'd talk about the difficult life on the road, the perseverance through failure and the recovery from injury.

Actually doing all this is tougher than tasks in the

---

[2] SHHHHHAAAAAAHHHHKKKKKKSSSS
[3] Yes, Prochnow spelled it that way.

CHAPTER 12

previous chapters, given our lack of rhetorical education. So this chapter, in the first edition, provided a list of some figurative language you might include, broken into two categories, inspired by Corbett (1971): *schemes*, which are word pattern alterations, and *tropes*, which alter the meanings of words. Both are effective, but schemes have the virtue of being less obvious, giving your words a more undetectable zing.

This chart, which you can still see,[4] if you really want to, was a bust.

In retrospect, this is not a surprise. Figurative language is hard to use in an extemporaneous speech. It feels dorky. It makes you nervous because it feels like a performance. Plus, I introduced my chart on the importance of interesting language with:

> The chart below will give some suggestions and examples that are relatively easy to use. Some you will already know. Most you will not. These definitions, many of which have existed for thousands of years, and these examples can all be found in Corbett (1971), Burton (2007), Cline (2011), Eidenmuller (2013), Harris (2010), Nordquist (2013), and Wheeler (2013). See Burton (2007) for a more exhaustive list from classical rhetoric if this is not enough.

Wow. Killer, right? Extra-motiavtional! So motivational that you might actually need to flip to the Reference List and find the Burton source's web address. I ended the chart and the chapter with:

---

[4] http://faculty.tlu.edu/svrooman/schemes.html.

Give it a try! Close your eyes and stab a finger at the chart. That one. Use that one.

The hits just keep on coming!

So our task, at the end of this chapter is to figure out how to get you, reluctant reader, to actually do this. Remember the beginning of the chapter? All the research that says we should do this? Or how about something new like Crespo-Fernandez (2013) arguing that Churchill's use of figurative language helped win the war? Or maybe I could mention Booth-Butterfield's WATTage metaphor again?

To motivate you to use figurative language, I will use some.

Ready?

Stand back.

Beware. This is a nerd metaphor.

Dungeons and Dragons time!

Even if you never played *D&D* (perhaps your Nana thought it was Satanic like mine did?), if you play video games, you've probably participated in the levelling up logic of RPG (role-playing game) design.

You are a wizard, maybe this guy . . .

CHAPTER 12

And, unlike "real" *D&D*, where you adventure with a group of friends, we'll do this computer-game-style, lone wizard.[5] It's just you! And all of the sudden:

---

[5] Yeah, I know he has a gun. This is a figure from Necromunda, a tabletop battle game. But he is a wizard with a giant staff of skulls. Come on!

THE ZOMBIE GUIDE TO PUBLIC SPEAKING

Zombies![6] This is going to be tough. You are still a noob.

---

[6] More precisely, this is just one zombie, and not all that scary. But it's the only undead minifig that I have finished the drybrushing on. See the part on his rags with the whitish highlights? That's important for figures like this, that are only an inch tall-------

Sorry. Back to the book, now . . .

CHAPTER 12

Level one![7] And wizards are not great on their own this early in their careers. As a level one wizard, you have the classic spell, Magic Missile, but that's only going to do 2d4+6 damage, which is not enough. Now, once you level up, you could learn how to cast Web, which could immobilize the zombie for a few turns while you cast more Magic Missiles at it or even go hit it with a stick (I mean, your magical staff). Or if you level up a few more times, Blast of Cold could do enough damage to destroy it outright, and it will immobilize it at the very least![8]

Those of you who are rolling your eyes (instead of dice!) at all of this should remember that this chapter (and really, any figurative language chapter in any of my *MOPSBOTS*) didn't really work before. So why not an extended metaphor comparing public speaking to *D&D*? You will, at the very least, remember it. And I think the idea that bits of figurative language are like tiny bits of mental magic you toss at the class is a useful way to think about them. A good *D&D* adventuring party usually has fighters and barbarians and other brutes to go up and punch things. It also usually has elves and halflings who can shoot arrows or stones from afar. But there are some challenges that require another approach. A well-placed Fireball is just the thing for a creature made of ice. If arguments are the

---

[7] Zombie rotters only have like 1 hit point, so this isn't scary at all, you think, but this is an actual zombie, not a rotter, your Dungeon Master has presented you with. 40 hit points! And you only have like 13. By the way, if this was your thinking, you are a nerd. You have no excuse not to use figurative language. If you can sit in a room with other people and say things like "I cast cure light wounds on Jesse before I ready my mace," you should have no problem mixing an anadiplosis into your next speech.

[8] This is all, by the way, 4th edition of *Dungeons & Dragons* (Heinsoo, Collins, & Wyatt, 2008). If you are a 3.5 edition fundamentalist or have moved on to the 5th edition, that's cool. But read the last half of the previous footnote again, please.

equivalent of swords and arrows are the other kinds of supporting material in these chapters in Part Two, figurative language is like this magic: tricky, risky and uncertain. But sometimes it is the only thing that will get you all out alive.

Does it really work? If you give another speech and even once think about wizards, I made an impact on your thinking I could not have made in any other way.

So let's make another kind of figurative language chart. I will present a small section of figurative language options in *D&D* character-creation order. Start off with Level One. They are the simplest, most familiar, and easiest to find examples of using the search suggestions in the previous section of this chapter. As you get more experience and level up as a speaker, try selecting ~~spells~~ tropes from the higher lists.

I mean, if you WANT the zombies to win, I guess you can ignore this advice. Some other adventuring party probably brought a cleric, and we know how good they are with spells against the undead, am I right? I'm sure they'll clear out this dungeon for you. I'm sure you didn't need the treasure or rare items the final boss was guarding, anyway.

CHAPTER 12

Wizard Powers Figurative Language Schemes and Tropes[9]

Level One Devices
You may already be at Level One, having experienced high school English class.

1. Alliteration
Repetition of consonant sounds
Progress is not a proclamation nor palaver – Warren G. Harding

2. Epizeuxis
Repetition of one word
Words, words, words – Hamlet

3. Isocolon
Parallelism with a similar number of words or syllables
For the end of a theoretical science is truth; but the end of a practical science is performance. – Aristotle

4. Metaphor
An implied comparison.
I am the bread of life – John 6:35

5. Simile
An explicit comparison.
He was like a cock who thought the sun had risen to hear him crow. – George Eliot

---

[9] These definitions and examples are drawn from the sources enumerated on page 207.

THE ZOMBIE GUIDE TO PUBLIC SPEAKING

6. Personification/Prosopoeia
Investing objects or abstractions with human qualities.
The ground thirsts for rain – Shakespeare

7. Climax
Ordered by increasing importance.
And from the crew of Apollo 8, we close with good night, good luck, a merry Christmas, and God bless all of you. . .
– Frank Borman

Level Two Devices

As your powers increase, you must be wary. Some of these devices can be used only once a speech before they need to be recharged with a "short rest" [Heinsoo, Collins & Wyatt, 2008, p. 263].

1. Anastrophe
Inversion of usual word order.
Strong am I with the Force – Yoda

2. Anticlimax
Ending a climactic structure with something of less importance.
He has seen the ravages of war, he has known natural catastrophes, he has been to singles bars. – Woody Allen

3. Anaphora
Repetition of words at the beginnings of successive clauses.
We shall fight on the beaches, we shall fight on the landing grounds, we shall fight . . . – Winston Churchill

4. Asyndeton
Omission of conjunctions.
Veni, vidi, vici. (I came, I saw, I conquered) –Caesar

5. Antithesis
Juxtaposition of contrasting ideas, often in parallel structure.
That's one small step for man, on giant leap for mankind.
– Neil Armstrong

6. Hyperbole
Using exaggerated terms for effect.
I haven't moved for five thousand years. – Thomas B. Aldrich

7. Enallage
Intentional grammatical error.
We was robbed – J Jacobs

Level Three Devices
Some of these devices need to be recharged with an "extended rest," which, as you know, consists of an uninterrupted 6 hours during which when you are not attacked [Heinsoo, Collins & Wyatt, 2008, p. 263].

1. Polysyndeton
Liberal use of conjunction.
And the people did feast upon the lambs and sloths and carp and anchovies and orangutans. . . – *Monty Python and The Holy Grail*

2. Synechdoche
A part stands in for the whole.
Give us this day our daily bread.[10] –Matthew 6:11

---

[10] "Daily bread" here stands in for "all the food we eat today."

THE ZOMBIE GUIDE TO PUBLIC SPEAKING

3. Metonymy
Substitution of an attribute or suggestive word.
Houston, we have a problem.[11] – Jim Lovell

4. Enumeratio
Detailing parts of arguments.
Who's gonna turn down a Junior Mint? It's chocolate; it's peppermint; it's delicious. –*Seinfeld*'s Kramer

5. Epistrophe
Repetition of words at the ends of successive clauses.
When I was a child, I spoke as a child, I understood as a child, I thought as a child –1 Corinthians 13:11

6. Antimetabole
Repetition of words, in successive clauses, in reverse grammatical order.
Ask not what your country can do for you; ask what you can do for your country. – John F. Kennedy

7. Chiasmus
Reversal of grammatical structures in successive clauses.
By the day, the frolic, and the dance by night. – Samuel Johnson

---

[11] "Houston" here stands for NASA.

CHAPTER 12

Level Four Devices

Although new spells are not acquired by wizards at the 4th level, <u>Dungeons & Dragons</u> is not real[12], so this should not constrain us.

1. Epanalepsis
Repetition of a word at the beginning and end of a clause.
Common sense is not so common. – Voltaire

2. Anadiplosis
Repetition of the last word of one clause at the beginning of the next.
Talent in an adornment; an adornment is also a concealment. – Friedrich Nietzsche

3. Scesis onomaton
A string of generally synonymous statements.
May God arise, may his enemies be scattered, may his foes flee before him –Psalm 68:1

4. Antanaclasis
A pun of repetition of a word in two different senses.
If we don't hang together, we'll hang separately. – Benjamin Franklin

5. Paranomasia
A pun which uses words that sound alike but have different meanings.
Atheism is a non-prophet institution. – George Carlin

---

[12] #themoreyouknow

THE ZOMBIE GUIDE TO PUBLIC SPEAKING

6. Auxesis[13]
Magnifying the importance of something by using a disproportionate name.
You will never find a more wretched hive of scum and villainy. – Ben Kenobi about Mos Esiley spaceport in *Star Wars*

7. Antiphrasis
Verbal irony of patent contradiction.
Thou wilt be condemned to everlasting redemption for this – Shakespeare

---

[13] You will also see this term defined as synonymous with climax. I know. Confusing. That's why it's level four!

CHAPTER 12

Dungeon Master's Guide

If you play enough *D&D*, you will have levelled many characters up to epic levels. By then someone will have asked you to Dungeon Master a game for them. They might even ask you sooner than that if they feel like you are creative, a good storyteller, detail-oriented and fair.

At its best, creative public speaking puts you in that role. What it says at the beginning of *the Dungeon Master's Guide* is a nice way to think about your role as a speaker. In Chapter 1 we admitted that the audience usually doesn't want to be there. But if you can level up enough to make the game interesting, perhaps you don't have to fail after all. And perhaps, instead of being the enemy your audience must defeat (or, at least, outlast), you can make that role more complicated. Remember, figurative language works by making cognition harder, but not *too* hard. If the extended *D&D* metaphor of this chapter had any impact on you at all, let that be a lesson. If you do not think it had an impact, well, just wait:

> Most games have a winner and a loser, but the *Dungeons & Dragons* Roleplaying Game is fundamentally a cooperative game. The Dungeon Master (DM) plays the role of the antagonists in the adventure, but the DM isn't playing against the player characters (PCs). . . . [The DM] doesn't want the player characters to fail . . . . The DM's goal is to make success taste the sweetest by presenting challenges that are just hard enough that the other players have to work to overcome them, but not so hard that they leave all the characters dead. (Wyatt, 2008, p. 4)

THE ZOMBIE GUIDE TO PUBLIC SPEAKING

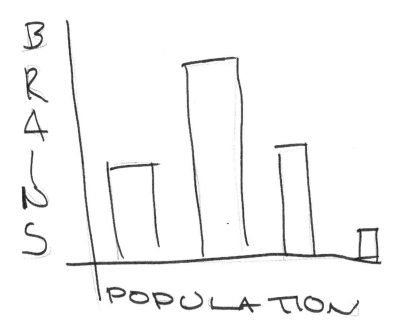

CHAPTER 13

Chapter 13: Slideworks

Fess up. Did you watch *Cargo* when Chapter 7 asked you to? If not, it's only 7 minutes. Go on. Please?

If you have, there's a good chance you cried or at least wanted to. That's what some visuals and some music and a good idea can do. When the dad pulls the little mommy stick figure off the back of the car, is there anything you could substitute for that that would be more powerful? If you're going to use a visual medium, USE IT!

In *Really Bad Power Point (And How to Avoid It)* Godin (2001) writes, "what you do now is lazy and ineffective. It bores people and doesn't communicate with them" (p. 6). Does this make you defensive? Even if you spent a lot of time on it, you were likely doing what Chapter 7 critiqued, you were making what Reynolds (2008) calls a "*slideument*" (p. 68), the lazy combination of three things that should all be separate:

- your speaking notes,
- slides the audience will see, and
- a take-home document you give them with details and information they might need to take notes on.

If we separate these functions, we can see what visual aids are for. Chapter 7 explained how to re-engineer the architecture of your Power Points to meet real audience needs. This chapter will focus on how to make decisions about what needs to be on each slide.

Think about that phrasing. It matters. What *needs* to be on each slide? What do you need to show the audience to get them to (remember the ELM) process your ideas? Really, there is not much when it comes down to it: textual data, numerical data and images. And you have to have a good variety of each (Civiello & Matthews, 2011).

Textual Data

Careful, now. This is where our laziness comes in. This is where you are going to run afoul of all the research on how poorly audiences do when confronted with masses of text thrown at them in this way. Reynolds (2008) argues that "no one can do a good presentation with slide after slide of bullet points. No one" (p. 130). Who exactly, in the audience, is good at and motivated to process that kind of information? Tufte (2003) argues this is what happened to the *Columbia*. Audiences couldn't process the butchered logic of a bulleted series of slides, and they made a deadly decision.

If students read the books, would we need lectures? If people came to meetings having read the reports, would we need bulleted Power Points?

Power Point's outline format is the intervention of a software model. The program starts up with a blank slide that suggests bulleting your information. Before this program was invented, what did we imagine visual aids were for? Winans (1920) suggested pictures, charts and maps might be needed by speakers. A textbook written right before Power Point hit it big suggests visual aids should include real objects, models, photographs, diagrams, maps, charts, cutaways and mockups (Wolvin, Berko & Wolvin, 1993). This was the age of chalkboards and overhead projectors, so it's not like it wasn't possible to display lots of words. It's that *no one thought it was a good idea until a program defaulted to that option*.

When I started teaching public speaking in 1995 at Arizona State University, most students used the technologies of posters and overheads. They created visual aids that were most often pictures or diagrams. Jenny Quackenbush made a poster for her speech on bulletproof vests with little Velcro guns she'd put up when she described an argument against vests and little vests she'd Velcro up when she gave her response. Students soon learned the ways of Power Point, though, and soon the typical Power Point style led to nonsensical posters like this that only make sense as an adaptation of the Power Point style to foam-core posterboard:

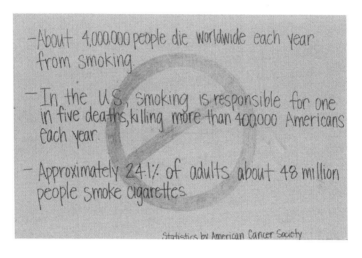

Instead of slides full or bulleted text (or a poster equivalent), wouldn't a handout (and NOT of your bulleted slides) be a more efficient way to give the audience that specific information?[1] Tufte (2003) suggests it. For one, the

---

[1] I know, I've used bulleted lists in this book. But only occasionally. I didn't write the whole book in bullets. Anything a person takes home to read should probably not be constrained to the bullet form. Even Roam's (2014) book, which is as close to a book composed entirely of bulleted lists as I've ever seen, still takes a break for longer prose when needed.

resolution of paper is so much higher that more dense text can be shown. Although old school *MOPSBOTS* often argue that you shouldn't give an audience a handout during your speech because their attention will wander to it (Lucas, 2001), Tufte (2004) thinks this is just an illusion of control. If your audience is reading your handout they are learning. They are processing. Sure, they may not be under your total sway, but they weren't anyway. And in the age of smart phones, perhaps you should just give up and give them the information, directing their attention to parts of it throughout your presentation, joking about their tendency to get lost in it along the way.

All of that said, sometimes you need to show some textual data. But make sure it is for a good reason. I don't need to read mission statements, definitions, long quotes, summary material we should already know, huge sections of the books/reports we should have already read (if you keep putting it on Power Points, will anyone ever read again?).

> "At this second appearing to take the oath of the presidential office, there is less occasion for an extended address than there was at the first. Then a statement, somewhat in detail, of a course to be pursued, seemed fitting and proper. Now, at the expiration of four years, during which public declarations have been constantly called forth on every point and phase of the great contest which still absorbs the attention, and engrosses the energies of the nation, little that is new could be presented. The progress of our arms, upon which all else chiefly depends, is as well known to the public as to myself; and it is, I trust, reasonably satisfactory and encouraging to all. With high hope for the future, no prediction in regard to it is ventured.
>
> On the occasion corresponding to this four years ago, all thoughts were anxiously directed to an impending civil war. All dreaded it—all sought to avert it. While the inaugural address was being delivered from this place, devoted altogether to saving the Union without war—seeking to dissolve the Union, and divide effects, by negotiation. Both parties deprecated war; but one of them would make war rather than let the nation survive; and the other would accept war rather than let it perish. And the war came.
>
> One eighth of the whole population were colored slaves, not distributed generally over the Union, but localized in the Southern part of it. These slaves constituted a peculiar and powerful interest. All knew that this interest was, somehow, the cause of the war. To strengthen, perpetuate, and extend this interest was the object for which the insurgents would rend the Union, even by war, while the government claimed no right to do more than to restrict the territorial enlargement of it. Neither party expected for the war, the magnitude, or the duration, which it has already attained. Neither anticipated that the cause of the conflict might cease with, or even before, the conflict itself should cease. Each looked for an easier triumph, and a result less fundamental and astounding. Both read the same Bible, and pray to the same God; and each invokes His aid against the other. It may seem strange that any men should dare to ask a just God's assistance in wringing their bread from the seat of other men's faces; but let us judge not that we be not judged. The prayers of both could not be answered; that of neither has been answered fully. The Almighty has His own purposes. 'Woe unto the world because of offences! for it must needs be that offences come; but woe to that man by whom the offence cometh!' If we shall suppose that American Slavery is one of those offences which, in the providence of God, must needs come, but which, having continued through His appointed time, He now wills to remove, and that He gives to both North and South, this terrible war, as the woe due to those by whom the offence came, shall we discern therein any departure from those divine attributes which the believers in a Living God always ascribe to Him? Fondly do we hope—fervently do we pray—that this mighty scourge of war may speedily pass away. Yet, if God wills that it continue, until all the wealth piled by the bond-man's two hundred and fifty years of unrequited toil shall be sunk, and until every drop of blood drawn with the lash, shall be paid by another drawn with the sword, as was said three thousand years ago, so still it must be said "the judgments of the Lord, are true and righteous altogether."
>
> With malice toward none; with charity for all; with firmness in the right, as God gives us to see the right, let us strive on to finish the work we are in; to bind up the nation's wounds; to care for him who shall have borne the battle, and for his widow, and his orphan — to do all which may achieve and cherish a just, and a lasting peace, among ourselves, and with all nations." — Lincoln's Second Inaugural

CHAPTER 13

Your goal in this case is to use the technology to help us read and process. For example, in my rhetoric class, in one class period, we discuss Leff's (1988) argument that Lincoln's (1865) change in verb tense, which leads to a particular shift toward theological instead of secular time, is the mainspring of his Second Inaugural Address. That's specific, kind of boring, and exactly the sort of room-full-of-experts minutia you'd imagine you'd need text for. Before I show them the slide I ask them to relax: "Don't try to read this next slide, just look":

> "At this second appearing to take the oath of the presidential office, there is less occasion for an extended address than there was at the first. Then a statement, somewhat in detail, of a course to be pursued, seemed fitting and proper. Now, at the expiration of four years, during which public declarations have been constantly called forth on every point and phase of the great contest which still absorbs the attention, and engrosses the energies of the nation, little that is new could be presented. The progress of our arms, upon which all else chiefly depends, is as well known to the public as to myself; and it is, I trust, reasonably satisfactory and encouraging to all. With high hope for the future, no prediction in regard to it is ventured.
> On the occasion corresponding to this four years ago, all thoughts were anxiously directed to an impending civil war. All dreaded it—all sought to avert it. While the inaugural address was being delivered from this place, devoted altogether to saving the Union without war—seeking to dissolve the Union, and divide effects, by negotiation. Both parties deprecated war; but one of them would make war rather than let the nation survive; and the other would accept war rather than let it perish. And the war came.
> One eighth of the whole population were coloured slaves, not distributed generally over the Union, but localized in the Southern part of it. These slaves constituted a peculiar and powerful interest. All knew that this interest was, somehow, the cause of the war. To strengthen, perpetuate, and extend this interest was the object for which the insurgents would rend the Union, even by war, while the government claimed no right to do more than to restrict the territorial enlargement of it. Neither party expected for the war, the magnitude, or the duration, which it has already attained. **Neither anticipated that the cause of the conflict might cease with, or even before, the conflict itself should cease. Each looked for an easier triumph, and a result less fundamental and astounding. Both read the same Bible, and pray to the same God; and each invokes His aid against the other. It may seem strange that any men should dare to ask a just God's assistance in wringing their bread from the sweat of other men's faces; but let us judge not that we be not judged.** The prayers of both could not be answered; that of neither has been answered fully. The Almighty has His own purposes. "Woe unto the world because of offences! for it must needs be that offences come; but woe to that man by whom the offence cometh!' If we shall suppose that American Slavery is one of those offences which, in the providence of God, must needs come, but which, having continued through His appointed time, He now wills to remove, and that He gives to both North and South, this terrible war, as the woe due to those by whom the offence came, shall we discern therein any departure from those divine attributes which the believers in a Living God always ascribe to Him? Fondly do we hope—fervently do we pray—that this mighty scourge of war may speedily pass away. Yet, if God wills that it continue, until all the wealth piled by the bond-man's two hundred and fifty years of unrequited toil shall be sunk, and until every drop of blood drawn with the lash, shall be paid by another drawn with the sword, as was said three thousand years ago, so still it must be said 'the judgments of the Lord are true and righteous altogether.'
> With malice toward none; with charity for all; with firmness in the right, as God gives us to see the right, let us strive on to finish the work we are in; to bind up the nation's wounds; to care for him who shall have borne the battle, and for his widow, and his orphan – to do all which may achieve and cherish a just, and a lasting peace, among ourselves, and with all nations." — Lincoln's Second Inaugural

Of course, they tried to read it. Audiences are obstinate. I then quickly move to my next slide, which focuses on the sentence where the verb tense transformation happens:

A few seconds pass. I say, "Let's make that bigger":

> Neither anticipated that the cause of the conflict might cease with, or even before, the conflict itself should cease. Each looked for an easier triumph, and a result less fundamental and astounding. Both read the same Bible, and pray to the same God; and each invokes His aid against the other. It may seem strange that any men should dare to ask a just God's assistance in wringing their bread from the seat of other men's faces; but let us judge not that we be not judged.

Then I highlight, in two different colors, the tense words that demonstrate the shift Leff is concerned with. I will simply highlight all those words for you, reader who paid a lot less for this book because the interior is not in color, and bold the past tense:

> Neither **anticipated** that the cause of the conflict might cease with, or even before, the conflict itself should cease. Each **looked** for an easier triumph, and a result less fundamental and astounding. Both **read** the same Bible, and pray to the same God; and each invokes His aid against the other. It may seem strange that any men should dare to ask a just God's assistance in wringing their bread from the seat of other men's faces; but let us judge not that we be not judged.

CHAPTER 13

All of this is to demonstrate a textual artifact and lead a discussion about the words themselves. There are many situations outside of teaching rhetoric or literature when this kind of thing would be relevant: meetings where the collective is learning, debating or wordsmithing everything from mission statements to marketing materials to survey data to press coverage to laws, policies and procedures.

If you are *not* using the Power Point to help audiences PROCESS the text in front of them AS TEXT, you have no business throwing blocks of it up there.

Numerical Data

The same holds true here. Process the numbers with the audience. Help them to understand. Reynolds (2008) is pretty sure few in the audience are understanding your graphs anyway.

Think back to Feynman trying to rethink the teaching of physics in the early 1960s. No Power Point existed. He still used a variety of visual aids and made extensive use of the chalkboard. But he did not assume that the visual aids were the entry to understanding for his audience. He understood that his primary goal was aided by the visual only after the ideas were clear and he'd helped them to figure out what they were going to see. In the audio of the lecture, you can hear a pause as he seems to roll his slide projector to the front and turn it on (Feynman, 2007). He doesn't even think of it until he felt he'd sufficiently explained and prepared his audience. His comparison, cited in Chapter 12, of molecules of water to fans at a football game, came before he showed his students the slide. He helped them process it first. He didn't assume that the image, which is actually very simple if you look in his book (Feynman, Leighton & Sands, 1963, p. *1*-2), would be enough. He finishes his discussion of three-atom water molecules crowded in an image with a closing explanation: "Another way to remember their size is this: if an apple is magnified to the size of the earth, then the atoms in the apple are approximately the size of the original apple" (p. *1*-3).

Feynman could have had the slides going the entire time. That was technically possible with those projectors, and there were teachers who did that. But he began with consideration of his goal, not with consideration of his technology.

It doesn't matter how technical your field is, or your audience. In fact, Feynman's audience in those lectures was also his expert Caltech faculty colleagues (Goodstein & Neugebauer, 1995).

So how do we help people understand? Tufte (2003) argues that we should use charts/tables of numbers instead of graphs. Wait before you scoff. People who make decisions based on numbers, like stock traders, fantasy football players and people shopping for cars use numerical tables. It does happen.

Let's work with some data and see . . .

CHAPTER 13

Here's a simpler version of a set of data which appeared as a too-busy bar graph:[2]

	Men	Women
Fate	53	70
Souls	54	69
Premonitions	47	68
God	49	63
Heaven	41	61
Life after Death	40	54
Telepathy	34	47
Guardian Angels	26	50
Ghosts	31	44
Hell	32	39
Reincarnation	18	27
Witches & Wizards	12	14

Yes, it takes a while for audiences to read through the material, but weren't you, Phantom Truculent Reader (PTR), just rejecting my ideas and thinking audiences would be just fine, thank you, with giant blocks of bulleted text?

Of course, if you are selecting bits and highlighting them along the way, it is easier for them, especially if your

---

[2] http://www.ipsos-mori.com/Assets/Images/Archive/ Polls/ schottsalmanac2.gif.

data is good. Kenny's (1982) notion from Chapter 7 of building up diagrams in stages can be easily reversed. Give them the big complexity and then take it away and build it further. McCandless (2010) does this in a fascinating way in his TED Talk by giving us a line graph with no labels and asking the audience if they can figure out what it represents before he starts adding labels to it. This is the cardinal rule of graphical representations of data: take your audience on a *multi-slide journey*.[3]

For a chart of beliefs multi-slide journey, what does it mean that more people believe in Heaven than Life after Death? I can blank the rest of the chart and just focus on that for a second. What exactly is Heaven supposed to be, anyway, if it does not count as Life after Death?

The part of your brain that might be rejecting this as too much for your audience is the part of you that assumes your own personal experience as an audience member is everyone's. Research on how people process graphs shows that graphs, because they are data metaphors, require additional processing time. They are HARDER to understand than a chart for many kinds of data and for many kinds of audience members. Pylar et al. (2007) found that even for people who reported they *liked* graphs and who had as much time as they liked with the graphs, less than half of them interpreted them accurately. This is close to ideal conditions for an audience's ability to process, right? Yet, the majority of them failed.

This is not like figurative language, where we wanted to increase difficulty. Numbers are already hard. We need to go the other way. Or, if we do want to increase the difficulty for them, we've got to do it in a step-by-step,

---

[3] This means you cannot harvest graphs from the Internet! You need to make your own versions so you can manipulate them!

CHAPTER 13

productive way that helps them to process.

This is why Borkin and associates' (2016) analysis of eye-tracking to show what we find memorable in graphs is used incorrectly as it is shared all over the blogosphere before it is even officially published. They conclude that people remember graph titles, labels/legends and accompanying text. They also suggested people look to pictograms (say, graph bars made of lightsabers) that Tufte (2001) suggests are often dishonest. But remember, that study is of what people look at and can remember, by themselves, at a computer, not in a speech. And the dependent variable here is what is memorable, not what impacts people, not what persuades. Viewers who find the graph hard to understand are looking for anything to hold onto. Titles and lightsabers provide them a way out. Do not give it to them. It's a trap. You have a purpose for your data, I hope, and that purpose cannot be achieved by them reading a title and then checking email.

Instead, give them a story that helps them through the tough parts but keeps them engaged. Peterson (1983) found that providing a narrative helped people to understand numerical information in all cases, but that tables with a narrative were easier to understand than graphs with a narrative. Your graphs need to have a relevant structure, a pattern which they reveal in the data (Porat, Oron-Gilad, & Meyer, 2009; Yates, 1985). This pattern or story has to be simple. Tufte (2003) cautions against the "chartjunk" that makes it so boggling to get through to find the meaning, the multiple levels of 3-D imaging, the compression of three or four graphs into one, etc., a finding supported by Porat, Oron-Gilad and Meyer's study. In a world heavy with infographics, many poorly designed template-things filled with clip art, optimized for scrolling down a laptop screen, we often try to pack in too much. But the infographic, when done well,[4] forces us to travel, via narrative line, through pieces of the data on the road to understanding the whole. Find the line that works for you, your data, and your slidedeck flow.

Summing up, we need to tell a coherent story with numbers. We need to have a good reason to use graphical transformations. We need to keep the numbers and graphs uncluttered. From my experience I would add the following key rules:

- Both graphs *and* tables should be used for each set of numbers to maximize avenues by which your audience can understand.
- Cite your sources immediately on the bottom of the slide, discretely. Do not have a Works Cited at the end or beginning. No one will care then, but I will be sniffing out your bogus data immediately, so add to your credibility with a citation.[5]
- Be sure not to create dishonest spatial representations, which is all too common in graphs (Tufte, 2001). Tufte points to pictographs as an especial problem, since they are often a proportional lie. This gives an inflated or deflated sense of size. Here's an example of another kind of dishonesty:

---

[4] For examples of good infographics see Leong's (2013) work in his book or at super-graphic.com and McCandless' (2012) book, TED Talk (2010) or at davidmcancdless.com.

[5] This is the third time I've mentioned this in this book. Has it sunk in yet? Just saying . . . . . . I always have students two-thirds of the way through the semester who get a bad grade on an assignment for leaving out immediate citations orally or on at the bottom of their slides, and they give me the "Wait, you mean we're supposed to say our sources? Out loud? AND on the slides?" as if they'd never heard of such a crazy thing before.

CHAPTER 13

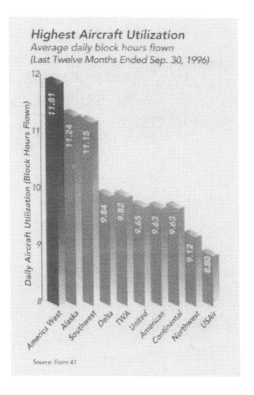

This chart was taken from an overhead used by a student 19 years ago for a speech on why America West Airlines was best. Visually, it looks like America West is about four times as efficient as US Air. That's only because the bar graph is arbitrarily sliced off at 8. If it went down to zero, it would not be so dramatic. This a lie. Beware!

Given all these rules, let's try some data visualization.

I might take the chart from a few pages ago and have it on the left side of a slide. The next slide would allow the following graph to appear (again, it would be in some color; pink and blue, actually ☺). I would explain the idea in connection with the chart, still visible on the other side, and then let it fade away, leaving only this:

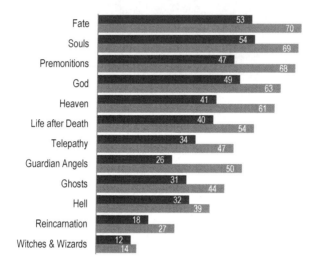

Whatever color the bars were, I'd explain it upfront. And I would omit the chartjunk of a key. If I did that sterotypical blue and pink for men and women, then I clearly don't need a key. If I choose to have Professors Snape and McGonagall as my avatars here, reasonable for the subject matter of the graph, I can easily choose black for the men and green for the women. This is possible for even larger sets of categories, as long as the story you tell about the colors is clear. It is, in my experience, easier for an audience to process that kind of story than a key with colors that have no meaning.

So what could we do with this data? A comparison I'd like to highlight for the audience might be the Heaven versus Hell, coupled with Life After Death, so I'd fade the full graph into this:

CHAPTER 13

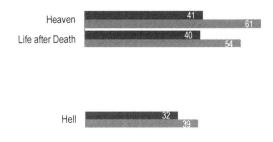

There are other comparisons I could illustrate, and I could even return to the chart when needed to explore the differences between men and women in a more precise way. I might even *sort* the chart or graph by the difference, which would put Guardian Angels and Premonitions at the top. I would make sure people had a good chance to see each version, and then I would move on. You could do a series of things, depending on your goals. All told, I would use 10 to 20 slides to work through this information with an audience if I wanted them to learn it or learn from it. Always move through the data in interesting ways.

The possibilities for making presentations that work are limitless. You can deepen the story by adding other bits of data from other sources to create an integrated argument. These are Brits. What if you found the data for Americans, or for, say, the other G20 countries on an element, like God, made the rest of the bars disappear except for the God line, faded the label to "British" and then made the other countries' bars appear alongside? Followed by a table, of course, etc.

Or perhaps you'd like to break it down further. You are interested in race or socioeconomic class and how that relates to beliefs in God. So you find that information, enlarge the bar for British women and then replace it with a bar with proportional, labeled segments for classes. Or, simpler, draw an arrow from the bar to an empty space where, on the next slide, another graph or table will appear to help explain.

There are so many ways to do this.

On the following page is the sequence of eight slides I took the TEDx audience through in an analysis of why we interact with a tweet (Vrooman, 2014b). Even without the original color, it communicates.

Here's the thing about on pie charts: usually they are a waste of time. Few's (2007) excellent analysis details the ways we just can't read these the way we think and how a small chart of numbers only works best. Even if we can read it, just give us the number. A semicircle does not communicate anything more meaningful than saying "50%."

In the case of my example, I wanted to take the audience through a numberless sense of big versus small, without asking anything more of the data. And I liked the narrative journey of revealing smaller pieces as I went. Does it matter what the exact figures are for the tiny slices? Nope. They are small and insignificant, and that is the point. Do you need the exact numbers on the bigger slices? Not really. In the end, I just want to help them compare the general importance of the phenomena I found, leading up toward the five categories of interaction I wanted to leave them with.

Always know where you are taking the audience before you start driving them there.

CHAPTER 13

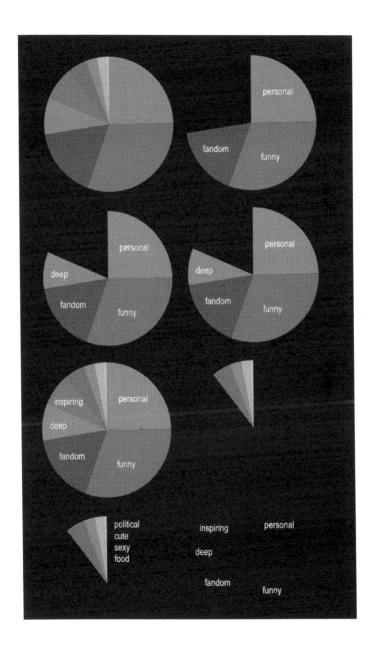

Interacting with your graph across multiple slides is the key. It's why people are willing to watch Al Gore do Power Point for two hours in *An Inconvenient Truth* (Guggenheim, 2006). Didn't that idea just sound like the most boring thing ever when you first heard about it?

If you are going to do graphs, make sure you do them right. Audiences will be amazed that they cared and understood.

Tell a story. Kill the clutter (Civiello & Matthews, 2008).

One suggestion to help stop the clutter is a kind of metaphor for the whole process of deciding what to keep and what to eliminate on a graph. And it is hard, because if you take too much away, it won't make sense, but if you have too much up there, it also won't make sense. Here's the suggestion: Label graphical units on or right near the unit, as I did with the beliefs bar graph above. Why make audiences track all the way to the y-axis or a graph legend to find the answer? Will they bother? And will they get lost trying to draw imaginary lines before they come back? Same thing with color legends off to the side.

Do you need those gridlines? How about all 15 of the slices of the pie or columns in the bar? *Everything on a slide distracts from everything else.*

Simplify *every* slide. Then use enough slides to clearly walk us through all of your information.

Images

For LeRoux and Corwin (2007), Godin (2001) and Reynolds (2008), this is really the only important function of Power Points. They would have us, in all places, do this instead of bullets, and, in almost all places, choose this instead of textual or numerical data. It is more powerful and it puts the focus back on you, which, from a business perspective, is the only way to use this technology to sell (Civiello & Matthews, 2008; LeRoux & Corwin, 2007; Witt, 2009)

But here is where we end up with pointless clip art (not one bit of it has ever done anything worthwhile!) and terrible, obvious (perhaps blurry) images grabbed from the web the night before your speech.

↙ There! Can you feel the persuasion flowing through you? If that guy was scratching his head in puzzlement at your bullet points, or pulling a wheelbarrow or reading a book, wouldn't that be just the thing to make your audience care? *Everything on a slide distracts from everything else.* Let's try a typical example of this kind of thing:

Yeah. Nope.

There's also plenty of use of photos that serve no real

point. Like this one you might pop onto a slidedeck when you talk about smartphones for a sec:

Wow! That was close! Without that picture you would have NO IDEA what a smartphone looks like! No way you have one right now in your pocket or on the desk.

If you have seen all the student-created Power Points I have or browsed slideshare.net as much as I have, you get the feeling that people are sitting at their computers and thinking, "Hmm, this is kind of boring right here. But I've got to get through this section. What about some kind of picture? Okay, what am I talking about again? Yeah, social media apps on phones. Okay, I can find a picture that goes with that." It is the same syndrome from Chapter 8, where we just look for a quote we can say some things about to pass the AP exam.

Everything distracts from everything else, on a slide and across slides.

If you ever played the video game *Dead Rising* (Inafune, 2006), you have a visceral sense of how difficult it is to do so many things at once. You had to decide which of the people on opposite sides of the mall you could save. Trying to save them all was generally impossible and would cause you to do a terrible job at each. The same thing is true as we

CHAPTER 13

process visual information. You can only do so much.

Reynolds (2008) takes pains to explain how important it is to get *good quality images* (pay for them at stock photo websites, suggests Godin [2001]) and *expand them to fill the frame* for maximum impact. A few pointers in how to get and use images, from a technical perspective, are in order before we move on to image functions.

First, be sure to get images that are big enough. In a Google image search, you can select the "Search tools" box on the right and then search only for images of large enough size so that you don't have to blow up a small photo and make it look blurry or pixelated. Also, be sure to wait until the image is fully loaded in the image preview pane that pops up when you click on an image or you will only copy a smaller, poorer-resolution version of the nice, big image you chose. Better yet, click to "View image" to get to its source, which you will need to use as a source citation on the bottom of your slides.[6]

Second, permissions are important, especially if your speech is going to be recorded in some form (which is only going to become increasingly common).[7] The Google image search page has an option for "Usage rights" that will allow you to find images that you can use and not get sued. Flickr is even better, because it is less likely someone swiped an image, threw it up on their blog and then popped a Creative Commons license on the content. After you search on flickr,

---

[6] Yes. CITE YOUR IMAGE SOURCES ON YOUR SLIDES! And if you *don't* click through, you will have this horrible thing for your citation, a thing that your audience couldn't use to find the image if they wanted to: https://www.google.com/search?q=shark&biw=1366&bih=599&source=lnms&tbm=isch&sa=X&ved=0CAYQ_AUoAWoVChMIwvSlzvCDxwIVjxSSCh1qqw6i#q=shark&tbm=isch&tbs=isz:l&imgrc=T_hUwhnJzvzNDM%3.

[7] And, honestly, some day you are going to wish you had video of yourself giving a good speech for your LinkedIn profile, YouTube channel and website when you apply for your next job.

there is a dropdown menu on the left that starts with "Any license" that you can change. Suing is unlikely, but in filming for TEDx and for TLU, I have had to make sure that my images can be freely reused or my speech won't be uploaded to YouTube. Even if your speech, which may very well be recorded for a class, doesn't seem like it will be uploaded, it is best to keep your options open.[8]

Third, Godin's stock photo directive is reasonable. There are terrific photos online that are free to reuse, but that simply will not make it to the top of a Google search. It is useful to develop a familiarity with sources of good photography online so that when you need a particular image you can find it. On my blog (Vrooman, 2015b) you can find a continually updated list of free photo resources.[9]

Finally, take your own photos. Your smartphone probably has a good camera. You might even own a better camera. Take pictures. Get better at it. Your pictures have a story with them that you know. It will enable you to use them better than a stranger's photo. You might also solicit permission to use pictures from friends on social media if the picture is what you need. Be sure to ask, though.

To sum up, find good, big, reusable photos and make them as big as possible on the slide, while adding a small citation at the bottom.

Now, let's talk about the functions of these images. Every image should have a function or it just distracts. Images without a clear rhetorical point are just that, pointless. There are three: emotion, humor and demonstration. They can overlap.

---

[8] You want to choose files that are okay for commercial use, as well. If you ever drop your speech video on your blog or YouTube channel and enable ads, well, um, that's pretty commercial.

[9] In case the Reference List at the end of the book is too far away, go here: bit.ly/freepicz. Or at the blog's search box type "photos."

CHAPTER 13

Emotion

This is my Grandpa:

He taught me how to use a band saw, hook up a trailer, parallel park, play poker, and how to just sit and have a beverage with the people you love. He died after years of emphysema and lung cancer from a lifetime of smoking. So I guess he taught me not to smoke, too. I might use his image to persuade you not to, as well.

Will it work? Will you quit? Probably not, but this is likely to have more impact than a list of bulleted reasons not to smoke. As Godin (2001) writes, "If all it took was logic, no one would smoke cigarettes. No one would be afraid to fly on airplanes" (p. 5). Give your presentations emotional resonance. Make us care. Tell us the story Chapter 9 told us was so important.

Your goal is to show pictures that elicit emotion, NOT try to show us a picture of an emotion. This picture is on the

THE ZOMBIE GUIDE TO PUBLIC SPEAKING

Wikipedia page for "Frustration":

I'm not sure that makes me feel anything. And most of the stock photos you find which try to show us an emotion are obviously fake, like this one:

CHAPTER 13

That almost ends up humorous, but not in a good way. I guess you could use it like I just did to demonstrate something, but unless you are giving a stock photos speech, probably not. How do you make your audience feel or empathize?

Try this instead: here's some pictures of seasides:

THE ZOMBIE GUIDE TO PUBLIC SPEAKING

Each of these has a different emotional valence. I don't think I need to show you a seaside in order to make you understand what one is. But I might want to give a speech on introversion and the need for solitude. I might suggest that for extroverts solitude feels like the first image, but for introverts it feels like the second when you don't have to deal with all those people in the third.[10] This is also a kind of demonstration, the third type of image. Remember, they overlap.

Emotion is tricky, especially if you are working with a topic that you haven't done deep enough work to find those connections. Does this image from Apollo 8 not stir emotions?

---

[10] All of this works better if you see the images in color, of course.

CHAPTER 13

Of course, we've seen this image used for all sorts of small, fragile planet sorts of speeches. New emotions are better than old.

We've also seen images like the following used as metaphors for struggle or success. That can work, especially if the image isn't overused. But at worst, it can all feel like one of those cheesy motivational posters about "SUCCESS" or "TEAMWORK":

THE ZOMBIE GUIDE TO PUBLIC SPEAKING

Is she going to make it? Is he? If you care about the answer, you are emotionally (or at least narratively, which is close enough, involved).

CHAPTER 13

Demonstration

This seems like the simplest of things. Sometimes we need to see an image to understand what something is or what it does. But often, we just get lazy here and assume people need to see a picture of everything. You've seen those slidedecks before. These are fine photos, but we don't really need to see a light switch (!) a ribbon for awareness (!!) or a chair (!!!)

THE ZOMBIE GUIDE TO PUBLIC SPEAKING

All of these images are fine for other purposes, but we don't need them in a speech. They don't add any new information if they are being used in this way.

Here are some things I might need a picture to demonstrate. How about the difference between arches? Romanesque:

And gothic:

CHAPTER 13

Or perhaps what the Chicago Mercantile Exchange looked like before electronic trading:

How about how a model rocket takes off?

THE ZOMBIE GUIDE TO PUBLIC SPEAKING

Or why my family makes cooler gingerbread houses than yours (yes, that's a pagoda):

Or I might use an image to show you something you haven't seen before in order to demonstrate an idea you need to consider. For example:

CHAPTER 13

Orator's Pulpit (Teket)
Middle Sepik River region, Papua New Guinea, late-19th-early-20th century
Painted wood, fishbone, and vegetable fiber, h. 32 in. (81.3 cm), 18 5/16 in. (46.5 cm)
San Antonio Museum of Art, gift of Gilbert M. Denman, Jr., 77.1025
Photography by Peggy Tenison
Courtesy of the San Antonio Museum of Art

This is not a chair (Bateson, 1932). This teket is the presence of an ancestor, or, in this case, a wagen, a spirit which "governs the spiritual affairs of the clan" (Misha, 2008, p. 51). Debates are important parts of traditional Iatmul society, which has no central leader (Bateson, 1972). These debates were, according to the San Antonio Museum of Art's label for this piece, noisily theatrical. Speakers would strike the pulpit with a bunch of Cordyline leaves they held for that purpose or place an individual leaf on the teket. This was to emphasize the point being made and, it seems, to invoke an ancestor or wagen as an arbiter of truth.

I'll bet you didn't know this before. I might use this image and share this information with my audience as I explain how this model of speaker-audience interaction, mediated through visual aids, differs so markedly from the "one damn thing after another" model (Tufte, 2004) of most Power Point presentations. I might suggest that perhaps this is could be an important thing to learn from Iatmul debating culture. If there is no clear hierarchy but what looks to us like an empty chair which represents previously agreed-upon truths, we need to understand that we are not the bosses of our audiences. Instead of inflicting a wholesale slidedeck wall, without pause, cowing them into submission, perhaps the idea that our visuals should be like Iatmul Cordyline leaves, occasional but exceptionally meaningful markers of emphasis or of our most precious truths, will help rethink our use of visual aids. A massive slidedeck is like a speaker constantly smacking those leaves on the teket. You can image how quickly that would lose impact and become a noisy distraction.

If you are going to show us things, show us something new. Give us a reason to care, or, at least, to feel kinda bad when we space out, like you might have halfway through that la

CHAPTER 13

st paragraph. You hit me with 134 slides like the one on page 124 and I really won't feel guilty at all when I ignore you. I guess it is, indeed, lowering our expectations to say that we should design visual aids to make the audience feel bad when they inevitably ignore you. But if we are honest with ourselves, in some rhetorical situations, that really is the best you can hope for.

One last example of demonstration. Perhaps I might need to show you what the Bronica camera looks like:

Remember that the categories of emotion, humor and demonstration overlap. This image, by Nic Jackson, is one I came across on his free photos webpage (littlevisuals.co). I scrolled through his images and liked this one. Only then did I read the language on the top of the page, which is a note from his family indicating that Nic Jackson died of Sudden Adult Death Syndrome, which I had never heard of before. They are encouraging charity donations to provide defibrillators to schools.

Find out more about the images you use. Pictures tell

stories beyond the obvious ones.

Humor

We already know how important this is. Remember Chapter 11. For example, here's how not to grout your tub:

CHAPTER 13

And what cold water feels like:

Visual humor can be in service of lots of things. If I were giving a speech about the ubiquity of social media, I could trot out this kind of thing and suggest the zombie apocalypse is already here, but you've seen that joke on Facebook already, so it will be a bit lame. I'll try a picture that makes fun of someone besides the teenagers who are always in those shots to freshen it up, but it is still not great:

THE ZOMBIE GUIDE TO PUBLIC SPEAKING

Or, I could announce the nature of the joke and promise a few images. A few bits like the golfers and then . . .

I guess that works. A bit of a surprise, maybe. But perhaps instead I want to tell a story about how obsessed I am with the idea that we are on our phones too much. I was so into

CHAPTER 13

this idea that last time I walked on the track at TLU, I saw this pipe with a broken bit of branch in it:

But when I first saw it, from far away:

Squirrel taking a selfie, right?
    If all else fails:

THE ZOMBIE GUIDE TO PUBLIC SPEAKING

Images are often a great way to lay into that joke one more, awkward, horrible, yet funny time. My dorm RA when I was an undergrad, a guy with the fantastic name of Travis Lawmaster, used to tell a sequence of horrible jokes. He'd preface it with something like:

> I'm going to tell you a sequence of three jokes. The most interesting thing about these jokes is that each joke is funnier than the previous joke. And also, each time you hear this sequence of three jokes, it will become funnier than the last time you heard them. Are you ready?

The jokes were pretty stupid.[11] But he was right about the repetition. Eventually, when Travis would do this in a

---

[11] The last joke in the series was "What does the hot dog say to the hamburger?" The answer is that Travis would just make a kind of soft whiny noise with his mouth closed.

CHAPTER 13

crowd, people who'd heard it all before were laughing before he finished the joke introduction.

Visual aids allow you to hit the joke repeat button one more time, quickly, without actually committing much to the joke (or even acknowledging what just happened on the screen).

Audio and Video

Sometimes you need audio and/or video to serve any or all of the functions in this chapter. But this stuff is really distracting.[12] I can't count the number of times, after showing some video, the students whined "AwwwwWWwwwwWWww," when I turned it off. Usually someone asks if they can watch more. When you play audiovisual stuff, you are giving the audience something that is immediately more engaging than you. You become the boring bad guy when you turn it off. So use this material judiciously. Remember, Clark's (1983) research has indicated that audiovisual material is actually not that great at increasing learning (so you don't owe it to your audience). If you use it:

- Keep it short. More than about 30 seconds, in my experience, and you start to lose them. If you need something longer, keep control of the volume, mute it when needed and talk to them over the video, at least occasionally, to keep them engaged with you. Or pause it. Often. Demand they return their attention to you. Train them. Don't let them

---

[12] I'm thinking of you, person who shows the Sarah McLachlan animal abuse video.

develop the illusion that if they are very very quiet you will forget and let the video run for the REST OF THE ALOTTED TIME!

- Learn how to embed the material into Power Point. It is more professional. If you don't know how to do that, well, perhaps you shouldn't be in the audiovisual business as a speaker. If we have to go to YouTube when you click on a big link in a slide, you are asking for it. You just told us you do not know how to do things. And you know something awful will show up on the YouTube sidebar that will derail everything. There are multiple ways to embed audio and video into Power Point, and they all have YouTube videos which demonstrate how to do each of them.

As with all visual aids, have a good reason or don't do it. Wanting to hide for a second while they look at something else is a bad reason. It impedes your goals and will actually make you more nervous.

Emotional, demonstrative or humorous images. Numerical or textual data. There really is not much else that you can accomplish with a visual aid. Add in the organizer lessons of Chapter 7, and you can do much better than the status quo, in whatever context you are speaking.

Part Four:
It's Alive! Alive!!

Usually, of course, it's not. Few of us leave a speech, lecture or presentation feeling energized, excited and happy. We often feel that way after good movies or meals or games. But speeches seem to kill us just a little bit. We shamble away, more undead than usual.

Now that we have the soul, bones and flesh of an undead speech, we need to zap it with the spark that will make it walk (or at least shuffle), talk (moan?), and look for BRRRRAAAIIINNNSSSZZZSS!

We leveled up, like in *D&D*, or in *Dead Rising* when you find the chainsaw. You can do the basics. Now for the last things. The hard things. Delivery and argument. Argument is so hard, in fact, that it gets 2 chapters. Scary, right? But you know as well as I do that when it comes to zombie movies, the sequels are usually just not as scary. So relax. I'm sure there's nothing to worry about. Nothing at all.

THE ZOMBIE GUIDE TO PUBLIC SPEAKING

CHAPTER 14

Chapter 14: Argument Basics

Throughout this book, a series of arguments have been made about how bad and unwilling we are to process argument. How should I proceed? Should I assume I've already persuaded you and move on? Should I re-explain about Fisher and Fiske and Taylor and Evans and the ELM and try to win you over again, maybe with some more paragraphs of evidence? Should I give up on you and not even try?

That's really the issue of importance for this chapter. At best, there are only so many things we can do to get our points across, only so many things we can do to change minds. I will try to boil down the vast and complicated field of argument study down into a few sets of guidelines you can follow to help improve your speeches, but in the end, the key is *knowing* whether or not your arguments are working.

Let's try zombie apocalypse arguments on for size. Do you have a plan? The CDCP thinks you might, which is why they are leveraging zombie preparedness to help teach you disaster preparedness. What arguments have you believed to develop this plan? Did Brooks (2003) persuade you to stay in your home and not try for the elusive fortress? Did he persuade you that you need a sword, not a gun, and that you should stay in your home, go upstairs and destroy the staircase? Of course he did. But, then, those are easy to believe. Perhaps you do not have a katana, but the rest of that is reasonably consequence-free to believe.

But what about the "rules" from *Zombieland* (Fleischer, 2009)? The first is cardio. You've got to be fast enough to not get eaten. Done that yet? Are you hitting the elliptical just in case? I thought not. That's asking too much for fantasy, right? But I'll bet you've made sure you can actually get up into the attic if you need to.

Knowing which arguments are likely to gain traction with a particular audience is the most important thing.

Yet we seem to portray this as a kind of unreachable magic in our culture. In *Night of the Living Dead* (Romero, 1968), the two parties in the house arguing about whether to try to keep the zombies out by barring and defending the windows or to just give up and reinforce the cellar never do much more than shout claims at each other with weapons in their hands. Ben shouts, "If you're dumb enough to go and die in that trap, it's your business. But I ain't dumb enough to go with you. It's just bad luck for the kid that her old man's so dumb." In other films, people just agree with no real reason or explanation. When Steve in *Dawn of the Dead* (Snyder, 2004) sarcastically suggests taking his boat to an island, and then heroine Ana unexpectedly agrees it is a decent idea because there will be less zombies on an island, hero Michael simply says, "That's a better plan than mine," and everyone goes along with it. Even C.J., who describes in detail how stupid it sounds, just pauses and says "I'm in."

Perhaps this lack of attention to making and understanding arguments is why all of the characters cited in the previous paragraph die.[1] When the zombies come, we have to do better.

Flipping the Enthymeme

Grounds and Claims

Corbett (1971) describes this argument concept from

---

[1] Spoiler alert. I guess. Sorry. That's probably too late to serve as a warning.

CHAPTER 14

Aristotle, the enthymeme, as an argument missing a premise. I think most arguments are of this type. If a friend asks if she should read this book, for example, you might say, "Yes, you should. It is incandescently brilliant" (Look, you are using figurative language! I'm very proud). You don't bother articulating the missing premise: "You like brilliant things." If you are conservative and watching Fox News, you don't really need a person to say "Taxes are bad because of X, Y, and Z." You already believe that as a self-selected audience member. It would be sufficient for them to say things like "Program X will raise taxes, so it's terrible."

This is such a common thing (Voss, 2005), and it may explain, in addition to everything else in Chapter 1, why we have such a hard time speaking to each other across great political divides. We are so much better at speaking to an intimate audience we share premises and values with. It doesn't always occur to us to go back to basics and explain. Evans (1989) makes a lot of sense, from this perspective. Since most of what we hear is missing parts, we get used to filling in those gaps ourselves with whatever we think a person like X would think.

Your audience is waiting to do this to you. And you have to stop it from happening. First, we need to learn how to fill in our enthymematic gaps. Second, we need to build a more strategic form of ambiguous enthymeme that works for us, not against us.

The simplest model of argument is that a claim needs to have two premises. One of these, which Toulmin (2003) calls the *grounds*, is a piece of specific, observable evidence. That's this book being brilliant and Program X raising taxes above. The other premise is the tricky part.

THE ZOMBIE GUIDE TO PUBLIC SPEAKING

Warrants

So how does this evidence link to the claim? This is the hard part. This part, which classical logic called the major premise (Corbett, 1971), is generally a statement which is *distributed* over many people or things. "You like brilliant things," for example, covers a lot. In classical logic this was something universal and true like "All men are mortal." But Toulmin (2003) points out, in his more complex model of argument, that we can't count on knowing so many universal truths shared by an audience. Instead, he defines this premise as a *warrant*, as something which authorizes the move from grounds to claim. We might also think of these things as rules or "agreements" (Perelman & Olbrechts-Tyteca, 1969, p. 66).

These are the basic three parts of argument, what ancient rhetoricians called the syllogism. To provide a few examples, here are some that my son Sam and his friend Maya lobbed back and forth in the back seat of the car while we were driving them to the LEGO store a few years ago:

Grounds: The *Word War Z* preview has fast zombies.
Warrant: In "real life' zombies are slow.
Claim: World War Z is not realistic.

Note the abstract nature of the warrant. We mocked Sam a bit for that warrant, as there are no zombies in real life.

(OR ARE THERE?!?!).

Here's another one:

Grounds: Spider-Man can't break plexiglass.
Warrant: Spider-Man is stronger than zombies.
Claim: Zombies can't break plexiglass.

CHAPTER 14

Maya gave him grief over this one, too. First, she wasn't sure that the grounds were true. Sam explained he'd seen that in a *Spider-Man* comic, which somehow seemed to convince her. But Maya was sure that Spider-Man's strength would, at some point, be eclipsed by the combined strength and weight of a lot of zombies. She eventually settled on 50 as the right number of zombies whose strength would collectively overwhelm Spidey's.

Sam remained unconvinced by her argument. Even though she had damaged his argument by pointing out the numerical vagary of his warrant, her return argument was vague and problematic at the grounds and warrant levels:

Grounds: 50 zombies are stronger than Spider-Man
Warrant: Anything stronger than Spider-Man could break plexiglass.
Claim: 50 zombies could break plexiglass.

There are two problems with this, and it meant they both abandoned the discussion and went on to looking up zombie jokes on her phone for the rest of the trip. First, the grounds is not a specific, observable fact, as it needs to be. It is a thought experiment, at best. Second, the warrant is not compelling at all. What we know about plexiglass, apparently, is that Spider-Man is not strong enough to break it. But we do not know how much stronger than Spider-Man something would have to be to break it. If you were twice as strong, would it be enough? Thor strong? The Hulk? We don't know, since the exact toughness of plexiglass has not been established in this discussion.

Both of them needed to do more work with warrants to convince the other side. As Perelman and Olbrechts-Tyteca argue, "every position taken is precarious; every argument is integrated into a perpetually changeable context" (qtd. In Bolduc & Frank, 2010, p. 318). It is never easy.

Working with Warrants

Because these warrants are ideas or rules or philosophies that are often shared within cultural groups, it is especially important to fix the common enthymeme gap that leaves them out if we are to ever persuade someone who doesn't already agree with us. Ye and Johnson (1995) have found that having these justifications leads to increased persuasion and that people prefer arguments that have warrants. Horne (2008), a theology teacher, gives the following example:

> It never occurs to my Christian students that a hypothetical Jewish student might not grant that a resurrection, even if such a thing happened, had anything to do with messianism per se, especially since said resurrection did not usher in any recognizable messianic age or messianic feast. In a word, for our Jewish student, there is no warrant for an assertion that resurrection might serve as a grounding for a messianic claim. (p. 205)

For Horne's Jewish student, the warrant that "Resurrection would make a person the Messiah" makes no sense. Jewish tradition has specific criteria, and that is not one.

How about another zombie example? In the *Warm Bodies* novel (Marion, 2011), in a scene not in the film, one of the elder zombies, a "bony," attempts to convince the hero, R, to abandon his burgeoning relationship with the living human he is protecting, Julie. Since the bonies are so

CHAPTER 14

rotten they have no lips or tongues, they are reduced to communicating through Polaroid pictures they take. The bony shows R images of humans being eaten by zombies and zombies being mowed down by human gunfire. R understands what this set of images, a grounds for an unspoken argument, is supposed to accomplish. R sees that the bony wants him to stop his relationship (claim) because every time humans and zombies mix there is inevitable carnage (warrant). But R rejects that warrant. His new experiences mean he no longer automatically fills in the warrant gap the way most members of the undead community would. He's been converted to something new and thinks he could fix or stop that conflict. He has left his old cultural warrants behind.

Different belief communities likely will not share your way of making sense of the world.

Additionally, sometimes things/ideas simply don't exist for nonspecialists. For example, a person trained in security or policing, like my brother, Gary, would likely notice behaviors that are common for someone about to commit a crime or become violent that I simply would not at a public event. The grounds are there (furtive glances, patting their pockets, whatever) but I don't see them because my background lacks those warrants. I'm probably just jealous of someone in the crowd's cool *Dead Alive* tee shirt.

To create those warrants we need to turn to Perelman (1982), who demonstrates that these elements of argument are almost always value structures. Our task is to find a way to access sets of values that have what he calls *presence* for our audience. How can we find a way to help them interpret a set of grounds the way we want them to?

The next section will explain how to do that more fully. If we can actually do that, we create a more productive model of the enthymeme. If I tell you "All men are mortal" and "Socrates is a man," you will likely provide the answer to this classic syllogism (Corbett, 1971): Socrates is mortal. If you leave off the conclusion, you force the audience to think of it first. This has to generate some goodwill toward the conclusion since it, in effect, is now their idea. Perelman (1982) suggests this type of argument itself gives presence. It short-circuits Evans' (1989) process by which we listen only for claims and then backfill with uncharitable warrants of our own devising because we leave off the claim. For Debois (1921), the energy of the audience is spent in thinking of the conclusion with this method. There is less chance of counter-argument.

That is how we flip the enthymeme.

Caesar's Bloody Tunic

There are many ways to analyze arguments, logically and practically. Toulmin is a helpful visualization for an argument novice. The "new rhetoric" of Perelman and Olbrechts-Tyteca is another. Warnick (2011) explains that they generated their analysis and categories of argument by rigorously studying arguments commonly used in various fields. So, for me, this means Perelman's approach is best suited to analysis of how to make arguments in the real world. All of the examples to follow could be analyzed in different ways. You've probably heard some of these argument categories called by different names. That's okay. We are looking for a means of analysis that can help us get better at argument. I think this one works. Let's give it a try.

CHAPTER 14

Presence

Perelman's (1982) prime example of presence is Caesar's bloody tunic, which is, of course, grounds. To create presence for what we'd call warrants he suggests investing premises with:

- Temporal urgency (time)
- Spatial closeness
- Repetition
- Amplification (dividing something into parts)
- Aggregation (pulling parts into a whole)
- Word choices that call attention to themselves

Teston (2012), in her study of how doctors used medical imaging technologies to make decisions about cancer patient care, shows that visual aids should be added to that list. And Crockett (2012) reports on research which shows that simply including a picture of a brain in a report about brain science makes it more believable to typical audiences.

Presence is also a question of the active search for ways to translate your own set of warranting values into that of the community you are speaking to. Or, better, it is about finding warrants that have presence for communities in your audience and then finding evidence or grounds that will work with those assumptions to help build persuasion. This is the reverse of the way we lazily, usually, do it, which is to try to figure out how to make the set of facts we already have work. Instead, we need to ask, "What do they need to be thinking about in order to have their minds changed?" And then we need to research the right set of facts to do that once we have the warrants clear.

This is so very hard to do. Keith and Beard (2008) argue that the whole concept of warrants is too slippery and murky to be of any use. But perhaps that is because what we are talking about here is the real slippery work of that rare thing called persuasion.

As a kid I helped my Dad coach my little brother's baseball team for a time. Our teams were never very good those last few years. My Dad never pushed to draft really good players. He liked to coach whoever came along. His job, so many times, was to convince the kids that they shouldn't be sad at the game they'd just lost. Instead, the loss was good. It had showed us all some important things about what we needed to work on if we were going to have a chance, at the end of the season, to make the playoffs. He was looking for another warrant the players possessed, "We want to make the playoffs" and trying to attach it to the grounds ("We just lost this game"). Their disappointed warrant, "Losers suck," would hopefully get set aside, at least for a little bit. Connecting "We just lost this game" with "We want to make the playoffs" almost leads to the following claim: "Losing this game might help us reach the playoffs." Almost. It's not really a good argument, and it didn't always work. But it worked just enough to perk us up after the game, as we sat eating our Twinkies and sucking down those fruit punches in the plastic, almost grenade-shaped bottles with the foil tops.

Martin Luther King, Jr. was able to do this in a number of ways. Selby (2008) shows how King used the Exodus narrative to help African Americans reinterpret the setbacks of the Civil Rights movement. The same suffering that you had been experiencing your whole life, before he began talking, is now reframed such that it makes you God's chosen people. Miller (1998) argues that King's use of some of the rhetoric of white preachers helped to make his message effective. Yancey (2001) talks of growing up a white racist in the South and the cognitive dissonance that

CHAPTER 14

King represented. His ordained status and his use of the gospel prodded against that wall of racism, seeking an entrance. Martin Luther King had more grounds than he could ever have used about the oppressions suffered by African Americans in the United States. His task, which he accomplished, was to find the right warrant that would unlock the door of white resistance.

Presumptions, Values, Hierarchies and Loci

A more specific way to work on this question is to use Perelman and Olbrecht-Tyteca's (1969) analysis of typical different kinds of premises. Aside from facts and truths, which would count as grounds in the Toulmin model, there are really only four different types we see in warrants: *presumptions, values, hierarchies* and *loci*. Each is processed differently, as each asks different things from the audience. Understanding how you are asking them to think is key to figuring out whether you will get what you are asking.

A *presumption* is something you and your audience can admit is a perhaps fictional assumption both you and your audience are willing to work with, like "Let's imagine we're all self-aware viruses. Which classroom would we want to infect next to spread the zombie plague most effectively?" If you ask your audience to pretend with you for a while, to play a game, it becomes a kind of story, and an enthymematic story structure may be one of the most effective routes to persuasion, according to Torronen (2000). To recall Horne's (2008) example about the messiah, giving students the details and asking them to try processing the information in a non-Christian way might produce a different kind of understanding.

What Perelman does with *values* is to break them up into different kinds. But as my rhetoric students have convinced me[2], all values make sense to us as parts of a Perelman's next category, *hierarchy*. You cannot get an audience to abandon a value like the right to bear arms. You can only ask them to increase their prioritization of the lives of victims of gun violence higher than freedoms in their hierarchy of values. That's still really hard to do, but it is a bit closer to possible.

Indeed, it is likely that the best strategies here will be developed in thinking through Perelman's concept of the *double hierarchy*, that is, the way different sets of hierarchies are so closely connected they begin to cue each other. Perelman (1982) uses the admonishment to children to stop behaving like pigs as an example. The hierarchy of people being better than animals is connected with the hierarchy about different kinds of behaviors being good or bad. Think of Martin Luther King's rhetoric and how it worked on Southern Christians. The more he used Christian rhetoric that spoke to them, the more their traditional double hierarchy was shifted. If God loves all people equally, it makes it harder to believe in the connected hierarchy about the superiority of beings racism taught: God-whites-blacks. The equal love prong of the hierarchy puts pressure on the racism hierarchy. In the end, the question must be posed in the white audience, "Can you love God and Jim Crow at the same time?"

The double hierarchy and the strategy around it are so key to persuasion that the entire next chapter will be focused on it.

The last kind of premises are what Perelman calls *loci*, which are premises that are traditionally argued. They have the weight of common belief, but they have the limitation

---

[2] I would especially like to cite Chelsea Craddock, Sarah Carmichael and Brett Bormann.

of being old saws, proverbs, pieces of common sense that people tend to believe, but not very strongly. For example, is more of a good thing better or is the rare and unique better? You can't really have both. Each proverb-style argument is useful in making a connection with an audience but is not likely to change minds alone. Political argument often employs these things: taxes reduce growth, business exploits workers, the death penalty deters crime, the death penalty is cruel and unusual. Loci like these rarely convince the other side alone.

Knowing which of these four kinds of premises you are using will help you understand how to position your arguments for an audience. At the very least have a variety.

Structures and Errors

The Toulmin diagram

There is a lot more to argument. Perelman's books try to outline all the possible kinds of arguments that might be made, and he does an exhaustingly thorough job of it. I could list them and you could try to find things that worked for you, but I'm not sure how helpful that would be.

Toulmin (2003) takes a different approach, focusing instead on the importance of the attempt to add three more parts to our model of argument, backing (*support*) for warrants, and an additional step where you state how sure you are your argument is true (a *modal* qualifier) and list exceptions (*rebuttals*) before a hostile audience can. For Toulmin, this is a reasonable response to a world of uncertainty, a world of fact, not truth. Kim and Benbasat (2006), in their study of arguments made on the checkout pages of Internet shopping sites, have found that the more of these details you include, the more persuasive your arguments are, so perhaps it is worth it to be reasonably specific and qualify your arguments.

His model looks like this:

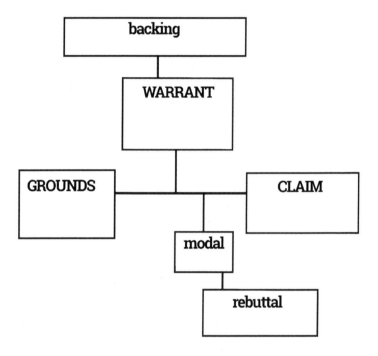

CHAPTER 14

Here's how an argument from Brooks's (2003) *Zombie Survival Guide* might look on it.

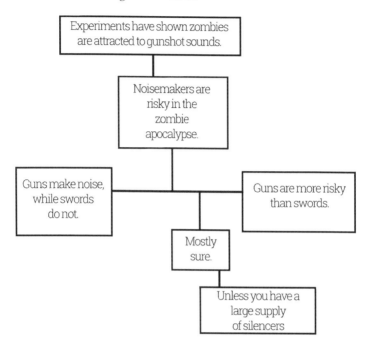

Knowing that we need to back up our warrants and understanding that we should admit that our arguments are not universally true is helpful. Why not admit right away to an idea your audience would otherwise be holding onto tightly so they can remember to pounce on you with it during Q&A? If you can name their rebuttals for them and still build a reasonable argument, you are, in terms of the ELM and HSM, directly reducing the audience's resources to generate counter-arguments.

This kind of knowledge is also helpful in seeing how arguments interact. Chains of reasoning generally involve the claim of what we feel is a proven argument being used as the grounds or warrant of a further argument, and so on. "Guns are more risky than swords" can be the grounds or warrant of a further argument, perhaps trying to prove that you should buy a sword before the zombies rise from the dead. And then that claim becomes the grounds for another argument, which might have the claim "I should go to the mall and buy a sword." This is how we prove a thing and then use that to build another argument. It is a tenuous process, "a succession of knots rather than a fluid flow" (Perelman & Olbrechts-Tyteca, qtd in Bolduc & Frank, 2010, p. 327)

The marshaling of various arguments toward a central thesis looks a bit like a flower, with a central claim bolstered by a series of arguments that all lead to the same place. You could argue, as Brooks does, that an oil platform is a good choice of a fortress against the zombie hordes. That claim can be bolstered by a fan of arguments based on all these different grounds: zombies don't swim, oil platforms tend to have a six-month food supply, zombies will move away from marinas toward population centers (making boats easier to get to), etc.

The more Toulmin-y details you give the audience about your arguments, the better you are able to connect arguments together into a persuasive whole.

Fallacies

This also helps us to understand why so many argumentative fallacies are such a problem. Fallacies are bad argument structures that become repeated styles or genres of argument (some, like the slippery slope, seem to have become terrible loci). Certainly these cheap-shot arguments feel effective when you make them, but since some of the fallacies listed below have been found to be

CHAPTER 14

heuristic cues by persuasion researchers (Ajzen, 1977; Baesler & Burgoon, 1994; Berman & Kenny, 1976; Bordiga & Nisbett, 1977), we know that this kind of persuasion isn't deep. It doesn't affect the ideas of the audience in a meaningful way.

For some people, like me, simply hearing one from a speaker can destroy so much credibility that it becomes an anti-persuasive heuristic.

A common example of a fallacy is the slippery slope, that action X will throw us down a metaphorical mountain and will snowball into a great catastrophe. One law, one action, one handshake, might be enough. A slippery slope is a shorthand for an argument chain that has a series of linked causal arguments. But the lazy arguer simply skips across all the steps in between and hopes you'll buy the shorthand version. It is the essence of a fallacy, poorly constructed and usually untrue.[3]

There are hundreds of types of fallacies out there. All of them have a structural gap or cheat. Most often, they contain an incorrect warranting assumption. The bandwagon fallacy, for example, always has an unspoken warrant that truth is determined by popular opinion. That sounds bad when you say it like that, which is why fallacies enthymematically hide their flaws. Because they are incomplete in terms of warrant and value, they don't help you strategically.

---

[3] You may believe some slippery slope logic, in spite of what I'm arguing here. You likely hold to at least one set of beliefs that suggests that "If we do X, it brings us closer to a world in which Y." Maybe it is about gun control or the environment or abortion or all sorts of things, depending on your politics. This does not mean a slippery slope is not a fallacy! It just means that, as *loci*, slippery slope arguments are often believed within a political culture. And you are a part of that. But it never really works to convince the other side, as it is a fallacy.

Some of these, like the appeals to pity and prejudice, are attempts to give presence to arguments, but they do so in such simplistic and generally wrong ways, that they reduce presence instead, at least for people who don't already believe the same as you do. That's part of the problem. These fallacies can be easily embraced by a belief community as slogans for their commitment, but they serve little value to convince others. We see this kind of rhetoric often from extremely partisan commentators whose audiences are almost entirely already in agreement with them: Rush Limbaugh, Keith Olbermann, etc.

And because people like me (rhetoricians) and anyone with some familiarity with the arguments on an issue (like just about anyone with strong beliefs on a subject) have heard them before and know their problems, they can be an immediate deal-breaker.

The reason I list these common fallacies is that when you research a topic, you will almost always find these things. And if you ever get into political arguments on Facebook, you see them a lot. Most of these were listed and understood thousands of years ago by classical rhetoricians. I've defined some I see a lot, "The Dirty Dozen," let's say, in the table below using Toulmin language. You can find explanations in Corbett (1971) as well as on a variety of places on the Internet. Curtis's (2012) "Fallacy Files," for example, has numerous examples and definitions and a really nice map of the relationships of dozens of fallacies to each other in his "Taxonomy" page. I made a simpler list (Vrooman, 2015a) with numerous examples if you'd like to dip into more complex waters but aren't ready to jump off the rhetorical deep end.

Avoid these! These will not help your case, and they may very well hurt it.

CHAPTER 14

Hasty Generalization
Making an unwarranted leap to a claim from too small a grounds.
Judging a book by its cover; knowing all geese are mean because one bit you as a child.

Appeal to Pity
A Hasty Generalization animated by sad emotional appeal.
One news story about a kid suffering from ____ in ____ country. And the kid is REALLY suffering. Therefore, ____ country is FALLING APART!!!

Appeal to Prejudice
A Hasty Generalization animated by cultural prejudice.
"*Here Comes Honey Boo Boo* is exactly why America is going down the tubes!"

Bandwagon
The unspoken warrant is that truth is determined by popular opinion or peer pressure.
"Most Americans believe in _____. Therefore it is true/the right thing to do."

Appeal to Tradition
A Bandwagon with old beliefs/practices.
"We've always used human sacrifice! We can't abandon it now that radicals all the sudden don't like it!"

Ad Hominem
If a person holds belief X, that belief is untrue if the person is bad for Y reasons, which have nothing to do with X.
"Vrooman says not to use ad hominems, but he doesn't know how to grout tile, so forget him!"

Bad Company
The unspoken warrant is that "Any idea also shared by a wrong person/group must be wrong."
"Hitler was a vegetarian, so . . . ."

Slippery Slope
A causal chain is established but not detailed or supported.
This is Yoda stuff: fear leads to blah blah blah . . . . .the DARK SIDE (that kind of argument only works in worlds with magical space wizards).

Cum Hoc or Post Hoc
A causal argument missing a logical warrant between the presumed cause and the either concurrent (cum) or later (post) effect
The "Redskins Rule" is supposed to predict election outcomes based on the performance of the football team.

Black or White/False Dilemma
The warrant is an absolute either/or when there are shades of grey.
"America: Love it or leave it!"

False Analogy
Two sets of grounds are linked by analogy, but the warrant connecting them is weak.
"Cars kill more people than guns, but no one wants to ban those" (Cars and guns serve vastly different purposes with

CHAPTER 14

different effects).[4]

Straw Man
An extreme form of an idea is refuted. The unspoken warrant is that refutation applies to all ideas from that perspective.
"Todd Akin thinks women who are raped can't get pregnant. Pro Life Republicans hate women."

Brockereide and Ehninger (1960) like the Toulmin model because it allows us to picture arguments moving and "working" to justify claims (p. 45). I guess that's why I like the model, too. Fallacies short-circuit that work. I agree with Hitchcock (2005) that arguers should use Toulmin's model to see what work their arguments really are doing. And I further think arguers need to explore how that work can connect with audiences, which is what application of Perelman's ideas allow us to do.

None of this is easy. Reed and Rowe (2005), in an academic journal called *Argumentation*, admit that it is hard "for experts too" (p. 267). But I really believe that if you are not doing some form of this work, you are just wasting everyone's time.

---

[4] This, of all the fallacies on these pages, gets the biggest negative reaction from readers. This is still a popular argument in the gun rights movement. But, like most fallacies, it sounds great if you already believe the conclusion, but it doesn't really work and it never convinces the other side. Look, if guns were banned, people could still get to work every day. And if we banned cars, you couldn't ride your AR-15 to your job. The calculus of danger for each thing is independent, since with cars we make a deal: "X people will die every year in a world with cars, but we have no other choice, so . . ." The calculus of danger for getting rid of guns leads to a whole different matrix of pros and cons, but the economy collapsing because people can't get to work is not one. If you believe the 2nd Amendment helps prevent tyranny, well, okay, but that is clearly a different kind of argument than how important cars are to the economy.

THE ZOMBIE GUIDE TO PUBLIC SPEAKING

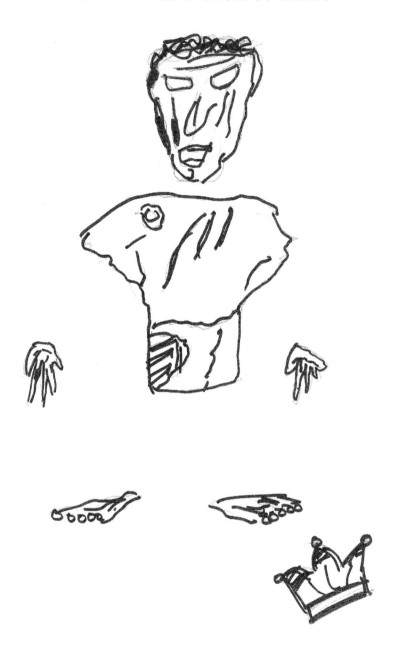

Chapter 15: Argument and the Double Hierarchy

If we think about persuasion as working to try to find a way to *appeal* to the value systems of others in order to move them toward our claim, that's one thing. But often, our goal is to actually *shift* the value systems of someone in order to move them toward a claim. Think of Sam and Maya arguing about Spider-Man and the zombies. It is all boiling down to a hierarchy of fictional strength which neither is fully investigating.

Thinking further about Perelman's double hierarchy concept, we can come up with a few strategies we might want to employ. It is important to note both how hard this task is in a practical sense and how often, seemingly paradoxically, it just sort of happens. Stewart, Smith and Denton (2012), in their textbook on social movement rhetoric, spend many chapters on the various ways this happens and fails to happen. Sometimes it takes decades.

But it does happen, in small ways, sometimes. As a teacher, I see it happen all the time.

I think of John F. Kennedy's (1962) "We Choose to Go to the Moon" speech. Delivered at Rice University, this address helped turned America's vision toward an eventual moon landing. The typical excerpt is a clear double hierarchy: "We choose to go to the moon. We choose to go to the moon in this decade and do the other things, not because they are easy, but because they are hard . . ." Americans typically have a hierarchy of difficult things. He establishes many points on that hierarchy in his speech, with examples of explorers and their deeds in America's past. We also, usually have a separate hierarchy that places easier to do things as more important or worth more focus than hard things, which might be why, in the early 60s, you might think this moon thing was just too much to attempt. This is one of the traditional, pragmatic American *loci*. Kennedy asks us to flip that around. He does it in lots of ways. He connects that with hierarchies of what makes great nations great, of fears of a Soviet-weaponized orbit, etc. But right before that famous quote, he provides another hierarchy for his audience, one that usually is not included in the video clips shown in documentaries: "Why does Rice play Texas?" Ahhh. He tells us to think through a sports analogy, a football analogy, especially in Texas. To get his audience to flip their hierarchy of easy and hard things in terms of government programs, he asks us to think about it in football terms. Rice plays Texas because losing that game is more important than never playing it. Sometimes we need to do things that are hard. It is a test of character. Kennedy does this by making connections, across value hierarchies, between, ultimately, space travel and football. He found a context where difficulty is more important than ease that was going to matter to his Texas audience. It worked. We went to the moon.

Can we simplify all of this down into a set of strategies to consider, strategies that might have a chance of working? I hope so. Let's try. We will look at two specific strategies, *transcendence* and what we'll call *the Checkers move*. We'll also consider a third, more radical strategy.

We choose to do this, not because it is easy, but because it is hard. (You saw that, right? A little double hierarchy there for you. Did it work?).

Hierarchy and Transcendence

The first step in persuasion based on value hierarchies is to see what hierarchies are already analogously linked in your audience's minds. Given how different people are, this is often hard. The *MOPSBOTS* generally have a chapter called "Audience Analysis," which is supposed to help us look out at an audience and try to figure out what will work with them given demographic variables (race, gender, class, etc.), expertise variables (are they all accountants?) and practical variables (are you speaking to them after they've had a big lunch?). But there are ways in which we often share larger sets of values with those around us. Perelman and Stewart, Smith and Denton make that abundantly clear. Given what we know about how people grow up in a society and the kinds of ideologies they learn there, it seems likely that we are not talking about complete idiosyncratic chaos here. Otherwise I could never sell people cars or colleges or coffee.

The best way to think about it is to imagine all the different hierarchies that are all connected on an issue. Think of the Kennedy example. At least four hierarchies are interacting there. What differentiates people is that for some, the easy-hard hierarchy mattered a bit more to them than the others. Some cared about little but football. Our first task as a persuader is to try to think through all those connections and provide what everyone needs in order to move them.

That's a lot of arguments, but if you really want to make an impact, you've got to do that work. Kennedy's entire speech is really just that work. No new facts or evidence. Not really. Just the work of *transcendence*.

It's like a whole chess game. But we can boil it down to the individual moves in that game, or at least the opening moves.

The smallest kind of impact you can make (and it is likely the best you can hope for in certain circumstances) is to accept both connected hierarchies an audience has and then shift a few rungs in the analogous one. Stewart, Smith and Denton (2012) describe this tactic in social movements as *transcendence*. Here's an example. . . .

Fahnestock (2002) describes a simple double hierarchy whereby medieval political theorists justified their absolute monarchies with an analogy to the human body. The king is the head. Presumably the lords are the torso and the serfs are the feet. Maybe the knights are the hands? Crawford (2002) summarizes some of the different ways this analogy works through the Middle Ages. But the king is always the head and the serfs the feet. We might visualize it like this:

Government	**Human Body**
king	head
lords	torso
knights	hands
serfs	feet

You can see how someone might defend the system using this hierarchy. If you cut off the head, the whole body dies, Feet are important, but decidedly less so. Plus, there are no brains there.

If you were a budding fan of democracy and wanted to get rid of kings, your task would be to alter the placement of the terms in the human body part of the analogy. Sure, you can live without feet, ideally, but given medicine at the time, isn't the loss of any of those body parts potentially fatal? Perhaps feet are not so unimportant after all. How would the head eat without the feet taking it where it needed to go? All parts are vital! The hierarchy of body is,

CHAPTER 15

in fact, flat!!

A more significant revision of this hierarchy comes with the concept of a mass. Friedland (2002) points out the ways that French political theorists in the centuries leading up to the French Revolution began to see the whole rest of the body as one large mass, the *body politic*. The heart was in there, which is key. The whole hierarchy shrinks to

Human Body
head
mass

The body's mass was bigger than the head. Much, much bigger. It was only a matter of time before the possibility of lopping off that unnecessary appendage to allow the body to live better would manifest itself in the guillotine.

How about another medieval example?

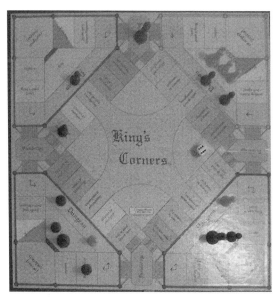

You probably know King's Corners as a card game. But this gem, published by "Family Fun Games" in the 70s, is a kind of low-rent version of Sorry! or Parcheesi. However, in those games, you can, you know, WIN, but in this game the "winner" is the person who dies from horrible things like poison, disease or moat monsters last.

Think about how that might work to try to teach kids about how awful it was to live in that time, perhaps, if that was your weird objective in making a game like this? Their normal hierarchy of having a fulfilling or happy life might involve a series of things they might get along the way, but since games rarely give us this stuff, we get used to imagining game rewards and connecting the hierarchies:

Happiness   Game Happiness
love   winning!
prestige   scoring
accomplishments   extra turns
money   power-ups
Twitter followers   tokens

But this game puts just "not dying" at the top of the new hierarchy of the game experience. Thus, what is there to bank as accomplishments in the game? One more turn without being poisoned? Various forms of death and destruction which normally would not be part of the typical hierarchies are now the new elements in a hierarchy between "death" and whatever the player's pervious lowest level of accomplishment might have been.

A more specific non-medieval example is from *World*

CHAPTER 15

War Z (Forster, 2013). Gerry, the UN investigator, has left his dangerous job so that he can make pancakes for his family. After the zombie apocalypse lands them on an aircraft carrier in the Atlantic (he called in some favors from a UN Undersecretary friend), he is asked to go investigate this zombie outbreak in South Korea. He refuses, not wanting to leave his family again in such emotionally challenging times. The military leader threatens to kick his family off the boat as "nonessential personnel" if he does not go. This directly manipulates Gerry's value hierarchy (family over job) by temporarily putting the job over the family (can't keep your family safe without doing the job). He says yes.

But that's a movie. It is likely that we have nested sets of value hierarchies and that our perspective on the relationship between, say, valuing life and the right to bear arms, is affected by a series of other value hierarchies that can be more or less relevant to us depending on circumstances. Questions of religion, personal responsibility, family safety, crime, mental illness and things as simple as what guns you like better than others all bear on how a gun rights advocate orders values in that central hierarchy. Our job, in persuading, is often to find the right hierarchy we can move people on and then finding the ways it intersects with those larger hierarchies.

To summarize, the goal is to specify the range of values we might use to interpret a piece of evidence and take the audience through a conversation about how they relate. Instead of skipping the warrant altogether, the bulk of our work should be about figuring out how to make those shifts and translations and transcendences. Ethics teachers do this all the time. We spent a vivid day in Professor Shanahan's philosophy class debating about exactly what precautions pool owners should take to prevent neighbor kids from using it and drowning when the owners weren't home. Any? A sign at least? How about a fence? A cover? Guard dogs and searchlights?

There are ways to take audiences along in these discussions. We just have to try harder.

The Checkers Move: Shifting Hierarchical Allegiance

The next way we might use these ideas is to try the Kennedy approach. We need to find another value hierarchy accepted by our audience (or a portion of it) that is usually not connected to the hierarchy we want to change them on and try to build a connection, which will hopefully lessen the connection between the two hierarchies we want to separate. In the Kennedy example, this is de-emphasizing the connection between the hard-easy *descriptive* hierarchy and the simple things are better than hard/complex things traditional American *value* hierarchy. He offers a series of other hierarchies, including one about the strength of nations and another one about sports. He tries to find ways to connect one or all of these hierarchies he thinks are already out there in his audience more securely to the easy-hard hierarchy. He wants to displace the simple-things-are-better hierarchy and replace it with another.

Campbell (1990) demonstrates how Charles Darwin was able to do this for himself as he built his earliest versions of his theories of evolution. Campbell analyzes Darwin's journals as he develops his ideas and points to the way that a double hierarchy connecting the development of animal life with Lyell's theory of geological development (a book he was reading on his famous *Beagle* voyage to the Galapagos) allowed Darwin to move beyond his existing

CHAPTER 15

assumptions about how animals should be categorized and, thus, how they evolved.

If this kind of thing is how *we* learn in our own minds, it must be relevant to working with the minds of others.

The last chapter pointed out how Martin Luther King was able to use religious hierarchies to shift attitudes about race and segregation, another example of this process.

But Coulson (2006) and Stewart, Smith and Denton (2012) describe numerous examples of the ways that the abortion controversy has been prolonged as each side's suggested hierarchies and suggested hierarchical transcendences are rejected by the other. And if you've been embroiled in a never-ending political debate, you've certainly seen this kind of thing happen. Shifting hierarchical allegiance is very hard.

Yet, Nixon (1952) was able to do this in his famous "Checkers" speech. He was accused of having a secret slush fund of cash from donors, and his position as candidate for Vice President was imperiled. He had to defend himself. He set out a list of his (modest) finances and claimed innocence. Later in the speech he accused the Democrats of being conveniently rich. Since he wasn't (his wife didn't have a mink coat, for example, but a "respectable Republican cloth coat"), he felt that he needed a fund to pay for his political travels, etc. This hierarchy, that the poor and middle classes are actually more important in America than the rich, is one that most Americans, especially at that time, would agree with. But the idea that it should be related to the moral and legal question of a political slush fund was the new hierarchical relation Nixon tried to establish.

He remained on the ticket and became Vice President, so it obviously worked. Another double hierarchy Nixon asks his audience to establish is when he admits that he did take a personal gift, which should be illegal. Earlier in the speech he says that even more important than the legal question is the moral question connected with it, an important hierarchical shift. It sounds like, in the beginning, he is going to be even harder on himself by establishing a moral standard above and beyond the legal one. But then he describes the gift of the dog, Checkers, that his kids received. Bullishly, he says, "regardless of what they say about it, we're gonna keep it." Do you want to take a puppy away from a little girl? It is, in fact, still illegal for him to keep that dog, theoretically. But since he's induced us to accept an alternate hierarchy that sets morality higher than the law, how then can we advocate what seems the bullying, immoral act of taking an innocent dog away from an innocent six year-old?

In two ways Nixon is able to save his political skin by asking America to apply a different set of value hierarchies to the facts than they were doing previously. Once he firmly roots the existing sets of hierarchies with the privileged elite like his rich political enemy Adlai Stevenson, he is able to succeed in his persuasive attempt. He does this by being sneaky, though (surprise, surprise). He gets us to agree to his new hierarchies in one context and then shifts the way he applies them later.

Another good example of how to argue this way that is not sneaky at all is Barbara Jordan's (1974) congressional testimony to try to explain to the American people why Nixon should be impeached two decades later, as President, after the Watergate incident. The impact of this speech on American public opinion about the possibility for impeachment was considerable (Rogers, 1998). In order to do this she makes both types of arguments we've seen in this chapter.

She accepts a hierarchy of acts, presumably established by the Republican defenders of Nixon, in terms of their seriousness/rightness. She simply argues that she and her Democratic colleagues are not on the bottom rung and suggests that where we are on the top three rungs is the question of the hour:

Seriousness of Acts
conviction
impeachment
accusations w/ cause
political lies

She also accepts, to some extent, the President's defenders' hierarchy of motivations/character:

Motivations
reason
passion
pettiness

She simply tries to move on that hierarchy. She rejects passion and pettiness and, with a huge number of citations from constitutional conventions and *The Federalist Papers*, demonstrates not only her reasonability, but also adds another, higher, prong to that hierarchy: expertise, which she has just amply demonstrated for herself. She is now higher than the highest value on the hierarchy that her audience is working with:

Motivations
EXPERTISE!
reason
passion
pettiness

Further, her additional work is to suggest a different hierarchy of motivation for the people who are accusing Nixon. She opens her speech by pointing out that, as an African American woman, when the Constitution was written, she was "not included in 'We the People.'" But through amendment she is no longer left out. This is followed by her statement of faith in that amended Constitution, which is "whole, it is complete, it is total." And she does not want to see it destroyed. This invokes a different American hierarchy, very similar to the class-based anti-Stevenson hierarchy Nixon had used twenty years before: earning it is better than having it given to you. Because the Constitution was unfair to her when written, it had to earn her respect. Now that it has, her feelings toward it are stronger than those of white men, who were always just casually included. That ends up almost making her the high priestess of the Constitution, an "Inquisitor," more than just a simple expert (of which, by the way, she seemed to have already established that she was the only one on Capitol Hill). She is the bearer of the deepest knowledge and, of course, and we feel the strength of her convictions, appropriate for an inquisitor:

CHAPTER 15

Motivations
INQUISITOR!
expertise
reason
passion
pettiness

Acts
conviction
impeachment
accusations w/ cause
political lies

In her few minutes in the air, working with the difficult to understand and boring material of Constitutional law, she demonstrates her expertise. She is able to raise the entire case for impeachment above the Republican argument, that it was filled with political lies from passion and pettiness. She demonstrates not only expertise, but a kind of righteous, special, inquisitory intensity, that inexorably links not only with the need for impeachment, but also for the real possibility of conviction.

All of this works in less dramatic realms, as well. Konstantinidou, Kastells and Cervero (nd) suggest that the best way to teach science is to have students explain the double hierarchies that underlie their thinking and then to interrogate and shift those hierarchies for them. If Nixon and Jordan can be successful persuaders in situations where they didn't know for sure what their audience was thinking (they were both editing their speeches right up until their speech times [Huebner, 2012; Rogers, 1998]), what would you be able to do in a long-term relationship with an audience, as a teacher, pastor, or manager, where you had a chance to find out for sure what an audience needed to revise their thinking about?

New Hierarchies

The final, most difficult tactic is to create an entirely new value hierarchy, persuade your audience to accept it, and then to persuade them to connect some other hierarchy we want them to shift something on to this new hierarchy we've given them.

This has got to be the most difficult thing of all. Perelman (2000), in his account of why he developed his theory of argumentation, looks back on World War 2 and suggests that we must have some form of alternative to that kind of argument practiced through war and tyranny: "is there a logic of value judgments that makes it possible for us to reason about values instead of making them depend solely on irrational choices, based on interest, passion, prejudice, and myth?" (p. 1389). Our existing value systems are perhaps too often the products of interest and myth. Wouldn't we hope we could be educated out of error?

The difficulty is that few examples of this kind of new hierarchy argument can be found. In places where it seems like new hierarchies of value pop up with new, separate categories, like the supposed invention of childhood in the Victorian era (Bryson, 2011, Cunningham, 2012), values and concepts from Christianity and Romanticism all seemed to simply shift in existing hierarchies. Something that seems super-new, like Kurzweil's (2005) controversial notion of the Singularity, at which technology will give our brains a kind of immortality, is still argued for with hierarchies of the epochs of past scientific change: evolution, Moore's law and mathematics. The closest example we can find in a text on social movements (Stewart, Smith & Denton, 2012) is when Robert Welch creates a fanciful alternative history of communism and the Illuminati to begin the John Birch Society. But even then, his metaphors and hierarchies are

CHAPTER 15

all about war, childhood and oppression.

Perhaps there really is nothing new under the sun. In fact, Perelman himself, as an activist in Jewish organizations in Belgium during WW2, was one of the first there to believe the new and outrageous claim that the Nazis were killing people, not just relocating them (Mattis, 2011). But even that huge belief shift when Perelman was an audience was accomplished based not on completely new hierarchies but on manipulation of existing ones.

When the big changes happen, rhetors like Martin Luther King use transcendence and hierarchical shifts.

So why have this last section at all, Vrooman? We've got better things we can do with our time! Well, you do now. You can stop looking for this magical set of new values you can deliver to your audience. I often see students give up when faced with the huge and seeming impossibility of persuasion. Perhaps understanding that you task is not to invent something new will help you not give up.

Tinker, do not invent.

In the end, Perelman's hope for intelligent conversations about values is really about giving up the hope of the new. It means giving up on inventing what you *want* to say and focusing instead on what audiences *need* to hear.

THE ZOMBIE GUIDE TO PUBLIC SPEAKING

CHAPTER 16

Chapter 16: Delivery and Credibility

My favorite character in *Dawn of the Dead* (Snyder, 2004) is C.J. He is a terrible person. But the film needs you to like him by the end. I credit the intensity and subtle energy of actor Michael Kelly's performance. C.J., a quasi-villain, gives the audience no other reason to feel bad for him when he dies. But you do.

That's the essence of what this chapter is trying to create. In most cases your audience would rather you not speak. They want to leave early or check their phones. You have to earn their connection.

Delivery, for Carnegie (1955) is how packages get to their destination. Speech delivery is much the same. He compares it to a window shining in light. No one should notice the window.

Delivery is there for you to accomplish something with your audience. It is a tool, a medium, a window. Too many of us think delivery is all there is. But even though many of the old speaking books were almost entirely about delivery (Houghton, 1916; Lee, 1900; Smith, 1858), today's *MOPSBOTS* correctly give delivery only one chapter in 18 or 19.

But how do we use this tool? I put this chapter in the back of the book because I wanted to emphasize that we should think about this question less than we do. We are afraid our delivery is bad and we obsess about it.

When I have students give speakers in class feedback, even when I tell them NOT to talk about delivery, I get a constant stream of comments like this: "Carried yourself well and had great enthusiasm" and "Lots of looking down on the paper instead of looking at the audience. Some reading off of your Power Point when it is right up there." We easily fall into the trap of thinking delivery is all there is. And since we know the audience is noticing it, we freak out.

The thing is, as discussed in Chapter 4, we can be naturally very interesting. But it's like an evil spell of notecards takes us over when preparing a speech, making us boring and horrible and inducing us to do ridiculous things, like when Ross on *Friends*, usually affable and interesting, gets so nervous while reading his notecards in a monotone that he adopts a British accent while teaching and doesn't quite know why. (Crane et al. 1999). So what do we do about that evil spell?

Energy

The trouble with delivery is also the solution. Carnegie (1955) suggests good delivery is your natural tones "enlarged a bit" (p. 144). Every one of the *MOPSBOTS* suggests something similar when they, like Naistadt (2005) in the business world, suggest an extemporaneous delivery. You are connecting with the audience and selling yourself.

If delivery is Carnegie's window, what they must see through it is the real you. Wheeler (1957), for example, emphasized simple things instead of listing a stack of different elements to focus on like Houghton, Lee and Smith do in their books. One of the most important was having normal and natural facial expressions so that people could connect with you as a real person.

It seems like a paradox. The real you. Except . . . not. More!

The "enlarged a bit" that Carnegie wants is *not* some big fake show, the used-car sales pitch, the carnival barker, Disneyland's Jungle Cruise ride operator, or most of the characters Phil Hartman played on *Saturday Night Live*.

The energy that animates you should come from your

CHAPTER 16

commitment to what you are doing. Lockwood and Thorpe (1922) write about how this energy is a passion from really having something to say, like Jane Addams, Booker T. Washington and William Jennings Bryan. Ailes and Kraushar (1988) list more contemporary figures who accomplish this: John F. Kennedy, Martin Luther King, and Winston Churchill. More interestingly, they list Barbara Walters, a person whose career has been about her ability to connect with others, to be so present as a person that she makes celebrities cry on their couches while interviewing them.

Lockwood and Thorpe (1922) argue that a speaker "cannot hope to stir and move others unless he tingles with life himself" (p. 51). Ailes and Kraushar (1988) write that it's:

> an inner flame that we all display when we sincerely believe something and we talk about it . . . . People in love have energy. People who truly relish their jobs have energy . . . . If you have no energy, you have no audience. (p. 123)

Ailes went on to become the head of Fox News. Part of the reason for that channel's success is that its personalities, people like Bill O'Reilly and Glenn Beck, have a personal energy that resonates with their audience.

This paradox is really a question of parallel processing, to use the language of the ELM and the HSM. We know some delivery and credibility elements are simple, pleasing heuristics. But this deep connection with a person who cares about their issues and the audience is what makes the communication have lasting impact. Burke (1969) posits that identification, or the connection made between the rhetor and the audience, is more important than argument.

THE ZOMBIE GUIDE TO PUBLIC SPEAKING

The job of delivery is to allow for that connection.

Credibility

We have generally assessed the connection between audience, speaker and the subject with this notion of speaker credibility, which Hovland and Weiss (1951) began researching heavily based on Aristotle's (2004) elements: competence, trustworthiness and goodwill toward audience.

In the 1960s, as charismatic communicators like Kennedy and King changed the world, Aristotle's second and third elements were combined together ("character"), and a new third element, dynamism, was added. Although McCroskey and Young (1981) find that dynamism is unstable and not clearly related to competence and character, most of the *MOPSBOTS* include all three elements in their discussion of speaker credibility to this day.

The trouble, perhaps, is that although McCroskey spends decades studying credibility, only in relatively rare instances in the living death of public speaking is the dynamic energy of a speaker something that flows directly from their subject (competence) and their commitment to it (character).

Dynamic energy, in most of the *MOPSBOTS*, becomes this magic thing that falls between the cracks. It is not delved into in the delivery chapters. And in the credibility section, it often has little but warnings about avoiding unethical manipulation. In Grice and Skinner (1998), for example, you can achieve competence by doing four things: (knowing the subject, documenting ideas [using supporting material], citing sources, and referencing personal involvement). You can achieve character (?!) with two:

CHAPTER 16

establishing common ground and objectivity. But dynamism has no steps. Perhaps we simply need to get out of our own way and be Carnegie's window.

As to Grice and Skinner on competence and character, I think credibility is more complex than that. Certainly cite your sources and have evidence, but I'm not sure that's enough. What I think is interesting is yet another paradox at the heart of these issues that their lists reveal: how does one achieve a sense of objectivity while demonstrating personal involvement? Grice and Skinner are not wrong. We need both. But isn't personal involvement the reason judges or attorneys recuse themselves from a case? Doesn't it by nature hamper objectivity?

The answer to this paradox is the same as the one about energy and the "real" you. In this case, your job is to explain the things the real you has done that make you an expert on the subject (or at least, as much as you can if you were assigned a topic) while still explaining how you can empathize with and understand the opposing side. Burke (1969) considered identification, or the almost paradoxical connection with the audience that can be created in those fleeting and fragile moments when we "get" each other and feel almost like we are the same, the key to persuasion. That connection with the audience is not something that can only happen with people who already agree. It has to happen with those on the opposite side. Because they hold strong beliefs, they will identify with your own strength of belief but be opposed in other, stronger ways. Only by demonstrating your empathy with their position can you begin to leverage toward persuasion.

This is what Ailes and Fox News, for all their energy, fail to do. Fox News is excellent at entertaining conservatives and reinforcing their beliefs. But it does not persuade liberals. If you watch the network for any period of time, you will be struck by how much it, like its liberal counterpart MSNBC, denigrates the ideas of its political adversaries. Straw man fallacies abound. We will not hear things like "What's good about liberalism is that it cares about the lives and resources of everyday people. But that's why the _____ [conservative proposal] is good. It achieves those goals while also achieving this other set of goals held by conservatives." Instead you'll hear things like "Liberals want the government to tell you what to do in every minute of your life. They don't trust you. They hate the idea of free choice." Is there any way that kind of rhetoric will have persuasive effect on a liberal viewer?

The ability to respect the other side of a debate by honoring your own personal involvement while also trying to objectively understand and respect the other is rare. Politicians who were able to (at least for a time) generate great bipartisan support were able to do just that: Eisenhower, Nixon, Reagan, Clinton. But credibility is not just about what you say (competence) and how you say it (dynamism). It is still connected to those issues of character. And when your honest commitment to this process wavers, as it did for Nixon and Clinton, it begins to fall apart. It always has to really be you, telling the truth and caring about your audience. Instead of a chapter on ethics, we can say just that.

The Details

Dynamically and honestly connect your knowledge, experience and commitment with an audience through common understanding and real, objective, commitment to being fair and balanced.

Sound impossible?

It's not. It only seems so because it happens so rarely.

CHAPTER 16

It's not rare because it is hard to do. It is rare because too few people care enough to really make it happen.

Assuming you do care, the function of all of the other parts of delivery is to allow for that connection to be made. Things like verbal stumbles, lack of gestures and eye contact, etc., make you appear less competent and distract from that connection (Natalle & Bodenheimer, 2004). We see flaws in delivery as questions of competence.

And this is one of the reasons why delivery is scary. But remember Motley from Chapter 2. Our goal is not to perform but to share content, just as this chapter has argued. We need to be as natural as possible and get out of the way of ourselves.

So instead of doing like the *MOPSBOTS* and listing all the elements of physical (posture! facial expression!!) and vocal (tone! pitch!!) delivery that you can obsess about, I will simply list some key things to work on from my experience. These are things that students have repeatedly asked about over the years, so perhaps they are hangups that afflict you, too.

Be animated. Remember energy? Let it show. Avoid the monotone, droning, unexcited ramble of Bob Dole, of Ben Stein in *Ferris Bueller's Day Off* (Hughes, 1986), of all of Al Gore's political career before *An Inconvenient Truth*.

You can never have too much eye contact. I know, it seems like it might be too much, too creepy. I guess, if you are just staring at someone in the front row, yes, or throwing evil glares at your audience like Ross does in that *Friends* episode.[1] But there's a reason teachers want eyes in the back of their heads. How can you tell if they are listening if you are not watching them? Ailes and Kraushar (1988) argue

---

[1] People keep putting this clip on You Tube, if you don't happen to remember 20 seconds of a TV show that aired 16 years ago.

that if you feel like the audience is a bunch of lions waiting to eat you, wouldn't you at least want to see what they are doing? Your eyes transmit your energy as much as anything. Use them.

Gesture more. Most people are paranoid that their gestures are distracting or rude or silly. Most people are wrong. Streeck (1993) has found that we use our peripheral vision's glances at our own gestures as a memory tool, so trying to stop gesturing makes you stop remembering. You don't want that. Bateson says we should talk with our hands. We are good at it. Do it. Maybe just avoid anything that pulls your hands together, like wringing them or grabbing a pen or twirling your rings. When your hands meet, they begin to betray you and secretly reveal your nerves.

Accept that you are kind of a spaz. I've spent 30 years trying to slow down my vocal speed and stop pacing around the room. Fail. You probably have other things that you do wrong, too. Maybe you can't stop a squeak? Maybe your posture stinks. Allow yourself flaws. Focus on what matters more (energy!) and these things will fall away or become less important. They might not be fixable, anyway. Apologize to your audience or make a joke about it. Move on.

Move closer. Get in your audience's space, if you can. It will wake up both you and them. It will remind you all that you are all real people. If you are stuck on a stage, see if you can get that podium moved closer. It really helps.

Video record yourself. Watching yourself on video is tough. But it will show you all the flaws. Then go watch some TED Talks. Then watch yourself again. There. See? Maybe those TED people are better than you. But maybe not, or maybe not by so much. I'll bet that things you hated about your delivery, like that thing you do with your left

CHAPTER 16

hand, you saw other do if you watched enough TEDs. Or maybe you saw something else one of them did. Pretty weird, but ultimately okay. Watch yourself. Improve. But don't be evil to yourself. Your delivery is better than you think. You just need more energy.

Finally, we need to deal with the dreaded verbal fillers, you know, like, the ums? First, you need to understand that these are somewhat inevitable and serve a memory function like gestures do. But sometimes people have a real problem here which needs resolution. I'm thinking of the person who speaks at a relatively normal tone but then ends every sentence with an ear- and nerve-shattering UUUUMMMMMMM that they plow into like my Grandpa did into his turkey dinner. To help alleviate this, we have to have two approaches because there are two kinds of fillers. But both are fundamentally the product of a lack of connection with your audience. Honor that connection and they will fade.

The first kind of filler is the um/uh/like thing, what we might call the *memory pause*. We say these things as we think. But they can become a ritualized habit that overwhelms everything else and leads people to start marking down a count of them in their notebooks. When these natural moments turn into long and intense LIIIIIKKKKKKEEEEs, etc., we are, I think, avoiding pauses. We are afraid of stopping our mouth for a second to find the words. This comes from a life of not being allowed to extemporaneously speak. You do not have to fill every gap. My students who are the biggest UUUUMMMMMers are cured after a semester of student teaching. Pauses can and should happen. Make yourself pause. Add silences. You will stop "um"ing.

To wean yourself off a big habit, though, consider forcing yourself to adopt another verbal filler that is not natural to you. Force yourself to say it after every sentence (put it on your outline!). You will slowly adopt, perhaps, an "uh" instead of UUMMMM, and you will never need either the same way. It will take the place of UUUMMMMM, but because it is not natural for you, you will eventually get rid of it. Dozens of my students I've trained in this way have found success.

The second kind of filler is the *audience call*: know what I mean, you feeling me, right, know what I'm saying, mmmmmm-kay? In this case, you want to know that your audience is listening, but you are a bit afraid to really ask. Interpersonally, KNOWWHATIMEANers tend to be monologuers who don't listen particularly well and who don't often pause to let someone else talk.[2] By constantly eliciting nods of recognition from their audience, perhaps it seems less so. To alleviate these fillers you need to reconnect with your audience and actually ask them.

Talk. To. Them.

Let the speech go for a second and just ask someone, "Did that explanation make sense?" Yes. Totally right in the middle of the speech! It is not a precious object with which you can rule Middle Earth or a hermetically sealed hyperbaric Beanie Baby chamber from 1993. There is no 4th wall. Talk to your audience!

Then pause and allow them to answer. If they tell you, "No," then explain it all again. Maybe ask again if you are doubtful. They may be so trained to nod at you that they need a second to understand you actually want their real opinion now, not the fake pseudolistening they are used to.

Dynamically and honestly connect your knowledge,

---

[2] Relax. I put myself in this category with you. I have had an "Okay?" problem in the past and am currently fighting through the last stages of an addition to "Right?"

experience and commitment with an audience through common understanding and real, objective, commitment to being fair and balanced.

A Few Concluding Thoughts on Group Presentations

You will inevitably make presentations as a group, committee or collective throughout your life. This provides a set of fairly significant challenges. Working with a group is tough. We expect there will always be, as in *Harry Potter* (Rowling, 1999), a Hermione who wants to do all the work and a Ron who will do nothing and barely show up. There are piles of textbooks on what to do about this situation. Most focus on the classic idea that there are task roles, maintenance roles and hindering roles in groups (see Porteus, n.d., for an example). Task roles are getting things done. Maintenance roles are all sorts of supportive and helpful kinds of encouraging communication. Hindering roles are the bad versions of both of those roles, from dominating conversations to degrading other members. All of that might be a useful taxonomy, and most people have been through some sort of training on that at some point, but I do not always find that as helpful as we'd hope.

I'd rather have a shorter solution, even if it is flawed. So here it is: there are task needs and social needs in every group. Although Hermione might only see the tasks and Ron might only see the social, both are important. Getting a class or work group to understand and verbally value the social tasks is, I think, the best way for the Ron Weasleys to avoid letting their unmet social needs drive them off the rails into hindering tasks. You can't just all hang out and then assign people individual tasks they will share when everyone meets up again. The same is true for fun-loving groups and the Hermione smoldering in the corner. You can't just focus on the job at hand and destroy all distracting sidetrack conversations. Group work should spend at least a little time, each time, on both sets of needs for both types of people.

This is not a complete answer to what you hate about group work, but it is a start. Every group has a set of unique dynamics depending on the various task and social needs. You have to find a way to work with that in as positive a way as you can.

From the perspective of this chapter, though, the real challenge of group presentations is during the presentation itself. Nothing is more stultifying to the perceived energy level of a group and its credibility than the tableau of a panel sitting or standing, bored, blank-eyed and clearly just waiting turns, not listening or engaging at all:

See how distracting that is?

In my defense, I was TOTALLY listening here! But you can't tell. I look like I am undergoing a zombie transformation. I've sat through decades of group speeches. Everyone always looks like that if you are sitting, without speaking, for a long enough period of time.

Finding a way not to do that is vital!

My favorite solution, which is not always possible, is to mix up the first one person, then the next, then the next structure. If, instead, every point of the speech has a constant interaction between group members, either in conversation, argument or interaction, it makes the entire

CHAPTER 16

thing feel more dynamic and makes you all look like you know everything you are talking about, not just the tiny portion you seem to have been assigned. I have been suggesting this to student groups for a decade now. It has, thus far, always been a good idea.

THE ZOMBIE GUIDE TO PUBLIC SPEAKING

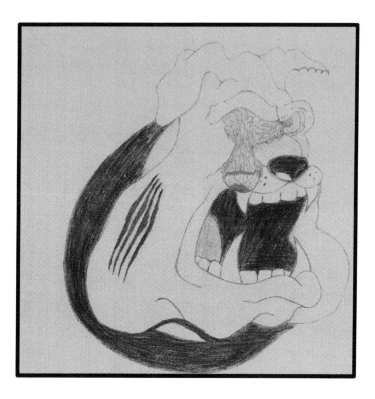

"Unlucky"

REFERENCES

Conclusion: Looking for Brains

This book was designed to help you find those needed brains at the podium. In the introduction I suggested it might be a cure for the living death of public speaking in our world. Of course, here now at the end, you realize that happy endings are hard to come by in a world of zombies.

Perhaps you feel like the lone survivor in a house surrounded by the undead, ready to practice your blank-slide Power Points and value hierarchies, but afraid of having the flesh stripped from your bones if you try.

This book has asked you to do a lot of things very differently than you might have been doing. Only some of you will bother to do so. Some of you will have long decided that I was simply wrong and that your manuscript speeches and recycled Power Points are just fine. Some of you will agree with me but balk at doing the harder work this book asks you to do, especially if you've gotten good feedback on speeches before.

As for me, I wrote this book to replace a series of *MOPSBOTS* I have used over the years which, in their typical 450+ pages, do exactly what bad speeches do: waste time. I hate wasted time: traffic, red lights, extra meetings, someone trying to get the projector to turn on, commercials, video buffering . . . most speeches.

We all can and should be better at this.

I know so many people who have a plan for a zombie apocalypse. I know some who seem to wish it would happen. Maybe they want to see if they'll survive. But maybe they just want the endless cycle of speeches and meetings and discussions and presentations to be over? They'd rather the society that wastes their time be laid to waste. In the zombie apocalypse, even a talky version of it like *The Walking Dead*, eventually the talk stops and you run, shoot, hammer or drive.

The cardinal virtue of zombies is that they don't speak. That might be our favorite thing about them.

Your task is to rescue your future audiences from the living death of the horde of bad speakers. Your task is to find a way to make your public speeches matter. It's time to make your public speeches live.

REFERENCES

References

Ace, T. (1992). You can check out any time you like ... *Diseased Pariah News, 5,* 3-4.

Adams, C. (2006). PowerPoint, habits of mind, and classroom culture. *Journal of Curriculum Studies, 38,* 389-411.

Addonizio, K. (2000). Night of the living, night of the dead. http://www.poemoftheweek.org/id148.html. And in, *Tell me.* New York: BOA.

Adler, R., & Towne, N. (1996). *Looking out / looking in: Interpersonal communication.* Fort Worth: Harcourt.

Agoramoorthy, G. (2012). Science teaching: From boring lecture to a performing art. *Current Science, 102,* 1620-1621.

Ailes, R., & Kraushar, J. (1988). *You are the message.* New York: Doubleday.

Ajzen, I. (1977). Intuitive theories of events and the effects of base-rate information on prediction. *Journal of Personality and Social Psychology, 35,* 303-314.

Alexander, M. (2012). *The new Jim Crow: Mass incarceration in the age of colorblindness.* New York: The New Press.

Amare, N. (2006). To slideware or not to slideware: Students' experiences with Powerpoint vs. lecture. *Journal of Technical Writing & Communication, 36,* 297-308.

American Psychiatric Association. (2013). Diagnostic and statistical manual of mental disorder (5th ed.). Washington, DC: Author.

Anderson, S. (nd). Why do writers use figurative language? *eHow.* http://www.ehow.com/facts_5170863_do-writers-use-figurative-language_.html.

Appel, M., & Richter, T. (2007). Persuasive effects of fictional narratives increase over time. *Media Psychology, 10,* 113-134.

Appel, M., & Richter, T. (2010). Transportation and the need for affect in narrative persuasion: A mediated moderation model. *Media Psychology, 13,* 101-135.

Arachakis, A., & Tsakona, V. (2005). Analyzing conversational data in GTVH terms: A new approach to the issue of identity construction via humor. *Humor, 18*(1), 41-68.

Areni, C. (2003). The effects of structural and grammatical variables on persuasion: An elaboration likelihood model perspective. *Psychology & Marketing, 20,* 349-375.

Aristotle. (1994). *Rhetoric.* Trans. W. Roberts. http://classics.mit.edu/Aristotle/rhetoric.html.

Austen, J. (1813). *Pride and prejudice.* http://www.pemberley.com/janeinfo/ppv1n11.html.

Baesler, E. J., & Burgoon, J. K. (1994). The temporal effects of story and statistical evidence on belief change. *Communication Research, 21,* 582-602.

Bateson G. (1932). Social structure of the Iatmul people of the Sepik River (Parts I and II). *Oceania, 2,* 245-91.

Bateson, G. (1972). *Steps to an Ecology of Mind.* New York: Ballantine.

Bebow, J. (2005, Apr. 22). Cornelius C. "Neal" Weed, Jr., 68: Game of golf brought business, pleasure." *Chicago Tribune.* http://articles.chicagotribune.com/2005-04-22/news/0504220107_1_mr-weed-advertising-club-golf.

Berger, A. A. (1999). *An anatomy of humor.* Piscataway, NJ: Transaction.

Berman, J. S., & Kenny, D. A. (1976). Correlational bias in observer ratings. *Journal of Personality and Social Psychology, 34,* 263-273.

THE ZOMBIE GUIDE TO PUBLIC SPEAKING

Betrus, A. (2014). *The corruption of Dale's cone of experience.* https://sites.google.com/site/thecorruptedconeoflearning/home.

Biderman, D. (2010, Jan. 15). 11 minutes of action. *The Wall Street Journal.* http://www.wsj.com/articles/ SB10001424052748704281204575002852055561406.

Bippus, A. (2007). Factors predicting the perceived effectiveness of politicians' use of humor during a debate. *Humor, 20*(2), 105-121.

Black, E. L., & Martin, G. L. (1980). A component analysis of public-speaking behaviors across individuals and categories. *Communication Education, 29,* 273-282.

Blakely, M. (2012). Changing course while losing altitude. *Vital Speeches of the Day, 78,* 282-286.

Bligh, D. A. (2000). *What's the use of lectures?* (2nd ed.) San Francisco: Jossey-Bass.

Bolduc, M. K., & Frank, D. A. (2010). Chaim Perelman and Lucie Olbrechts-Tyteca's "On temporality as a characteristic of argumentation': Commentary and translation. *Philosophy and Rhetoric, 43,* 308-336.

Booth-Buttefield, S. (2009a). *The complete idiot's guide to persuasion.* Royersford, PA: Alpha.

Booth-Butterfield, S. (2009b, Jun. 20). WATTage: How brightly burns your light? *Persuasion Blog.* http://healthyinfluence.com/wordpress/2009/06/20/ wattage-how-brightly-burns-your-light/.

Booth-Butterfield, S. (2011, Feb. 14). Pretty persuasion pictures. *Persuasion Blog.* http://healthyinfluence.com/wordpress/ 2011/02/14/pretty-persuasion-pictures/.

Bordiga, E., & Nisbett, R. E. (1977). The differential impact of abstract vs. concrete information on decisions. *Journal of Applied Social Psychology, 7,* 258-271.

Borkin, M. A., Bylinskii, Z., Nam Wook Kim, Bainbridge, C. M., Yeh, C. S., Borkin, D., Pfister, H., & Oliva, A. (2016). Beyond memorability: Visualization recognition and recall. Visualization and Computer Graphics, 22, 519-528. http://vcg.seas.harvard.edu/files/pfister/files/ infovis_submission251-camera.pdf.

Bosman, J. (1987). Persuasive effects of political metaphor. *Metaphor & Symbolic Activity, 2,* 97-114.

Bosman, J., & Hagendoorn, L. (1991). Effects of literal and metaphorical persuasive messages. *Metaphor & Symbolic Activity, 6,* 271-293.

Bostdorff, D. (1987). Making light of James Watt: A Burkean approach to the form and attitude of political cartoons. *Quarterly Journal of Speech, 73,* 43-59.

Bouvard, M. (1994). *Revolutionizing motherhood: The mothers of the Plaza de Mayo.* Wilmington, DE: SR Books.

Bowers, J., & Osborn, M. (1966). Attitudinal effects of selected types of concluding metaphors in persuasive speeches. *Speech Monographs, 33,* 147-155.

Boyle, D. (Director). (2002). *28 days later.* UK: DNA Films.

Brings, L. (1954). *Clever introductions for chairmen.* Minneapolis: Denison.

Brooks, M. (2003). *The zombie survival guide.* New York: Three Rivers.

Brooks, M. (2007). *World war Z.* New York: Broadway.

Brosh, A. (2013). Hyperbole and a half. New York: Simon & Schuster.

Bruner, J. (1990). *Acts of meaning.* Cambridge, MA: Harvard Univ. Press.

Bryant, J., Comisky, P., & Zillmann, D. (1979). Teachers' humor in the college classroom. *Communication Education, 28,* 110-118.

Brydon, S., & Scott, M. (1994). *Between one and many: The art and science of public speaking.* Mountain View, CA: Mayfield.

REFERENCES

Bryson, B. (2011). *At home: A short history of private life*. New York: Anchor.

Buchko, A., Buchko, K., & Meyer, J. (2013). Perceived efficacy and the actual effectiveness of PowerPoint on the retention and recall of religious messages in the weekly sermon: An empirical field study. *Journal of Communication & Religion, 36,* 149-165.

Buck, C., & Lee. J. (Directors) (2013). *Frozen* [Motion picture]. USA: Disney.

Buijzen, M., & Valkenberg, P. M. (2004). Developing as typology of humor in audiovisual media. *Media Psychology, 6,* 147-167.

Burke, K. (1969). *A rhetoric of motives*. Berkeley: University of California Press.

Burke, K. (1984). *Attitudes toward history*. 3rd ed. Berkeley: University of California Press.

Burton, G. (2007). Silva rhetoricae. http://humanities.byu.edu/rhetoric/silva.htm.

Buselle, R., & Bilandzib, H. (2009). Measuring narrative engagement. *Media Psychology, 12,* 321-347.

Campbell, J. (1990). Scientific discovery and rhetorical invention: The path to Darwin's *Origin*. In H. Simons (Ed.), *The rhetorical turn: Invention and persuasion in the conduct of inquiry* (pp. 58-90). Chicago: University of Chicago Press.

Carnegie, D. (1955). *Public speaking and influencing men in business*. New York: Association Press.

Carroll, L. (1939). *Conversation, please*. Cleveland: World.

Carroll, N. (2001). *Beyond aesthetics: Philosophical essays*. Cambridge, UK: Cambridge Univ. Press.

Carter, J. (2012). Russell H. Conwell. http://www.temple.edu/about/RussellConwell.htm.

Chaiken, S. (1980). Heuristic versus systematic information processing and the use of source versus message cues in persuasion. *Journal of Personality and Social Psychology, 39,* 752-766.

Chaiken, S. (1987). The heuristic model of persuasion. In M. P. Zanna, J. M. Olson, & C. P. Herman (Eds.), *Social influence: The Ontario symposium, volume 5* (pp. 3-39). Hillsdale, NJ: Erlbaum.

Chaiken, S., & Maheswaran, D. (1994). Heuristic processing can bias systematic processing: Effects of source credibility, argument ambiguity, and task importance on attitude judgment. *Journal of Personality and Social Psychology, 66,* 460-472.

Chestek, K. (2010). Judging by the numbers: An empirical study of the power of story. *Journal of the Association of Legal Writing Directors, 7,* 1-35.

Civiello, M., & Matthews, A. (2008). *Communication counts: Business presentations for busy people*. New York: Wiley.

Clark, R. E. (1983). Reconsidering research on learning from media. *Review of Education Research, 53,* 445-459.

Cline, A. R. (2001). *Rhetorica: Tropes and schemes*. http://rhetorica.net/tropes.htm.

Cline, E. (2011). *Ready player one*. New York: Random House.

Cocker, F., Nicholson, J. M., Graves, N., Oldenburg, B., Palmer, A. J., Scorr, J., Venn, A., & Sanderson, K. (2014). Depression in working adults: Comparing the costs and health outcomes of working when ill. *PLoS ONE 9*(9): e105430. doi:10.1371/journal.pone.0105430.

Construction Safety and Health Outreach Program. (1996). Presenting effective presentations with visual aids. *U.S. Department of Labor OSHA Office of Training and Education.* Retrieved July 7, 2015 at http://www.rufwork.com/110/mats/oshaVisualAids.html.

Conwell, R. (2012). *Acres of diamonds.* http://www.temple.edu/about/Acres_of_Diamonds.htm.

Corbett, E. (1971). *Classical rhetoric for the modern student.* NY: Oxford.

Cork, J., & Van Eyssen, L. (Directors). (2008).The ultimate romance: The making of *Notorious* [Documentary].United States: Fox.

Coulson, S. (2006). *Semantic leaps: Frame-shifting and conceptual blending in meaning construction.* Cambridge, UK: Cambridge University Press.

Crabtree, S. (2007, Aug. 30). Book uncovers a lonely, spiritually desolate Mother Teresa. *Christianity Today.* http://www.christianitytoday.com/ct/2007/augustweb-only/135-43.0.html.

Craig, R., & Amernic, J. (2006). Power Point presentation technology and the dynamics of teaching. *Innovative Higher Education, 31,* 147-160.

Crane, D., Kaufman, M., Reich, A., & Cohen, T. (Writers) & Halverson, G. (Director). (1999, Oct. 14). The one where Joey loses his insurance [television episode]. *Friends.* Los Angeles: Warner.

Crawford, D. (2002). The vulnerable body of Havelok the Dane. *Medieval Forum,* http://www.sfsu.edu/~medieval/Volume%201/ Crawford.html.

Crockett, M. (2012, Nov.). Beware neuro-bunk. *TED.* http://www.ted.com/talks/molly_crockett_beware_neuro_bunk.html.

Cuddy, A. (2012). Your body language shapers who you are. *TED.* http://www.ted.com/talks/amy_cuddy_your_body_language_shapes_who_you_are?

Cunninghman, H. (2012). *The invention of childhood.* New York: Random House.

Curtis, G. (2012). *The Fallacy Files.* http://www.fallacyfiles.org/ aboutgnc.html.

Djafarova, E. (2008). Why do advertisers use puns? A linguistic perspective. *Journal of Advertising Research, 48,* 267-275.

Djonev, E., & Van Leeuwen, T. (2013). Between the grid and composition: Layout in PowerPoint's design and use. *Semiotica, 197,* 1-34.

Dolman, J. (1922). *A handbook of public speaking.* New York: Harcourt.

Doumont, J-L. (2005). The cognitive style of PowerPoint: Slides are not all evil. *Technical Communication, 52,* 64-70.

Eaton, L. (2006, Oct. 2). Zombies spreading like a virus: *PW* talks with Max Brooks. *Publisher's Weekly,* 57.

Eidenmuller, M. E. (2013). *American rhetoric: Rhetorical figures in sound.* http://www.americanrhetoric.com/rhetoricaldevicesinsound.htm.

"Elevate." (2015). *Dictionary.com.* http://dictionary.reference.com/browse/elevate.

Ellis, A. 1962. *Reason and emotion in psychotherapy.* New York: Lyle Stuart.

Ephron, N. (2006). *I feel bad about my neck: And other thoughts on being a woman.* New York: Knopf.

Escalas, J. (2004). Imagine yourself in the product: Mental stimulation, narrative transportation, and persuasion. *Journal of Advertising, 33* (20), 37-48.

Escalas, J. (2007). Self-referencing and persuasion: Narrative transportation versus analytical elaboration. *Journal of Consumer Research, 33,* 421-429.

Evans, J. (1989). *Biases in reasoning: Causes and consequences.* Hove, UK:

REFERENCES

Erlbaum.

Fahnestock, J. (2002). *Rhetorical figures in science*. New York: Oxford University Press.

Fahnestock, J (2011). "No neutral choices": The art of style in *The New Rhetoric*. In J. Gage (Ed.), *The promise of reason: Studies in The New Rhetoric* (pp. 29-47). Carbondale: Southern Illinois University Press.

Farkhas, D. K. (2006). Toward a better understanding of PowerPoint deck design. *Information Design Journal + Document Design, 14*(2), 162-171.

Feinberg, D. (1994). *Queer and loathing: Rants and raves of a raging AIDS clone*. New York: Viking.

Few, S. (2007, Aug.). *Save the pies for dessert*. http://www.perceptualedge.com/articles/visual_business_intelligence/save_the_pies_for_dessert.pdf.

Feynman, R. (2007). *The Feynman lectures on physics volumes 11-12* [audio recording]. New York: Basic Books.

Feynman, R., Leighton, R., & Hutchings, E. (1986). *"Surely you're joking, Mr. Feynman": Adventures of a curious character*. Toronto: Bantam.

Feynman, R., Leighton, R., & Sands, M. (1963). *The Feynman lectures on physics: Volume I: Mainly mechanics, radiation, and heat*. Reading, MA: Addison-Wesley.

Fisher, W (1984). Narration as human communication paradigm: The case of public moral argument. *Communication Monographs, 51*, 1–22.

Fiske, S., & Taylor, S. (1991). *Social cognition*. New York: McGraw Hill.

"The Five Paragraph Essay" (n.d.). http://olympia.osd.wednet.edu/media/olympia/departments/social_studies/kabat__dh/a.p._u.s._history/ap0test0study0help/frq__dbq_structure__needs.pdf.

Fleischer, R. (Director). (2009). *Zombieland* [Motion picture]. USA: Columbia.

Flaming, J. (2004). The art & science of signs and graphics. *Complete Campaign*. http://www.completecampaigns.com/article.asp?articleid=30.

Fleming, J., & Hunt, S. (1996). Winning graphics. *Campaigns & Elections, 19*(6), 50-56.

Fluharty, G. W., & Ross, H. R. (1981). *Public speaking and other forms of speech communication*. 2nd ed. New York: Barnes and Noble.

Forster, M. (Director). (2013). *World War Z* [Motion picture]. USA: Paramount.

Foss, S., & Foss, K. (2003). *Inviting transformation: Presentational speaking for a changing world*. Prospect Heights, IL: Waveland.

Fraleigh, D., & Tuman, J. (2009). *Speak up!: An illustrated guide to public speaking*. Boston: Bedford.

Frank, D., & Bolduc, M. (2011). Lucie Olbrecht-Tyteca's new rhetoric. In J. Gage (Ed.), *The promise of reason: Studies in The New Rhetoric* (pp. 55-79). Carbondale: Southern Illinois University Press.

Freddi, M. (2011). Analogical reasoning in the teaching of science: The case of Richard Feynman's physics. In J. Gage (Ed.), *The promise of reason: Studies in The New Rhetoric* (pp. 206-222). Carbondale: Southern Illinois University Press.

Frentz, T. (2006). Ashes of love. *Southern Communication Journal, 71*, 195-203.

Friedland, P. (2002). Parallel stages: Theatrical and political representation in early modern and revolutionary France. In C. Jones & D. Wahrman (eds.), *The age of cultural revolutions: Britain and France, 1750-1820*. Berkeley, University of California Press.

Fulci, L. (Director). (1979). *Zombi 2* [Motion picture]. Italy: Variety Film

Production.

Gadamer, H. (1994). *Truth and method.* (Trans., J. Weinsheimer & D. G. Marshall). 2nd Ed. New York: Continuum.

Gardner, S. A. (2003). The unrecognized exceptionality: Teaching gifted adolescents with depression. *English Journal, 92,* 28-32.

Gaskins, R. (2012). *Sweating bullets: Notes about inventing Power Point.* San Francisco: Vinland.

Geary, J. (2009). Metaphorically speaking. *TED.* http://www.ted.com/talks/james_geary_metaphorically_speaking.

Gebroe, D. (Director). (1985). *Zombie Honeymoon* [Motion picture]. USA: Showtime.

Gehring, R. E., & Togglia, M. P. (1988). Relative retention of verbal and audiovisual information in a national training programme. *Applied Cognitive Psychology, 2,* 213-221.

Gelinas-Chebat, C., & Chebat, J. (1992). Effects of two voice characteristics on the attitudes toward advertising messages. *The Journal of Social Psychology, 132,* 447-459.

Gillham, J., & Reivich, K. (2004). Cultivating optimism in childhood and adolescence. *The Annals of the American Academy of Political and Social Science, 591* (10), 146-163.

Gillham, J., & Reivich, K. (2007). Resilience in children: The Penn resiliency project. http://www.ppc.sas.upenn.edu/prpsum.htm.

Glaser, S. R, (1981). Oral communication apprehension and avoidance: The current status of treatment research. *Communication Education, 30,* 321-341.

Godin, S. (2001). *Really bad Power Point (And how to avoid it).* http://www.sethgodin.com/freeprize/reallybad-1.pdf.

Godin, S. (2003). How to get your ideas to spread. *TED.* http://www.ted.com/talks/seth_godin_on_sliced_bread.

Godin, S. (2006). This is broken. *TED.* http://www.ted.com/talks/seth_godin_this_is_broken_1.

Godin, S. (2009). The tribes we lead. *TED.* http://www.ted.com/talks/seth_godin_on_the_tribes_we_lead.

Goel, V., & Dolan, R. (2001). The functional anatomy of humor: Segregating cognitive and affective components. *Nature Neuroscience, 4,* 237-238.

Goodstein, D., & Neugebauer, G. (1995). Special preface. In R. Feynman, R. Leighton, & M. Sands, *Six Easy Pieces* (pp. xix-xxiii). Cambridge, MA: Perseus.

Green, M. (2004). Transportation into narrative worlds: The role of prior knowledge and perceived realism. *Discourse Processes, 38,* 247-266.

Green, M. (2006). Narratives and cancer communication. *Journal of Communication, 56,* 163-183.

Green, M., Garst, J., & Brock, T. (2004). The power of fiction: Determinants and boundaries. In L. Shrum (ed.), *The psychology of entertainment media: Blurring the lines between entertainment and persuasion* (pp. 161-176). New York: Erlbaum

Green, M., Garst, J., Brock, T., & Chung, S. (2006). Fact versus fiction labeling: Persuasion parity despite heightened scrutiny of fact. *Media Psychology, 8,* 267-285.

Grice, G., & Skinner, J. (1998). *Mastering public speaking.* Boston: Allyn & Bacon.

Grohl, D. (2014, Apr. 11). Rock and Roll Hall of Fame, Nirvana induction acceptance speech. https://www.youtube.com/ watch?v=SdN7CPqXKHE.

REFERENCES

Guggenheim, D. (Director). (2006). *An inconvenient truth* [Documentary]. United States: Lawrence Bender.

Hagney, M. (2014, Oct. 18). Distributed urban agriculture. *TEDxSanAntonio*. https://www.youtube.com/watch?v=z7KBTt9q4nE.

Halperin,V. (Director). (1932). *White zombie* [Motion picture]. USA: United Artists.

Hardin, E. E. (2007). Technology in teaching: Presentation software in the college classroom: don't forget the instructor. *Teaching of Psychology, 34*(1), 53-57.

Harris, R. A. (2010). *Virtual salt: A handbook of rhetorical devices.* http://www.virtualsalt.com.

Hartsock, E. (1929). In defense of punning. *American Speech, 4,* 224-227.

Hasling, J. (1998). *The audience, the message, the speaker.* 6th ed. Boston: McGraw-Hill.

Hazel, P. (2008). Toward a narrative pedagogy for interactive learning environments. *Interactive Learning Environments, 3,* 199-213.

Heinsoo, R., Collins, A., & Wyatt, J. (2008). *Dungeons & Dragons player's handbook: Arcane, divine and martial heroes.* Renton, WA: Wizards of the Coast.

Henderson, G. (2006). The cost of persuasion: Figure, story, and eloquence in the rhetoric of judicial discourse. *University of Toronto Quarterly, 75,* 905-924.

Henson, B. (Director). (1992). *The Muppet Christmas Carol* [Motion picture]. United States: Disney.

History of OOH (n.d.). *OAAA.* http://www.oaaa.org/OutofHomeAdvertising/HistoryofOOH.aspx.

Hitchcock, D. (2005). Good reasoning on the Toulmin model. *Argumentation, 19,* 373-391.

Hobbs, P. (2007). Lawyers' use of humor as persuasion. *Humor, 20*(2), 123-156.

Hoeken, H., & Hustinx, L. (2009). When is statistical evidence superior to anecdotal evidence in supporting probability claims? The role of argument type. *Human Communication Research, 35,* 491-510.

Horne, M. (2008). Teaching religious doubt with Toulmin's model of reasoning. *Teaching Theology and Religion, 11*(4), 203-212.

Horninx, J. (2008). Comparing the actual and expected persuasiveness of evidence types: How good are lay people at selecting persuasive evidence? *Argumentation, 22,* 555-569.

Houghton, H. (1916). *The elements of public speaking.* Boston: Ginn.

Hovland, C. & Weiss, W. (1951). The influence of source credibility on communication effectiveness, *Public Opinion Quarterly, 15,* 635-650.

Howling, B, & Ramke, Y. (Directors). (2013). *Cargo* [Short film]. USA: http://www.youtube.com/watch?v=gryenlQKTbE.

Huebner, L. (2012, Sep 22.). The Checkers speech after 60 year. *The Atlantic.* http://www.theatlantic.com/politics/archive/2012/09/the-checkers-speech-after-60-years/262172/.

Hughes, J. (Director). (1986). *Ferris Bueller's Day Off* [Motion picture]. United States: Paramount.

Hughes, J. (Director). (1987). *Planes, Trains & Automobiles* [Motion picture]. United States: Paramount.

Hunt, G. (1987). *Public speaking.* 2nd ed. Englewood Cliffs, NJ: Prentice-Hall.

Inafune, K. (Producer). (2006) *Dead rising* [video game]. Japan: Capcom.

Ingraham, J. C. (1958, Jan. 27). White-on-green signs chosen by autoists in U.

THE ZOMBIE GUIDE TO PUBLIC SPEAKING

S. poll. *New York Times*, L29.

Jandaghi, G., & Matin, H. (2009). Achievement and satisfaction in a computer-assisted versus a traditional lecturing of an introductory statistics course. *Australian Journal of Basic & Applied Sciences, 3*, 1875-1878.

Jay, J. K. (2015, Jan. 28). The innovative learning strategy used by leading Fortune 500 companies. *Inc.* http://www.inc.com/joelle-k-jay/the-top-learning-strategy-used-by-leading-fortune-500-companies.html.

Jennings, W. (2012). The story of the lost corpse. *Vital Speeches of the Day, 78,* 359-361.

Jobs, S. (2005, Jun, 12). You've got to find what you love [Commencement address]. Stanford University. http://news.stanford.edu/news/2005/june15/jobs-061505.html.

Johnson, R., & Barr., A. (2012, Dec. 5). Graphic: Stopping the dead – a statistical look back at the *Walking Dead* series so far. *National Post,* http://news.nationalpost.com/2012/12/05/graphic-stopping-the-dead-a-statistical-look-back-at-the-walking-dead-series-so-far/.

Jonsson, U., Goodman, A., von Knorring, A., von Knorring, L., & Koupil, I. (2012). School performance and hospital admission due to unipolar depression: A three-generational study of social causation and social selection. *Social Psychiatry & Psychiatric Epidemiology, 47,* 1695-1706.

Jordan, B. (1974, Jul. 25). Speech on impeachment. *Watergate Hearings, Washington, D. C.* http://watergate.info/1974/07/25/barbara-jordan-speech-on-impeachment.html.

Jordan, B. (1976, Jul. 12). Keynote address. *Democratic National Convention, New York.* https://www.youtube.com/watch?v=Bg7gLIx__-k.

Jorm, A., Allen, N., Morgan, A., & Purcell, R. (2009). *A guide to what works for depression.* Melbourne: beyondblue. http://fwtdp.org.au/wp-content/uploads/2013/05/What-works-for-depression.pdf.

Junker, D. (2013, Feb.). In defense of puns: How to use them effectively. *Public Relations Tactics, 20*(2), 18.

Kahan, D., & Braman, D. (2003). More statistics, less persuasion: A cultural theory of gun-risk perceptions. *University of Pennsylvania Law Review, 151,* 1291-1327.

Kawasaki, G. (2005). The 10/20/30 rule of PowerPoint. *Guy Kawasaki.* http://guykawasaki.com/the_102030_rule/.

Kazoleas, D. (1993). A comparison of the persuasive effectiveness of qualitative versus quantitative evidence: A test of exploratory hypotheses. *Communication Quarterly, 41,* 40-50.

Keith, W., & Beard, D. (2008). Toulmin's rhetorical logic: What's the warrant for warrants? *Philosophy & Rhetoric, 41,* 22-50.

Kennedy, J. F. (1962, Sep. 12). Speech at Rice University. http://er.jsc.nasa.gov/seh/ricetalk.htm.

Kenny, P. (1982). *A handbook of public speaking for scientists & engineers.* Bristol, UK: Adam Hilger.

Kim, D., & Benbasat, I. (2006). The effects of trust-assuring arguments on consumer trust in Internet stores: Application of Toulmin's model of argumentation. *Information Systems Research, 17,* 286-300.

Klibert, J., Lamis, D. A., Collina, W., Smalley, K. B., Warren, J. C., Yancey, C. T., & Winterowd, C. (2014). Resilience mediates the relations between perfectionism

REFERENCES

and college student distress. *Journal of Counseling & Development, 92*, 75-82.

Konstantinidou, A., Castells, M., & Cervero, J. (nd). Argumentation and science education: Argument schemes as a physics teaching instrument. http://www.hpdst.gr/system/files/1203-workshop-science-education.doc.

Kopfman, J, Smith, A., Yun, J., & Hodges, A. (1998). Affective and cognitive reactions to narrative versus statistical evidence in organ donation messages. *Journal of Applied Communication Research, 26*, 279-300.

Kozy, J. (1970). The argumentative use of rhetorical figures. *Philosophy & Rhetoric, 3*, 141-151.

Krug, S. (2000). *Don't make me think!: A common sense approach to web usability.* Indianapolis: New Riders.

Kurzweil, R. (2005). *The singularity is near: When humans transcend biology.* New York: Penguin.

Layfield, E. (2015). What are the effects of figurative language on a short story? *Seattle PI.* http://education.seattlepi.com/effects-figurative-language-short-story-6288.html.

Lee, G. (1900). *Principles of public speaking.* New York: Putnam.

Leff, M. (1988). Dimensions of temporality in Lincoln's Second Inaugural. *Communication Reports, 1*, 26-31.

Leigh, J. (1994). The use of figures of speech in print ad headlines. *Journal of Advertising, 23*, 17-33.

Leong, T. (2013). *Super-graphic: A visual guide to the comic book universe.* New York: Chronicle.

LeRoux, P., & Corwin, M. (2007). *Visual selling: Capture the eye and the customer will follow.* Hoboken, NJ: Wiley.

Letterman, D. (2011, Sep. 17). 9/11 monologue. https://www.youtube.com/watch?v=DBLgp1qTCTg.

Levassuer, D. G., & Sawyer, J. K. (2006). Pedagogy meets Power Point: A research review of the effects of computer—generated slides in the classroom. *The Review of Communication, 6*, 101-123.

Levine, J. (Director). (2013). *Warm bodies* [Motion picture]. USA: Summit.

Lincoln, A. (1865, Mar. 4). *Second Inaugural Address.* Washington, D. C. http://www.bartleby.com/124/pres32.html.

Lloyd, D. H. (1968, October). A concept of improvement of learning response in the taught lesson. *Visual Education*, 23-25.

Lockwood, F., & Thorpe, C. (1922). *Public speaking today: A high school manual.* Chicago: Sanborn.

Lomax, R. G., & Moosavi, S. A. (2002). Using humor to teach statistics: Must they be orthogonal? *Understanding Statistics 1*(2), 113-130.

Lucas, S. (2001). *The art of public speaking.* 7th ed. Boston: McGraw Hill.

Lyons, C. (1931). Audience consciousness. *Quarterly Journal of Speech, 17*(3), 375-385.

Lyttle, J. (2001). The effectiveness of humor in persuasion: The case of business ethics training. *Journal of General Psychology, 128*, 206-217.

Mackiewicz, J. (2008). Comparing PowerPoint experts' and university students' opinions about PowerPoint presentations. *Journal of Technical Writing & Communication, 38*(2), 149-165.

Marion, I. (2011). *Warm bodies.* New York: Atria.

Martin, K. C. (2015, Jun. 25). Twerking since 1820: An *OED* antedating.

OxfordWords. http://blog.oxforddictionaries.com/ 2015/06/twerk-origin-oed/.

Mattis, N. (2011). Chaïm Perelman: A life well lived. In J. Gage (Ed.), *The promise of reason: Studies in The New Rhetoric* (pp. 8-18). Carbondale: Southern Illinois University Press.

McCabe, A. (1988). Effect of different contexts on memory for metaphor. *Metaphor & Symbolic Activity, 3,* 105-133.

McCandless, D. (2010). The beauty of data visualization. *TED.* http://www.ted.com/talks/david_mccandless_the_beauty_of_data_visualization.

McCandless, D. (2012). *The visual miscellaneum.* New York: Harper.

McLaren, M. (Director). (2010). Guts. In F. Darabont (Producer), *The Walking Dead.* USA: AMC.

McClure, K. (2009). Resurrecting the narrative paradigm: Identification and the case of young earth creationism. *Rhetoric Society Quarterly, 39,* 189-211.

McCroskey, J., & Young, T. (1981). Ethos and credibility: The construct and its measurement after three decades. *Central States Speech Journal, 32,* 24-34.

McGee, M. C. (1980). The "ideograph": A link between rhetoric and ideology. *Quarterly Journal of Speech, 66,* 1-16.

McGrath, C. (2015, Feb. 4). Communication & learning cmg. *Slideshare.* http://www.slideshare.net/CormacMcGrath/communication-learning-cmg.

McQuarrie, E., & Mick, D. (2003). Visual and verbal rhetorical figures under directed processing versus incidental exposure to advertising. *Journal of Consumer Research, 29,* 579-587.

MichCommunication. (2012, Feb. 16). Attention curve for presentations. *MichCommunication.* http://michcommunication.com/ ?attachment_id=1012.

Migiel, M. (1998). Encrypted messages: Men, women, and figurative language in Decameron 5.4. *Philological Quarterly, 77,* 1-13.

Mikkelson, B. (2013, Aug. 14). Daydream deceiver. *Snopes.* http://www.snopes.com/science/stats/thinksex.asp.

Miller, K. (1988). *Voice of deliverance: The language of Martin Luther King, Jr., and its sources.* Athens: Univ. of Georgia Press.

Mills, H. R. (1977). *Techniques of technical training.* (3rd ed.). London: Macmillan.

Misha, T. (2008). Case study: the impact of the Middle Sepik River People's cultural practices and spiritworship on their Christian worship. *Melanesian Journal of Theology, 24*(1), 43-80.

Montessori, M. (1912). The Montessori method. (Trans. A. E. George). New York: Stokes. http://digital.library.upenn.edu/women/montessori/method/method.html.

Morgan, S., & Reichert, T. (1999). The message is in the metaphor: Assessing the comprehension of metaphors and analogies in advertisements. *Journal of Advertising, 28,* 1-12.

Morris, M. (1901). The Lane Lectures on the social aspects of dermatology. *American Medicine, 2,* 413-417.

Mosher, J. (1917). *Effective public speaking: The essentials of extempore speaking and of gesture.* New York: Macmillan.

Mothersbaugh, D., Huhmann, B., & Franke, G. (2002). Combinatory and separative elements of rhetorical figures on consumers' effort and focus in print advertising. *Journal of Consumer Research, 28,* 589-602.

Motley, M. (1997). *Overcoming your fear of public speaking: A proven method.* Boston: Houghton.

REFERENCES

Nabi, R., Moyer-Guse, E., & Byrne, S. (2007). All joking aside: A serious investigation into the persuasive effect of funny social issue messages. *Communication Monographs, 74,* 29-54.

Naistadt, I. (2005). *Speak without fear: A total system for becoming a natural, confident communicator.* New York: Harper.

Natalle, E., & Bodenheimer, F. (2004). *The woman's public speaking handbook.* Southbank, Australia: Thompson.

Nehmy, T. J. (2010). School-based prevention of depression and anxiety in Australia: Current state and future directions. *Clinical Psychologist, 14* (3), 74-83.

Niemantsverdreit, J. W. (n.d.). How to give a successful oral presentation. *EFCATS.* http://presentations.catalysis.nl/presentations/presentation.php.

Nixon, R. (1952, Sep. 23). "Checkers" speech. http://watergate.info/1952/09/23/nixon-checkers-speech.html

Nordquist, R. (2013). *Glossary of grammatical & rhetorical terms.* http://grammar.about.com/od/terms/Glossary_of_Grammatical_Rhetorical_Terms.htm.

Notaro, T. (2012). *Live.* United States: iTunes/Amazon.

O'Keefe, D. J. (2008). Elaboration likelihood model. In W. Donsbach (Ed.), *International encyclopedia of communication* (Vol. 4, pp. 1475-1480).Oxford, UK, and Malden, MA: Wiley-Blackwell. http://www.dokeefe.net/pub/OKeefe08IEC-ELM.pdf.

Obama, B. (2013, Jul. 19). President Obama speaks on Trayvon Martin. https://www.youtube.com/watch?v=MHBdZWbncXI.

"Outdoor advertising—How to get maximum results." (1950, July). *Duke University Libraries Digital Collections.* http://library.duke.edu/digitalcollections/oaaaarchives_BBB4049/, http://library.duke.edu/digitalcollections/oaaaarchives_BBB4050/, http://library.duke.edu/digitalcollections/oaaaarchives_BBB4051/.

Pawlowski, D., Badzinski, D, & Mithcell, N. (1988). Effects of metaphors on children's comprehension and perception of print advertisements. *Journal of Advertising, 27,* 83-98.

Paralumun (n.d.). American rape statistics. *Paralumun.* http://www.paralumun.com/issuesrapestats.htm.

Perelman, C. (1982). *The realm of rhetoric.* Notre Dame: Univ. of Notre Dame Press.

Perelman, C. (2000). "The new rhetoric: A theory of practical reasoning. In P. Bizzell & B. Herzberg (Eds.), *The rhetorical tradition: Readings for classical times to the present* (pp. 1384-1409). New York: Bedford.

Perelman, C., & Olbrechts-Tyteca, L. (1969). *The new rhetoric: A treatise on argumentation.* Notre Dame: Univ. of Notre Dame Press.

Peterson, H. (1954). *A treasury of the world's great speeches.* New York: Grolier.

Peterson, B. (1983). Tables and graphs improve reader performance and reader retention. *Journal of Business Communication, 20,* 47-55.

Petty, R., & Cacioppo, J. (1981). *Attitudes and persuasion: Classic and contemporary approaches.* Dubuque: IA: Brown.

Petty, R., Kasmer, J., Haugvedt, C., & Cacioppo, J. (1987). Source and message factors in communication: A reply to Stiff's critique of the elaboration likelihood model. *Communication Monographs, 54,* 233-249.

Phelan, J. (1991). *Beyond the tenure track: Fifteen months in the life of an English*

Professor. Columbus: Ohio State University Press.

Phelan, J. (2010). Teaching narrative as rhetoric: The example of time's arrow. *Pedagogy, 10,* 217-228.

Phillips, B. (1997). Thinking into it: Customer interpretation of complex advertising images. *The Journal of Advertising, 26*(2), 77-87.

Phillips-Anderson, M. A. (2007). *A theory of rhetorical humor in American political discourse* [Doctoral dissertation]. http://drum.lib.umd.edu/bitstream/1903/7739/1/umi-umd-5020.pdf.

Porat, T., Oran-Gilad, T., & Meyer, J. (2009). Task-dependent processing of tables and graphs. *Behaviour & Information Technology, 28,* 293-307.

Polk, J., Young, D., & Holbert, R. (2009). Humor complexity and political influence: An elaboration likelihood approach to the effects of humor type on The Daily Show with Jon Stewart. *Atlantic Journal of Communication, 17,* 202-219.

Polyorat, K, Alden, D., & Kim, E. (2007). Impact of narrative versus factual print ad copy on product evaluation: The mediating role of ad message involvement. *Psychology & Marketing, 24,* 539-554.

Porteus, A. (n.d.). Roles people play in groups. http://web.stanford.edu/group/resed/resed/staffresources/RM/training/grouproles.html.

Prochnow, H. (1942). *The public speaker's treasure chest.* New York: Harper.

Pylar, J., Wills, C., Lillie, J., Rovner, D., Kelly-Blake, K, & Holmes-Rovner, M. (2007). Men's interpretations of graphical information in a videotape decision aid. *Health Expectations, 10,* 184-193.

Radford, B. (2015, Jul. 24). The ten-percent myth. *Snopes.* http://www.snopes.com/science/stats/10percent.asp.

RAINN (2009). How often does sexual assault occur? *Rape, Abuse & Incest National Network.* http://www.rainn.org/get-information/statistics/frequency-of-sexual-assault.

Red Magma. (2009, Aug. 7). eLearning sucks. *Slideshare.* http://www.slideshare.net/redmagma/elearning-sucks.

Reed, C., & Rowe, G. (2005). Translating Toulmin diagrams: Theory neutrality in argument representation. *Argument, 19,* 267-286.

Rees, J. (2014, Jul. 30). Do you really use six metaphors a minute? *XrayListening.* http://www.xraylistening.com/do-you-really-use-six-metaphors-a-minute/.

Reid, R. (2012, Mar.). The $8 billion iPod. *TED.* http://www.ted.com/talks/rob_reid_the_8_billion_ipod.

Reimold, C., & Reimold, P. M. (2003). *The short road to great presentations : how to reach any audience through focussed preparation, inspired delivery, and smart use of technology*. Piscataway, NJ: IEEE.

Rener, F. (1989). *Interpretatio: Language and translation from Cicero to Tytler.* Amsterdam: Rodopi, 1989.

Reynolds, G. (2008). *Presentation zen: Simple ideas on presentation design and delivery.* Berkeley, CA: New Riders.

Ricer, R. E., Filak, A. T., & Short, J. (2005). Does a high tech (Computerized, animated, Powerpoint) presentation increase retention of material compared to a low tech (Black on clear overheads) presentation?. *Teaching & Learning in Medicine, 17*(2), 107-111.

Richmond, V., & McCroskey, J. (1995). *Communication: Apprehension, avoidance,*

REFERENCES

and effectiveness. Scottsdale, AZ: Gorsuch.

Roam, D. (2014). *Show and tell: How everybody can make extraordinary presentations.* New York: Penguin.

Roberson, C., & Allred, M. (2011). *Dead to the world (I, zombie).* New York: Vertigo.

Rogers, M. (1998). *Barbara Jordan: American hero.* New York: Bantam.

Romero, G. (Writer & Director). (1968). *Night of the living dead* [Motion picture]. USA: Image Ten.

Romero, G. (Writer & Director). (1978). *Dawn of the dead* [Motion picture]. USA: MKR.

Romero, G. (Writer & Director). (1985). *Day of the dead* [Motion picture]. USA: UFDC.

Rose, S. B., Spalek, K., Rahman, R. A. (2015). Listening to puns elicits the co-activation of alternative homophone meanings during language production. *PLoS One, 10*(6), 10(6): e0130853. doi:10.1371/journal.pone.0130853.

Rowland, R. (1989). On limiting the narrative paradigm: Three case studies. *Communication Monographs, 56,* 39-54.

Rowling, J. (1999). *Harry Potter and the sorcerer's stone.* New York: scholastic.

Rubenstein Library (n.d.). Guide to the Outdoor Advertising Association of America (OAAA) Archives, 1885-1990s. *Duke University Libraries.* http://library.duke.edu/rubenstein/findingaids/ oaaaarchives/#c01_21.

"Rumpled brains." (1961, Mar. 20). *Eugene Register-Guard.* https://news.google.com/newspapers?id=av9VAAAAIBAJ&sjid=0uIDAAAAIBAJ&pg=1012%2C3375181.

Sandberg, S, & Scovell, N. (2013). *Lean in: Women, work, and the will to lead.* New York: Knopf.

Santos, E. (2014, Oct. 13). Coloring isn't just for kids. It can actually help adults combat stress. *Huffington Post.* http://www.huffingtonpost.com /2014/10/13/coloring-for-stress_n_5975832.html.

Sawyer, M. G., Pfeiffer, S., Spence, S. H., Bond, L., Graetz, B., Kay, D., Patton, G., & Sheffield, J. (2010). School-based prevention of depression: A randomzed controlled study of the beyondblue schools research initiative. *Journal of Child Psychology & Psychiatry, 51,* 199-209.

Schank, R.C. & Abelson, R. (1977). *Scripts, plans, goals, and understanding.* Hillsdale, NJ: Erlbaum.

Seife, C. (2010). *Proofiness: The dark arts of mathematical deception.* New York: Viking.

Selby, G. (2008). *Martin Luther King and the rhetoric of freedom: The Exodus narrative in America's struggle for civil rights.* Waco: Baylor Univ. Press.

Sellnow, D. (2005). *Confident public speaking.* 2nd ed. Belmont, CA: Thompson.

Sharpe, R. (2012, May 17). Rhona Sharpe on lecturing. https://www.youtube.com/watch?v=JnMfo4iUgks#t=911.

Sheldon, E. K. (1956). Some pun among the hucksters. *American Speech, 31,* 13-20.

Shelnut, S. (2015). An exam reader's advice on writing. *College Board.* http://apcentral.collegeboard.com/apc/members/courses/ teachers_corner/17306.html.

Shepard, J. (2013, Jan. 30). Lecture conducted at Texas Lutheran University, Seguin, TX.

Shurter, E. (1903). *Public speaking: A treatise on delivery*. Boston: Allyn & Bacon.

Skalski, P., Tamborini, R., Glazer, E., & Smith, S. (2009). Effects of humor on presence and recall of persuasive messages. *Communication Quarterly, 57*, 136-153.

Smith, C. (1858). *Hints on elocution and public speaking*. London: Ward.

Smith, R. (2000). Requiem shark. *Poetry Foundation*. http://www.poetryfoundation.org/poetrymagazine/poem/30030.

Snyder, Z. (Director). (2004). *Dawn of the dead* [Motion picture]. USA: Universal.

Sopory, P. (2008). Metaphor and intra-attitudinal structural coherence. *Communication Studies, 59*, 164-181.

Sprague, J., & Stuart, D. (1996). *The speaker's handbook*. 4th ed. Fort Worth: Harcourt.

Sprague, J., & Stuart, D. (2000). *The speaker's handbook*. 5th ed. Fort Worth: Harcourt.

Stanton, A., & Unkrich, L. (Directors). (2003). *Finding Nemo* [motion picture]. USA: Disney.

Steel, E., & Somaiya, R. (2015, Feb. 10). Brian Williams suspended for 6 months from NBC without pay. *The New York Times*. http://www.nytimes.com/2015/02/11/business/media/brian-williams-suspended-by-nbc-news-for-six-months.html.

Stewart, C., Smith, R., & Denton, C. (2012). *Persuasion and social movements*. 6th ed. Long Grove, IL: Waveland.

Stiff, J. (1986). Cognitive processing of persuasive message cues: A meta-analytic review of the effects of supporting information on attitudes. *Communication Monographs, 53*, 75-89.

Stratton, C. (1920). *Public speaking*. New York: Holt.

Streeck, J. (1993). Gesture as communication I: Its coordination with gaze and speech. *Communication Monographs, 60*, 275-299.

Summerfelt, H., Lippman L., & Hyman, Jr., I. E. (2010). The effect of humor on memory: Constrained by pun. *The Journal of General Psychology, 137*(4), 376-394.

Tarkovsky, A. (Director). (1972). *Solaris* [Motion picture]. USSR: Mosfilm.

Teston, C. (2012). Moving from artifact to action: A grounded investigation of visual displays of evidence during medical deliberations. *Technical Communication Quarterly, 21*, 187-209.

Thalhaimer, W. (2006, May 1). People remember 10%, 20%...oh really? *Will at Work Learning*. http://www.willatworklearning.com/2006/05/people_remember.html.

Thalhaimer, W. (2015, Jan. 05). Mythical retention data & the corrupted cone. *Will at Work Learning*. http://www.willatworklearning.com/2015/01/mythical-retention-data-the-corrupted-cone.html.

Thorne, B. (1992). Cranky words. *Diseased Pariah News, 4*, 3-6.

Tippee, B. (2012). The energy industry is like a B-52 pilot. *Vital Speeches of the Day, 78*, 388-392.

Todorov, T. (1984). *Theories of the symbol*. Trans. C. Porter. New York: Cornell Univ. Press, 1984.

Torronen, J. (2000). The passionate text: The pending narrative as a macrostructure of persuasion. *Social Semiotics, 10*, 81-98.

Toulmin, S. (2003). *The uses of argument*. Updated ed. Cambridge, UK: Cambridge Univ. Press.

REFERENCES

Tosey, P., Sullivan, W., & Meyer, M. (2013). Clean sources: Six metaphors a minute? *Academia.edu*. http://www.academia.edu/9774145/Clean_Sources_Six_metaphors_a_minute.

Tufte, E. (2001). *The visual display of quantitative information*. CT: Graphics Press.

Tufte, E. (2003). *The cognitive style of Power Point*. Cheshire, CT: Graphics Press.

Tufte, E. (2004, Oct. 7). Presenting data and information. Lecture conducted in Austin, TX.

Voss, J. (2005). Toulmin's model and the solving of ill-structured problems. *Argumentation, 19*, 321-329.

Vrooman, S., & Egan, C. (2009). *Speak up! An illustrated guide to public speaking – instructor's resource manual*. New York: Bedford.

Vrooman, S. (2014a, May 22). Twitter's favorite joke about broken legs and public speaking is a problem. *MoreBrainz: The Zombie Guide to Public Speaking*. http://morebrainz.blogspot.com/2014/05/twitters-favorite-joke-about-broken.html.

Vrooman, S. (2014b, Oct. 18). Our brains are a-twitter. *TEDxSanAntonio*. https://www.youtube.com/watch?v=k6c5eeOCZ7E.

Vrooman, S. (2015a, Feb. 12). Some informal argumentative fallacies. *MoreBrainz: The Zombie Guide to Public Speaking*. http://morebrainz.blogspot.com/2015/02/informal-argumentative-fallacies.html.

Vrooman, S. (2015b, Jul. 30). Good, free sources for photos that you can reuse. *MoreBrainz: The Zombie Guide to Public Speaking*. http://morebrainz.blogspot.com/2015/07/good-free-sources-for-photos-that-you.html.

Vrooman, S. (2015c, Aug. 3). Activities for nervous speakers, part 1. *MoreBrainz: The Zombie Guide to Public Speaking*. http://morebrainz.blogspot.com/2015/08/activities-for-nervous-speakers-part-1.html.

Wachowski, A., & Wachowski, L. (1999). *The Matrix* [Motion picture]. USA: Warner.

Wachtel, J. (2007, Oct. 18). A critical, comprehensive review of two studies recently released by the Outdoor Advertising Association of America. *Maryland State Highway Administration*, Project No. AX137A51. Hanover, MD. Obtained from https://www.toaks.org/civica/filebank/ blobdload.asp?BlobID=19580.

Wanzer, M., Frymier, A., & Irwin, J. (2010). An explanation of the relationship between instructor humor and student learning: Instructional humor processing theory. *Communication Education, 59*, 1-18.

Warnick, B. (2011). Empiricism, securement and *The New Rhetoric*. In J. Gage (Ed.), *The promise of reason: Studies in* <u>The New Rhetoric</u> (pp. 21-28). Carbondale: Southern Illinois University Press.

Wayman, R. (Director). (1959). *Signal 30* [Motion picture]. USA: Highway Safety Films.

Weingroff, R. (2013). Shields and signs. *Highway history*. http://www.fhwa.dot.gov/infrastructure/50sheild.cfm.

Wheeler, E. (1957). *How I mastered my fear of public speaking*. New York: Harper.

Wheeler, L. K. (2013). Rhetoric. http://web.cn.edu/kwheeler/ resource_rhet.html.

Whitehead, C. (2011). *Zone one*. New York: Doubleday.

"Why do writers use figurative language?" (2015). *Yahoo! Answers*.

THE ZOMBIE GUIDE TO PUBLIC SPEAKING

https://in.answers.yahoo.com/question/index?qid=20100225213807AAOcZPG.

Wilson, K, & Korn, J. H. (2007). Attention during lectures: Beyond ten minutes. *Teaching of Psychology, 34*, 85-98.

Winans, J. (1920). *Public speaking*. Rev. ed. New York: Century.

Winter, I. (1913). *Public speaking: Principles and practice*. New York: Macmillan.

Witt, C. (2009). *Real leaders don't do powerpoint*. New York: Crown.

Witt, P., Roberts, M. L., & Behnke, R. R. (2008). Comparative patterns of anxiety and depression in a public speaking context. *Human Communication, 11*, 219-230. http://www.uab.edu/Communicationstudies/humancommunication/11.2.7.pdf.

Wolvin, A., Berko, R., & Wolvin, D. (1993). *The public speaker/ the public listener*. Dallas: Houghton.

Wright, E. (Director). (2004). *Shaun of the dead* [Motion picture]. USA: Universal.

Wyatt, J. (2008). *Dungeons & Dragons dungeon master's guide*. Renton, WA: Wizards of the Coast.

Yancey, P. (2001). *Soul survivor: How my faith survived the church*. New York: Doubleday.

Ye, L., & Johnson, P. (1995). The impact of explanation facilities on user acceptance of expert systems advice. *MIS Quarterly, 19*, 157-172.

Young, D. (2008). The privileged role of the late-night joke: Exploring humor's role in disrupting argument scrutiny. *Media Psychology, 11*, 119-142.

Young, J. (2012, Mar. 24). Box office update: The Hunger Games scores best opening day ever for a non-sequel with $68.3 mil. *Entertainment Weekly*, http://insidemovies.ew.com/2012/03/23/the-hunger-games-midnight-box-office/.

ACKNOWLEDGMENTS

Acknowledgments and Thanks

This book would not be any good without the help of many.

First, thanks to Texas Lutheran University and the Summer Development Grant that provided what I needed to start the first edition of this book.

Second, thanks to my son, Sam Johnson-Vrooman, for the art. I have a sinking suspicion that the cover zombie is me.

Third, thanks to the great teachers I've had whose techniques taught me something I needed to learn about communication (in theory or practice). At Buena Park High School (Go, Coyotes!): Kevin Fawley, Rick Foley, John Hufferd, Rochelle Lubin, Cynthia Martini, and Joe Parrish. At LMU (Go, Lions!): Linda Bannister, Mel Bertolozzi, Jasper Blystone, Barbara Busse, Jay Busse, James Hanink, Paul Harris, Marie Anne Mayeski, Chuck Rosenthal, Dean Scheibel, Tim Shanahan, and Gail Wronsky. At ASU (Go, Sun Devils!): Cheree Carlson, Fred Corey, Kathleen Ferraro, Marouf Hasian, Marsha Houston, Tom Nakayama, Clark Olson, Jim Stiff, and Kristin Valentine.

Fourth, thanks to everyone whose conversations about the ideas in this book and about public speaking or rhetoric in general over these many years have been so vital. Over twenty years ago, I met Michelle Johnson, and she taught me to be a scholar in all the ways that were most important. Many of the ideas in this book came from conversations with her. Chris Bollinger and I have been troubling each other about how to teach public speaking for a more than a decade. He is responsible for a large stack of these ideas, too. A variety of other colleagues and/or friends have been helpful, as well. Sometimes it was the smallest bit of a conversation that sparked an idea. Sometimes it was more. Most specifically, I'd like to single out Carolyn Austin, Jann Barber, Beth Barry, Jason Berke, Robin Bisha, Collin Bost, Dane Boyle, Wesley Buerkle, Doug Chapin, Annette Citzler, Linda Clark, Rebecca Clark, Jean Constable, Sally Cook, Mike Czuchry, Mark Dibble, Etsuko Fujimoto, Laura Galloway, Margaret Gonzales, Philip Grace, Todd Graham, Will Hager, Rona Halualani, Michele Hammers, Judy Hoffmann, Michelle Holling, Donna Hopkins-Smith, Bryan Hubbard, Joel Iverson, Pam Johnston, Susanne Jones, Amelia Koford, Pam Krippner, Cathy Marston, Jennifer Mata, Jean-Pierre Metereau, Omedi Ochieng, Michael Olstad, Melanie Payne, Joey Pogue, Terry Price, Dean Rader, Tracey Rhodes, Martha Rinn, Phil Ruge-Jones, Carolyn Schneider, Tiffiny Sia, John Sieben, Sara Sliter-Hays, Kevin Smith, Jennifer Spencer, Chris Stage, Melanie Thompson, and Carol Turner for thanks. There are probably others I've forgotten. Sorry about that. I'm sure none of the folks listed (or unlisted) agrees with everything in here, so don't blame them.

Fifth, thanks to everyone at TedxSanAntonio, especially those whose advice and conversation taught me, the guy who thought I knew everything, so much about public speaking: Jeff Adams, Shari Albright, Kori Ashton, Molly Cox, Laurie Ann Guerrero, Mitch Hagney, Harry Max, Chris Sandoval, Suzanne Scott, Victor Landa and Chacho & Brance.

Sixth, thanks to my students over the years, whose challenges and conversations have been so helpful in this book's development. There are too many of you to list (and if you are reading this page, looking for names, well, come on, guys! ☺). But there were a few classes who took a larger role in the development and testing of these ideas, so I would like to thank them here. My Spring 2013 Professional

ACKNOWLEDGMENTS

Speaking classes, who were the guinea pigs for this book, are owed thanks for their helpful strategic feedback, as well as their enthusiastic test runs of a different style of visual aids. I will single out April Estes, Chaney Hill, Bryan Mittelstadt, Arthur Munoz, David Soop, and Laura Torres, especially. I will name my May 2013 class, specifically, for thanks, as they were co-strugglers with me on questions of argument for many hours. For better or worse, there would be no Chapter 15 without them: Arthur Babcock, Briana Burnett, Nathaniel Haynes, Allison May, Angelynn May, Maigon O'Reilly, Machell Petri, and Sarah Richard. Thanks to my Summer 2015 class for being such great sports when assigned so much revision. I learned more from their work this summer than I have been able to include here (3rd edition, one day?): Sarah Baldridge, Liz Bosse, Elmer Catalan, Kathrene Fitzpatrick, Alex Hall, Chelsea Kalina, Marcos Lerma, Victoria Martinez, Oksana Pfennig, Megan Riley, Robert Senter, Lori Wiese and Madison Wilks. To all the students whose ideas I cite in this book and to all of those who read and improved the chapter on depression, sometimes by sharing their own experiences, my enduring thanks. Finally, although I said I would not single any students out, I have to admit, at the end of this long paragraph, that that was a lie. In addition to all of the students thanked thus far, I would be remiss if left off a few more whose dedication to innovating, especially when it comes to visual aids, in the two years since the publication of the first edition of this book, contributed in important ways to the developments of my thought in these areas: Mason Allenger, Anna Midkiff, Danielle Ruckman, Spencer Stephens, and Brittany Waltman

Seventh, thanks to the Superthinkers, a Destination Imagination team that Michelle Johnson and I coach. Their obsession with zombies and their superior skills at improv have helped my thinking on communication issues in all sorts of ways: Maya Clark, Sam Johnson-Vrooman, Luke Krueger, Roman Ruiz, Sheldon Scholl, and Rushton Skinner.

Eighth, thanks to the librarians who helped me gather needed resources for this book, in some cases, with preternaturally good timing: Elizabeth McArthur and Claudia Shaw.

Ninth, thanks to Kimberley Mirelez at the San Antionio Museum of Art and Richard Weingroff at the Department of Transportation for their help and information.

Tenth, thanks to all who helped me with the difficult work of figuring out how to publish this thing: Beth Barry, Chris Bollinger, Phil Ruge-Jones, and Lana Urbanek.

Finally, thank you for reading. If you got this far, you must really like the book (or really hate it). Tell me about it. I'm easy to find.

Photo/Art Credits

Cover
Art: Sam Johnson-Vrooman
Design: Steven S. Vrooman
Font: "Redneck Zombies" by Josh Wilhelm.
http://lifewithouttaffy.com/taffy/blog/

Interior
All images/artwork © Sam Johnson-Vrooman, except:

Introduction
p. 4: Steven S. Vrooman
p. 8: Stephen Dann.
https://www.flickr.com/photos/stephendann/
p. 14: Shari Albright

Chapter 1
p. 27: Steven S. Vrooman
p. 29: Steven S. Vrooman

Chapter 2
p. 46 Steven S. Vrooman

Chapter 3
p. 51: Paul L. Witt.
p. 64: Thierry Ehrmann.
https://www.flickr.com/photos/home_of_chaos/, cropped.

Chapter 5
p. 88: Dominic Alves.
https://www.flickr.com/photos/dominicspics/
p. 91: April Estes

THE ZOMBIE GUIDE TO PUBLIC SPEAKING

Chapter 7
p. 124: Ryan McGuire: gratisography.com
p. 129: Steven S. Vrooman
p. 132: Spencer Stephens
p. 133: Spencer Stephens
p. 135: pixabay.com

Chapter 8
p. 156: Dico Royce Calingal: https://www.flickr.com/photos/dicocalingal/

Chapter 9
p. 185: Ben Howling & Yolanda Ramke. Courtesy of Dreaming Tree Productions

Chapter 11
p. 198: Elias Levy: https://www.flickr.com/photos/elevy/

Chapter 12
p. 208: Elias Levy: https://www.flickr.com/photos/elevy/
p. 211: Steven S. Vrooman
p. 212: Steven S. Vrooman

Chapter 13
p. 233: Steven S. Vrooman
p. 237: Steven S. Vrooman
p. 239. Radacina. Public Domain Files
p. 240: Bokeh Images. Publicdomainarchive.com
p. 243: Gary Vrooman
p. 244: LaurMG. https://upload.wikimedia.org/wikipedia/commons/c/c5/Frustrated_man_at_a_desk.jpg
p. 244: Jon Collier. https://www.flickr.com/photos/imnotquitejack/

p. 245: Henry Hemming.
https://www.flickr.com/photos/henry_hemming/
p. 245: Phalinn Ooi.
https://www.flickr.com/photos/phalinn/ unsplash.com
p. 246: LetsGoOutBournemouth.
https://www.flickr.com/photos/letsgoout-bournemouthandpoole/
p. 247: Bill Anders, NASA.
https://en.wikipedia.org/wiki/File:NASA-Apollo8-Dec24-Earthrise.jpg9
p. 248: New Old Stock.
http://nos.twnsnd.co/image/118702568047
p. 248: Tom Eversley. http://isorepublic.com/airtime-london/
p. 249: Steven S. Vrooman
p. 249: Gary van der Merwe.
https://commons.wikimedia.org/wiki/File:Red_Ribbon.svg
p. 249: Dan Machold.
https://www.flickr.com/photos/mybloodyself/
p. 250: Larry Wentzel.
https://www.flickr.com/photos/wentzelepsy/
p. 250: Spencer Means.
https://www.flickr.com/photos/hunky_punk/
p. 251: Baer Tierkel.
https://www.flickr.com/photos/sweetmojo/
p. 251: Michelle Johnson
p. 252: Michelle Johnson
p. 253: Peggy Tenison. Courtesy of the San Antonio Museum of Art
p. 255: Nic Jackson. littlevisuals.co
p. 256: Michelle Johnson
p. 257: Michelle Johnson
p. 258: Jim Larrison.
https://www.flickr.com/photos/larrison/

p. 258: Steve Baker.
https://www.flickr.com/photos/littlebiglens/
p. 259: Steven S. Vrooman
p. 259: Steven S. Vrooman
p. 259: Elias Levy: https://www.flickr.com/photos/elevy/

Chapter 15
p. 293: Steven S. Vrooman

Chapter 16
p. 314: Terry Price

Conclusion
p. 316: Jacob Wilmunen

About the Author

Steven S. Vrooman, Ph.D., is a Professor of Communication Studies at Texas Lutheran University.

He has taught courses on public speaking, research methods, popular culture and communication technology for 20 years.

He appeared in the documentary film *The People Versus George Lucas,* spoke at TEDxSanAntonio, and filmed still yet-to-be-used footage for the upcoming found-footage zombie film, *Virus of the Dead* (he's in the official trailer, anyway). He has published articles on popular culture and the rhetoric of the Internet. He has presented on diverse topics at numerous conferences around the country.

He is the creator of the *Every Speaker Has A Story* podcast, which interviews professional speakers from around the world and curates thematic episodes like "Technical Difficulties" and "Superheroes." Find it at morebrainz.simplecast.fm or by searching it on whatever podcast app you use.

He blogs at morebrainz.blogspot.com. He consults at stevenvrooman.com. He Facebooks as "MoreBrainz." He tweets and Instagrams @MoreBrainz, where you can see his green-fonted critiques of bad visual aids.

Made in the USA
Columbia, SC
26 July 2019